From Charity to Social Change

From Charity to Social Change

Trends in Arab Philanthropy

Edited by
Barbara Lethem Ibrahim
Dina H. Sherif

The American University in Cairo Press
Cairo • New York

Dar el Kutub No. 4608/08
ISBN 978 977 416 207 7

Dar el Kutub Cataloging-in-Publication Data

Ibrahim, Barbara
        From Charity to Social Change: Trends in Arab Philanthropy / Edited by Barbara Lethem
Ibrahim and Dina H. Sherif.—Cairo: The American University in Cairo Press, 2008
        p.   cm.
        ISBN 977 416 207 2
        1. Social change   I. Ibrahim, Barbara Lethem (ed.)   II. Sherif, Dina H. (jt. ed.)
        303.4

1 2 3 4 5 6 7 8 14 13 12 11 10 09 08

Designed by Sally Boylan
Printed in Egypt

Contents

Acknowledgments

It is impossible to thank by name all those who contributed to this publication. For that reason, we wish to broadly recognize the efforts of all who have contributed from its conceptualization to final production. The John D. Gerhart Center for Philanthropy and Civic Engagement is indebted to the philanthropists, executives of foundations, members of community service organizations, activists, and business leaders who generously took time from busy schedules to share their knowledge and insight and to provide us with the information upon which this book is based.

First and foremost, we acknowledge the invaluable efforts and intellectual contributions of the authors, including Mona Atia, PhD (Egypt), Mahi Khallaf (Qatar and Kuwait), Hadeel Qazzaz, PhD (Palestine), Fadi Sharaiha (Lebanon), and Gerhart Center staff members Karim Shalaby (Saudi Arabia), Dina H. Sherif (Jordan, the United Arab Emirates, and Conclusion), and Barbara Lethem Ibrahim PhD (Introduction and Conclusion). Valerie Kirk, an American University in Cairo (AUC) graduate student and research assistant, deserves acknowledgment for conducting background research and contributing writing and editing for the country chapters. Special thanks to her for endless hours of work and dedication.

The center would like to thank the following institutions and individuals whose contributions to the book have been invaluable: Her Majesty Queen Rania Al Abdullah for giving generously of her time and providing insight on the state of philanthropy in Jordan; Her Royal Highness Princess Haya Bint Al Hussein for generously granting us time, support, and valuable insight into the state of philanthropy in Jordan and the UAE; and Barry Gaberman, former senior vice president of the Ford Foundation and distinguished visiting professor at AUC, for offering his broad expertise to help develop the research methodology of this study.

In Qatar, we thank Her Highness Mozah bint Nasser al Missned of Qatar for her leadership of philanthropy in her country, for having a regional vision of social transformation, and believing in the work of the Gerhart Center. Thanks to the Qatar Foundation for research support and Mr. Salman Sheikh for valuable insights.

In the UAE, we thank Yasar Jarrar, former executive dean of the Dubai School of Government, for reviewing the chapters on Jordan and the UAE and for opening important doors for our UAE fieldwork, as well as Samar Abdulhadi of Young Arab Leaders for facilitating research.

In Jordan, we thank Fadi Sharaiha for facilitating research in Jordan and conducting fieldwork in Lebanon under difficult circumstances, and Atallah Kuttab, director general of the Welfare Association, for collegial advice and friendship. We offer special thanks to Fadi Ghandour, the chief executive officer of Aramex, whose insights facilitated research in Jordan, for his continued support and confidence in our work.

In Lebanon, we thank Dania Refai, program manager of UN Habitat, for reviewing the chapter on Lebanon and facilitating field research in that country, and Sallama Namani, program manager of the Makhzoumi Foundation, for facilitating research. Thanks also to May al-Makhzoumi, Paul Salem, and Cynthia Myntti for valuable advice.

In Egypt, we thank Mahmoud Fathalla, professor at Assiut University, for his wise guidance; Moataz al-Alfi, for his encouragement and belief in the power of giving; Ehaab Abdou, chairperson of Nahdet El Mahrousa, for his careful reading of the Egypt chapter; Marwa El-Daly of Waqfeyat al-Maadi for sharing her knowledge of Egyptian philanthropy; and Mohamed Nabil Hayek for his assistance throughout the research process.

In Kuwait, we thank His Excellency Hassan al-Ebraheem, chair of the Kuwait Society for Childhood; Mohamed al-Rumaihi, professor of Sociology at Kuwait University; Rola Dashti, president of the Kuwait Economic Society; and Farahnaz Rezaei of F&N Consultancy.

In Palestine, we thank Nora Lester Murad for her insights and review of the Palestine chapter; Amal Ghadban, Mohammad Masrouji, and Iyad Masrougi for the valuable information they provided during the research; and Sufian Mushashaa for insightful comments about philanthropy not only in Palestine but also in the Arab region. We offer special thanks to our field researchers in Gaza, Haneen Samak and Azza Saadallah.

In Saudi Arabia, we offer warm appreciation to Prince Bandar Bin AbdAllah Bin Abdulrahman for facilitating many aspects of the research effort in KSA; Mohamed Salahuddin Aldundarawy, journalist and publisher, for his guidance and the valuable material he offered; Malik Dahlan, esq., for his insights into legal and civil society environments; Turki bin Khaled al-Sudairy, chairman of the Human Rights Commission, for useful contacts; the Help Center staff, children, and board for information and inspiration; Khaled Ahmed Nahas, executive manager of the National Society for Human Rights; and Matoug al-Shereef, journalist.

We are indebted to Tagreid Hassabo for her tireless work over many weeks to transform the draft report into one coherent document, and to Hanifa Sadek, who contributed to the editing of this publication with admirable professionalism.

Last but not least, we thank a group of special individuals who provided moral and material support in the early stages of the Gerhart Center's work. We are grateful to AUC President David Arnold for believing in the idea of the center long before it existed. We also are grateful to Tim (Earl) Sullivan, former AUC Provost for offering unfailing support and constructive criticism—you will be missed—and Emma Playfair, former regional representative for MENA, Ford Foundation, who has for a number of years been laying the groundwork for a strong Arab philanthropy sector.

The research, drafting, and production of this first-ever study of Arab philanthropy was made possible by a grant from Boeing International Corporation in Dubai, UAE. We applaud their interest and investment in Arab philanthropy and their commitment to social responsibility. The center would like to give special thanks to Anna Roosevelt, vice president of Global Citizenship, John B. Craig, former vice-president of Boeing International (Middle East Region), and Aisha al-Kharusi, deputy director of strategic analysis for Boeing International (Middle East Region).

We hope that this mapping study will stimulate and inspire others to invest in developing resources and documentation for the sector. This is an exciting time to be part of the renaissance of Arab philanthropy, and we all feel grateful for the opportunity to make a contribution to that effort.

About the Contributors

Mona Atia

Mona Atia is assistant professor of geography and international affairs at George Washington University in Washington, DC. She recently completed her dissertation, titled *Building a House in Heaven: Islamic Charity in Neoliberal Egypt*, at the University of Washington, Seattle. Her research has been supported by the Nancy Bell Evans Center on Nonprofits and Philanthropy, the University of Washington Graduate School Dissertation Fellowship, and the Institute of International Education Fulbright Fellowship. In 2006, Atia was a fellow at the John D. Gerhart Center for Philanthropy and Civic Engagement. Her work has appeared in several academic journals, including *Environment and Planning D*, *Environment and Planning A*, *Geografiska Annaler B*, *Housing Policy Debate*, and *Antipode*. She holds an MSc in Cities, Space, and Society from the London School of Economics and a BS in Business Administration from the University of California at Berkeley.

Barbara Lethem Ibrahim

Barbara Lethem Ibrahim is the founding director of the John D. Gerhart Center for Philanthropy and Civic Engagement, established in 2006 at the American University in Cairo. Prior to that, she served for fourteen years as regional director for West Asia and North Africa of the Population Council. From 1982 to 1990, she was a program officer at the Ford Foundation regional office in Cairo, responsible for programs in urban poverty, microenterprise lending, and gender studies. In 1990, she was a senior research associate at the Center for the Study of Philanthropy at the City University of New York. She has an MA in Sociology from the American University of Beirut (1975) and a PhD in Sociology from Indiana University (1980). Her publications are in the fields of women's employment, youth transitions to adulthood, gender and health, and Arab philanthropy. In 1999, she was inducted into the International Educators' Hall of Fame. She received the Lifetime Achievement Award of the Association of Middle East Women's Studies in 2003.

Mahi Khallaf

Mahi Khallaf is a senior project officer at CIVICUS: World Alliance for Civil Participation and a consultant at the John D. Gerhart Center for Philanthropy and Civic Engagement. Khallaf has also done consulting work for several other organizations, including the Aga Khan Foundation, the United States Agency for International Development (USAID), and the Egyptian Center for Development Services (CDS). She has designed training workshops for NGO development practitioners, developed handbooks on advocacy issues for Egyptian NGOs, and worked on setting up a countrywide system for monitoring and evaluating the activities of civil society. Khallaf has researched and published on civil society in Egypt, the Middle East, and internationally. She holds a BA in Political Science from the American University in Cairo and an MA in International Relations from Carleton University's Norman Patterson School of International Affairs.

Hadeel Qazzaz

Hadeel Qazzaz is the program coordinator at the Heinrich-Boll Foundation Office in Ramallah. Her responsibilities include the development and steering of program areas, in addition to monitoring and evaluating projects and representing the foundation in different activities. Qazzaz's area of expertise is gender and development. She was born in the Gaza Strip, but after studying at al-Quds University in Jerusalem and the University of Leeds in the UK, she now resides in Ramallah.

Karim Shalaby

Karim Shalaby is the philanthropy advisor at the John D. Gerhart Center for Philanthropy and Civic Engagement. Prior to his appointment at the center, he accumulated fourteen years experience in the field of community development in Egypt as a practitioner and policy advisor. His engagements included tackling community development through education initiatives and natural resource management pilot programs. He holds a BA in Economics and an MSc in Rural Development. His areas of expertise include finance in the banking sector, as well as change management and institutional reform.

Fadi Sharaiha

Fadi Sharaiha is the executive director of the Royal Marine Conservation Society of Jordan (JREDS), the only NGO working in the field of sustainable development and the marine environment in Jordan. Prior to his engagement with JREDS, he worked with various international organizations, including Creative Associates International, Save the Children, Care International, and the Agricultural Credit Corporation. Sharaiha holds a BSc in Agriculture and Plant Production from the University of Jordan, an MBS from JETS, in addition to a diploma of Permaculture (Permanent Agriculture) Design in the fields of Site Development, Site Design, and Community Service from the Permaculture Research Institute in Australia.

Dina H. Sherif

Dina H. Sherif is the associate director of the John D. Gerhart Center for Philanthropy and Civic Engagement at the American University in Cairo. Prior to that, she was deputy director of projects at Financial Technical Consulting Services, a consultancy firm that specializes in rural development in Sub-Saharan Africa. Sherif has wide-ranging experience in development at the local level in Egypt through her work at the Institute for Cultural Affairs in the Middle East and North Africa and at Environmental Quality International. She serves on the board of several NGOs in Egypt. She holds a BA in Political Science and an MA in Development Studies, both from the American University in Cairo, in addition to a Project Management Professional (PMP) certificate.

Introduction
Arab Philanthropy in Transition

Barbara Lethem Ibrahim

Overview

The Arab region is currently generating unprecedented wealth and creating new generations of wealthy citizens. For the second time in half a century, rapid economic expansion is underway, fueled in part by high oil prices and growth in related sectors. National economies today are more diverse, however, than during the first oil boom of the 1970s. The petroleum and gas exporting countries of the Gulf now have policies in place to capture resource wealth for sounder long-term growth. Arab companies have become globally competitive, including in non-extractive sectors such as telecommunications, construction, and transportation. Meanwhile, economic growth is strong in emerging capital markets like Egypt and Jordan. As a result, current wealth creation is far more diversified than in any previous decade and appears set to continue independent of global oil pricing.

Meanwhile, demographic shifts and political conflicts are exacerbating some of the region's longstanding socioeconomic problems. Youth unemployment, intractable poverty, substandard public services in health and education, environmental degradation, wars, and sectarian strife are among the critical challenges facing Arab societies. Whereas in the past, foreign donors or governments would have been looked to for solutions, the wide consensus today is that they alone cannot bring about desired change. Arab governments have an uneven track record in responding to the major challenges, but all have been forced to open up spaces for greater citizen participation. The most progressive leaders are creating incentives for stronger partnerships between private and public sector actors. Throughout the region, individuals, families, and companies are seeking new ways to make use of their wealth and expertise to improve life for their fellow citizens, and increasingly for those in need beyond their borders.

This book explores the ways in which persistent societal problems coupled with rapid wealth creation in the Arab region are driving a new generation of private citizens to commit resources for the greater public welfare. Widely known as philanthropy, voluntary contributions to causes that serve a public good are a longstanding and important aspect of cultures in the Arab region. What is of particular interest today is the proliferation of ways in which private giving is taking on new institutional forms. While contemporary philanthropy remains strongly grounded in religious frameworks, in some cases it is becoming more *strategic* in its aims, utilizing resources effectively to address the underlying causes of social problems, and ultimately to resolve them.

The interplay between more traditional forms of giving and 'new philanthropy' in the Arab region is creating a dynamic and rapidly changing field. Lack of documentation has kept the focus on only a few of the largest initiatives and prevented analysis of broader trends and their implications. The research that informs this book is an effort to begin that process.

This book focuses on the ways that philanthropic giving currently is formalized into institutions. This is important because of the potential impact institutions can have over time. They serve as models with a higher visibility and likelihood of being replicated. Institutions are more sustainable than individual actions and have greater potential for long-term effectiveness. These are assumptions that need to be tested, but our initial findings suggest that increasing numbers of individual philanthropists are seeking to institutionalize their giving. They see it as a way to achieve greater scale and leave a legacy that will survive their lifetime. Institutions are more likely (though not always successful) to have a cumulative impact, form alliances, and take a long-term view of social change. Therefore, the present study focuses on the landscape of philanthropic organizations and the founders and executives behind them.

The idea of philanthropy does not have a single accepted Arabic translation but instead is expressed through many terms around the region. Yet the meaning underlying the concept is easily understood by everyone; it holds positive valence regardless of class, religion, education, or place of residence. Giving of one's material wealth to benefit those in need is a fundamental tenet of both Islam and Christianity. Studies consistently find that this form of giving is widely practiced at all levels of society and in countries across the region.[1] It is so fundamental that most people who give take it for granted, though they are unlikely to put one label on their actions.

Many people would simply say "li-llah" (for God), a phrase that reflects the religious underpinnings of giving. Other terms in use include *'ata' khayri* (charitable giving), *zakat* or *'ushr* (religious tithing among Muslims and Christians, respectively), *birr* or *mabarra* (good works), or *zakat* and *sadaqa* (obligatory and voluntary beneficence). Recent attempts by writers to capture the idea of modern philanthropy in Arabic include *'ata' al-igtima'i* (social giving) and *takaful insani* (humanitarian solidarity), but neither of these phrases is in wide usage at this time.

Definitions are further complicated by ideas that recently have gained currency in the private sector. Corporate philanthropy and corporate social responsibility (CSR) are increasingly attractive concepts that identify the ways in which private business marshals its assets to serve the community or broader public good. These initiatives, along with governmental efforts to partner with private actors for philanthropic aims, create a boundary area that blurs the lines between private, corporate, and public philanthropy.

For the purposes of this study, the authors developed a working definition of philanthropy as *the institutionalized pooling and distribution of private resources with the goal of building capacity, sustainable financing, and expertise for long-term societal benefit.*[2] Our definition of philanthropy, therefore, is somewhat narrower than the utilization of private wealth for the public good. It places emphasis not only on the act of giving but also on the outcomes of giving. Not all of the examples given in this book meet each of the criteria above, but we found a growing consensus concerning their importance as worthy objectives for the sector.

Important Traditions of Giving[*]

The idea of philanthropic giving is deeply rooted in tradition and closely linked to the Arabic concept of *takaful*, or social solidarity.[3] For Christian Arabs, *'ushr* is the practice of giving a tenth of one's wealth or income to those less fortunate in the community. This is often accompanied by the giving of time for voluntary service to others. For Muslim Arabs, *zakat* is one of the five pillars of the faith—a practice that is seen as both a spiritual and a social obligation. *Zakat* falls under the wider umbrella of charity referred to as *sadaqa. Sadaqa jariya* encompasses benevolent acts with an ongoing life, such as distributing religious books or tapes, making educational materials freely available, or planting fruit trees in a public square. *Waqf* is an important institutionalized form of *sadaqa jariya* that is described below.

---

* This section was contributed by Mona Atia.

Zakat

Zakat is the third pillar of Islam and a requirement for all believers. The word *zakat*, which appears in eighty-two verses of the Quran, is most often translated as alms or charitable giving. The social importance of *zakat* is its role in helping to ease the burdens of poverty. It is seen as a tool for more equitable distribution of wealth, achieving social stability and solidarity, discouraging hoarding, and encouraging the circulation of capital in the economy.[4] *Zakat* also is seen as a way to spiritually cleanse oneself and purify wealth.[5]

Zakat requires that the donor's intention is to give solely as an act of piety. In many countries, *zakat* is an entirely private matter. A desire not to humiliate the poor underlies the practice of giving anonymously, and many believe that "special religious merit is gained by giving alms in secret."[6]

There are various forms of *zakat*, including on money, on trade, on merchandise, and so forth. A Muslim is responsible for paying *zakat al-mal* (alms on money) equivalent to 2.5 percent of net worth if, after meeting his needs, the believer possesses the equivalent of 85 grams of gold or 600 grams of silver for a period of one year.[7]

The Quran mentions eight categories of people as entitled to receive *zakat*.[8] This issue is of utmost importance because it underlies the organizational structure of charity in all of the countries included in this study. The list includes the poor, the needy or vulnerable, administrators of *zakat* funds, recent or potential converts, freed slaves or those in bondage, overburdened debtors, those following the cause of God, and travelers who need to return to their homes. The seventh category is the most open to interpretation and discussion because while *fi-sabil-Illah* literally means "following the cause of God," this has in some circumstances been interpreted as supporting *jihad* (struggle in the name of Islam) and as funding the travel of those who cannot afford to perform the *hajj*, or pilgrimage to Mecca.

Today, a great deal of discussion occurs about whether *zakat* can be used to contribute to other causes, such as providing support to strengthen charitable institutions, environmental organizations, development projects, and cultural institutions. For example, Mufti Nasr Farid Wasel in Egypt issued a *fatwa* that contributing to the building of a cancer treatment center is a form of *zakat*.[9] The legal scholar Abd-Allah interprets category eight to include the subcategory of refugees,[10] but this opinion is not widely held because of debates over whether recipients of *zakat* must be Muslim. Islamic scholarly opinions on this topic are often confusing and at odds. Regardless of the area of giving, however, the responsibility exists to reserve a portion of one's *zakat* for the poor and the needy. Therefore, most *zakat*-supported organizations distribute primarily to these categories, including orphans and those widows who have no male support and are most clearly identifiable as the 'deserving poor.'

Sadaqa

Sadaqa is translated as benevolence. The main difference between *zakat* and *sadaqa* is that *zakat* is obligatory while *sadaqa,* the broader concept, usually refers to voluntary giving of all types. *Sadaqa* can take many different forms, material and nonmaterial. According to *hadith*, or traditions attributed to the Prophet, every good deed is a form of *sadaqa*; a kind word and a smile are both considered forms of *sadaqa*.[11] The best form of *sadaqa*, according to another *hadith*, is passing on knowledge.[12] *Sadaqa* is often performed through voluntary work, in-kind contributions, and free services. It can be given to anyone, with no specific groups designated as recipients.

Because most charitable organizations are sustained through the receipt of *zakat* funds, spending priorities tend to be in line with the eight *zakat* categories. Since *sadaqa* is less structured, it recently has been explored as a way to extend Muslim civil society organization (CSO) work to more development-oriented approaches and support for art, culture, or environmental protection. In addition, *sadaqa* has been utilized as a means of reviving volunteerism, especially among pious youth. In countries like Egypt, with large populations in poverty, *sadaqa* is increasingly mobilized to finance microenterprise and microfinance credit programs.

Waqf

Waqf is an Arabic term that means to stop, confine, isolate, or preserve in perpetuity certain revenue or property for religious or philanthropic purposes. Thus, it is one of the oldest examples of an endowment. The act of establishing a *waqf* may be performed personally or on behalf of someone who has passed away, through the endowment of a public water fountain or the construction of a mosque.

A *waqf* endowment (pl., *awqaf*) is a form of ongoing public service that utilizes private wealth to establish projects of public benefit. An individual, a family, a group of individuals, or an entity can accumulate the capital for a *waqf*. *Waqf* funds may derive from assets such as real estate, land (usually agricultural), buildings, cars, machinery, books, and money. There were traditionally three kinds of *waqf*: charitable *waqf*, familial (heirs) *waqf*, and mixed *waqf*, or *waqf* that serves both purposes.

The purpose of a *waqf* is set by the endower and should only be changed in accordance with his/her will. There are numerous ways to allocate *waqf* money, including through direct benefit (for example, housing people or building a mosque) and investments (financial or agricultural). Historically, most *awqaf* took the form of real estate, and this may still be the case in some Arab Gulf countries. Other ways of financing *awqaf* exist, including shares, stocks, bonds, and other instruments that have been established by Islamic financial institutions.[13]

Waqf as an institution has changed dramatically over time.[14] Historically, *awqaf* were an important source of funding for and played a critical role in the provision of public services, including support for the building of mosques, schools, libraries, hospitals, water supply, cemeteries, gardens, windmills, public transport facilities, parks, roads, and the provision of healthcare services for the needy and disabled.[15] Often, revenues from farms, gardens, buildings, shops, and industrial plants were channeled toward charitable purposes in the form of *awqaf*. During the Mamluk period, after the mid-thirteenth century, more than half of Egypt's agricultural land and the majority of buildings in Cairo were *awqaf*.[16] At the start of the nineteenth century, between half and two-thirds of all property in the Ottoman Empire was held as *awqaf*.

As modern states emerged over the course of the next 150 years, some governments either took over control of *waqf* properties or heavily regulated them. In the countries included in this study, the *waqf* institution was found to be thriving in some but completely frozen in others. With its important features of sustainability and generation of ongoing funding streams for public causes, *waqf* is a promising model for reinvigoration in the present.[17]

Mapping Arab Philanthropy Today

Arab philanthropy is rich in history and contemporary complexity. An entire book has been written about a single charitable endowment in thirteenth-century Jerusalem that continues to feed the poor to this day.[18] Thousands of comparable *waqf* endowments persist and continue to increase across the region, while registered *mu'assasat* (asset-bearing foundations) in just one country, Egypt, now number over four hundred.[19] Clearly, given the depth of traditions of giving in Arab countries, any initial attempt to cover contemporary trends in the region must be in some respects incomplete.

What is novel today is the ways some actors are structuring and targeting their giving. These include revamping older forms, like the centuries-old *waqf* endowment model, creative uses of religiously mandated donations (*zakat* and *'ushr*), and a variety of other modalities, such as social investing, corporate philanthropy, and the establishment of modern grant-making foundations. Another promising trend is toward regional funding institutions based in one country but governed by a pan-Arab board of directors.

The authors have selected eight Arab countries for study that together represent a range of historic and contemporary profiles.[20] They include oil and gas producers such as Saudi Arabia, Kuwait, Qatar, and the United Arab Emirates (UAE). The other selected countries—Egypt, Jordan, Lebanon, and Palestine—have fewer oil resources but longer histories of CSOs involved in social development. These eight countries display a wide diversity in the contexts in which philanthropy developed. At one end of the spectrum is Palestine, where the lack of a functioning government for many decades led to a proliferation of CSOs providing basic services to the Palestinian people. At the other end is Egypt, which is emerging from over half a century of tight control over the activities of private social actors. Egypt at one point nationalized *waqf* endowments and state actors appropriated the sole mandate to address social problems. In other Arab countries, ruling elites used their influence and private wealth to stimulate additional giving among fellow citizens. In all cases, we found a dynamic situation, with new forms of giving emerging and larger scales of philanthropy than at any other time in recent history.

While this emerging sector is not yet fully documented, it is an increasingly potent actor on the national and regional scene. Newer entrants are less likely to follow the models of previous generations. Charity is viewed by some as necessary but not sufficient to address the challenges of poverty and underdevelopment. This view inspired the title of the book, *From Charity to Social Change*. Nonetheless, newer institutions and alliances will never replace charitable giving, nor do they intend to do so.

The leaders behind newer philanthropic projects may be somewhat impatient with modalities that they believe are inefficient in effecting social change. In some cases, they are in dialogue with colleagues in charitable institutions, working to widen the permissible targets for religious giving. Among many philanthropic actors, there is healthy debate regarding the ethics and conduct of their field. It is a vibrant moment for Arab philanthropy, and the authors hope that their first efforts at documentation will contribute to the work being carried forward.

Study Approach

As this is an initial mapping exercise, the authors aimed for breadth of coverage. Each of the eight countries included in the volume merits a fuller survey to convey the diversity of its organized philanthropy. Some settings have a longer history of civil society institutions and therefore more research and written material were readily available. Where there has been longer international involvement in philanthropy, the available documentation was sometimes greater. Authors found people in some settings more used to responding to the requests of social researchers for information and therefore more forthcoming. For all of these reasons, country coverage is in some respects uneven. This volume should be read as a 'map' of the major contours of giving in each country, with examples to illustrate the diversity of giving in each context.

The authors aimed to identify factors that contribute to a particular national giving scene and the institutional forms of philanthropy found there. For each form identified, examples are given that offer insight into the areas of work and modes of operation of contemporary giving. Where a number of organizations belong in a single category, such as family foundations, authors included just one or two examples per country to illustrate the category. These may not be the oldest, largest, or 'best' examples, but they reflect an effort to provide broad coverage of the range of types of giving in each country.

Study Design

Because corporate social responsibility is a burgeoning field, and one that others, such as the United Nations Development Programme (UNDP),[21] are in the process of documenting, it is not covered extensively in this volume. Where it overlaps significantly with individual philanthropic initiatives, the authors have given one or two examples in several country chapters.

Data presented here was collected over a nine-month period in 2007 by a team of six researchers coordinated by the John D. Gerhart Center for Philanthropy and Civic Engagement at the American University in Cairo. The premise that guided the study's design was that the field of philanthropy is changing rapidly in the Arab region and that those changes are poorly documented and often too new to be widely understood. The goal was to create an initial 'map' of the major trends and types of organizations comprising philanthropy in the eight selected countries. We recognized at the outset that this is the first effort of its kind, and that our initial report would be preliminary and indicative rather than definitive and complete.

A core research group consisting of Dina H. Sherif, the project coordinator, and Barbara Lethem Ibrahim, Mahi Khallaf, and Mona Atia met to develop a set of key issue areas around the structure, management, giving philosophy, and programs of philanthropic organizations.[22] They developed a set of questions around the national culture of giving and the legal, political, and economic factors that shape local philanthropy. This became the basis for an interview guide used by individual researchers, who made one or more visits to each country to conduct interviews and make field visits.[23] Researchers authored their country chapters, having been chosen because of extensive prior knowledge of the country under study and/or of civil society institutions in the region.

Prior to field visits, each researcher compiled secondary data and conducted a desk review of published material on philanthropy for each country. Based on this, data gaps were identified and a study strategy developed for each country. In addition, a common set of country-level statistics were compiled, as well as historical profiles and thumbnail sketches of the contemporary political, economic, and relevant legal contexts in the selected countries. Once in the field, a combination of key informant interviews and case studies of institutions were completed, notes reviewed, and write-ups shared with other authors for comment.

In each country, key advisors were involved from an early stage in framing the central questions for that setting and in arranging interviews with major actors. They provided pivotal information and, in some cases, acted as readers for the draft chapters. They also generally facilitated the completion of the study. Country chapters were reviewed by other members of the research team and by experts selected for their knowledge of the national scene. We are grateful to all of those who facilitated our work, often under tight time pressures and in environments where there is considerable reluctance to reveal financial or other information about philanthropic giving.

From the outset, it was planned that the results of this first round of data collection would be shared with important stakeholders in a regional consultation. The intent was to invite key actors in the field to respond to the study findings and to reflect on the implications for forward action to enhance the field.

A preliminary version of this volume was presented to over four hundred participants in Dubai at a consultation co-hosted by the Mohamed Bin Rashid Al Maktoum Foundation and the Gerhart Center. It was attended by a range of important stakeholders in the emerging philanthropy field, including business leaders, members of ruling families, *waqf* and foundation executives, and those engaged in research and media coverage of the field. Suggestions arising from that meeting were incorporated into this volume, as well as into the Arabic translation.

Research Constraints

A number of factors complicated data collection, which is not uncommon for research efforts in the region. Planned study trips had to be postponed more than once when an election or other national event made interviewing impracticable. In particular, political conditions in Lebanon restricted travel and limited data collection, and Gaza could not be covered as the authors had envisioned.

While the historic record is extensive, documentation of patterns of contemporary giving is scarce. Few governments publish or make available the data they collect on private philanthropic giving. Thus, we relied on senior advisors in each locale to point researchers to important institutions and actors. These individuals provided crucial assistance in gaining the confidence of those needed for interviews. Still, the authors found that the realm of philanthropy is surrounded by a great deal of secrecy, especially with regard to finance and the volume of assistance offered. Public disclosure in the form of published annual reports and independent audits of organizations is increasing, but it is still rare in some places. The management of traditional giving practices such as tithe, *zakat*, *mabarrat*, and *waqf* is typically the purview of religious bodies, many of which are only starting to publish information on their holdings.

In addition, a history of nationalizing private assets and other forms of official interference has made people in some countries wary of disclosing information. In other instances, organizations operate in a segmented fashion so that executive managers are not fully aware of the full financial picture, especially with respect to the contributions of the founder or other benefactors.

Another important reason for lack of respondent openness is rooted in religious belief. Both Christian and Muslim traditions discourage giving that is announced so as to bring acclaim to the giver. Muslim practice is to be discreet in order to protect the dignity of those receiving the gift.[24] Some philanthropists organize their giving so that it is completely anonymous. One national survey of philanthropy in Egypt estimated the overall volume of private philanthropic giving to be over EGP 5 billion (nearly USD 1 billion). The authors noted, however, that secrecy and underreporting make that figure unreliably low.[25] We found these attitudes and practices to be widespread across the countries studied.

While reluctance to share information made the task of compiling this study difficult, secrecy around philanthropy may have wider implications. By not sharing information, philanthropic organizations remain isolated and do not benefit from the learning that is possible through the exchange of best practices and the formation of professional networks. It is more difficult to gain public trust when philanthropic activities are not transparent. Fortunately, the trend toward increasing openness and disclosure is gaining ground, which is one of the positive findings of this study.

One aspect of secrecy that is not addressed directly in the present study is post-9/11 reticence to report activities that might expose philanthropists to legal or security-related scrutiny. The international atmosphere of suspicion affected authors' ability to access information. In countries like Kuwait and Saudi Arabia, post-9/11 pressures have resulted in regulations that restrict spontaneous giving and create distrust. We found that some foundations that would have registered in the Arab region are now based in Europe as a strategy to avoid the local scrutiny that increased after 2001.

Secrecy also surrounds philanthropic activity that may be tied to oppositional politics. The line between funding social services and funding political loyalty is not firmly drawn in a number of countries.[26] In Lebanon and Palestine, our informants pointed to the prevalence of sectarian and political identities as a source of philanthropic initiative. Egypt has a tradition of social services for the poor, university students, and others provided by philanthropists with ties to the outlawed Muslim Brotherhood. The study does not include activities or groups whose objectives are overtly religious or political in nature.[27]

Emerging Themes in the Study Findings

The Arab world, with its long and deep traditions of giving and beneficence, is one of the last regions in the world to develop a vigorous modern sector of philanthropic institutions. The region has a high volume of individual generosity, often conducted in private, but a relatively low prevalence of institutionalized philanthropy. Nonetheless, traditional giving practices are widespread and historically rooted in every country in the study.[28] Arabs have been and remain generous and philanthropically inclined people. Islamic and Christian principles provide the bedrock for giving that is supported by even older traditions of Bedouin hospitality to strangers and guests. And yet, institutions that aim to make this giving cumulative and effective are often isolated and only a few decades old.

Why should these disparities exist in a region where benevolent giving has its earliest origins? The search for answers turned up several important factors that this book explores. One is that some venerable religious traditions of institutionalized giving failed to make a robust transition to modern circumstances. Another is the prevalence of foreign donor contributions (both public and private), which for decades have dominated the development scene in places like Egypt and Palestine. Yet another is the relative weakness of modern civil society institutions generally. Finally, governments in the region have not always been friendly to private, homegrown institutionalized giving, or they have attempted to meet the need for public goods and services without assistance from private sources.

A primary factor that has both stimulated giving and inhibited new expressions of it is the religiously motivated drive to make charitable contributions. Far from waning in recent decades, religious charitable giving has grown stronger as part of a resurgence of religiosity across the region. *By charitable giving, we mean contributions to causes that alleviate the immediate suffering or wants of people in need.* Both Islam and Christianity call on believers to give from their material wealth in order to share their good fortune and reduce the suffering of others. This is both a spiritual and social command. Abdullahi An-Na'im has referred to this type of giving as the provision of consumables, because once the offering of food, clothing, medicine, or similar support is depleted, the beneficiary finds himself/herself in the same position of want.[29] When communities were smaller and the need for subsistence less monetized, this system probably functioned well.

This study finds that the devotion to religious giving practices is strong and drives ever-increasing scales of giving. Commitment to these practices and the sense of having completed one's religious obligations may deflect impulses toward other forms of giving. Most giving to fulfill religious obligations remains charitable rather than developmental in the choice of targets and therefore is relatively short term in its effects.[30]

As societies have become more complex, the problems of poverty, displacement, exclusion, and discrimination have become more intractable. Governments that once tried to fulfill the basic needs of citizens are withdrawing from this role, in some cases leaving a growing sector of the population unable to achieve minimal standards of healthcare, education, shelter, and so forth. In this study, we found a growing consensus around the Arab region that longstanding inequities cannot be solved through charity alone. Significant progress toward the solution of the 'big issue' problems of our day will require new approaches and more collective and strategic pooling of resources.

States and Private Philanthropy

Relationships between states and philanthropy in the Arab region historically have been complex. Under the centuries of Ottoman rule, Mashreq countries with urban centers (Lebanon, Jordan, Syria, and Palestine) and the Saudi Arabian peninsula as well as Egypt, developed a vast system of private *waqf* endowments to fund good works and prevent property from dissipation or taxation. By and large, these arrangements were respected by generations of rulers. In the twentieth century, modern states attempted various degrees of control and appropriation of *waqf* property. This led, in Egypt, for example, to nationalization and a stop to the formation of new *awqaf*. More important, these actions generated a good deal of reluctance to establish other forms of private endowments for fear of interference.[31]

Other countries have managed to revive and modernize the *waqf* model, so that in Kuwait, Saudi Arabia, and Qatar, rulers serve as important role models for their establishment. Alternatively, the lack of a recognized government for many years in Palestine created a large vacuum in public services. CSOs and foundations proliferated to fill the gaps. Internal political struggles there are undermining philanthropic organizations just as they impact all aspects of Palestinian society. Private diaspora philanthropy has been and continues to be of high importance in Palestine.

As a general observation, governments in the region are rarely active in the promotion of foundations or endowed philanthropic organizations. Recent studies have shown the serious obstacles governments place in the way of registering an independent foundation and protecting its assets across the region.[32] In late 2007, a draft law in Egypt proposed reducing the tax advantages previously reserved for charitable foundations. Proactive measures need to be taken in all of the Arab countries covered in this study to create more effective public–private partnerships, to improve the legal climate, and to encourage institutionalized private giving.

One hopeful sign is the way in which hereditary rulers are proving strong role models for philanthropic giving in a number of Arab countries of the Gulf and in Jordan. Their high-profile support for institutions and causes helps to legitimize expanded forms of philanthropic giving. Commitments of time and talents are modeled by 'royals,' as well as the giving of wealth. In Lebanon, a former prime minister, Rafiq Hariri, was a major benefactor of that country's reconstruction during and after fifteen years of destructive civil war.

Wealth Creation and Citizen Business Leaders

Perhaps at no time since the economic and social surge of the 1920s have businessmen and women played such key roles in public life. During much of the last half of the twentieth century, the business community remained somewhat aloof from public life, seeking to avoid the state or currying favor only as much as necessary to gain business advantages. Today, some Arab business leaders are redefining their roles as public actors, increasingly seeing themselves as partners with governments and with civil society. The impetus for this new activism is not altogether altruistic. Many have come to recognize that social and economic development for all sectors of society is "good for business." At the same time, success in the corporate sphere gives these individuals confidence in their ability to make a positive difference beyond their own commercial interests. They are emerging as founders of nonprofit associations and foundations, outspoken advocates for social issues such as the environment, and advisors to government on social, economic, and political reform.

Earlier pioneers in this spirit, whom we call 'citizen business leaders,' were great philanthropists such as Abdul Hameed Shoman, founder of the Arab Bank.[33] Their counterparts today have become active for a variety of reasons. Some may feel pangs of conscience over their large personal fortunes. Many are motivated to engage in public life by religious convictions. However, they are unlikely to speak outwardly in religious terms. Business leaders interviewed for this volume spoke about identifying with the welfare of their country or the region, which is a motivation that Asef Bayat calls 'nativism.'[34] Many expressed an impulse to share their gains with those less fortunate. Some said that their personal philosophy parallels that of global 'corporate social responsibility' (CSR), which posits a mutual benefit to business and the country from corporate engagement in the long-term solution of pressing social problems.

A small but growing number of citizen business leaders seeks to be more strategic in deploying wealth to address large systemic problems. They are concerned about the effects of poor public policy or burgeoning poverty on long-term business prospects. They also see clearly that governments, regardless of the size of their coffers, cannot fix all of the complex problems of modern societies. Some worry about the growth of corruption as a corollary of government stagnation. They often share a conviction that success in the private sector gives them a set of skills and methods that would enhance the efforts of civic groups and government bodies.

Varieties of Philanthropic Institutions

We found that when business and professional leaders engage in philanthropy, they fairly rapidly see the advantages of institutionalizing their involvement. Many do so with a registered fund or endowment established in the name of their family or a parent. We have termed this category 'family foundations,' a widespread practice in all of the countries presented in this book.

Another trend is to establish a department inside privately owned firms to handle giving or CSR activities. Over time, these departments may spin off into legally independent foundations in the name of the companies, operated through a share of annual profits. Throughout this volume, these are referred to as 'corporate foundations.' Some variant on this pattern was found in every country surveyed.

Revivals of traditional institutions also are vibrant in some settings. Where *waqf* structures are viable and not too closely controlled, as in Kuwait and Qatar, this is a preferred form of endowing private philanthropy. In countries such as Egypt, Lebanon, and the UAE, *mu'assasat* (asset-bearing foundations) are gaining popularity. In a few cases, business entrepreneurs have become impatient with the structures they have set in place, preferring to return to spontaneous giving that they can control individually. Most, however, are convinced of the advantages of continuity, impact, and professionalism that are afforded by organized programs of giving.

An interesting modality we identified emerges when two or more entrepreneurs partner closely with each other on the basis of trust and a common social goal. Because these arrangements can be an outgrowth of longstanding business relations, elsewhere this author has called this form of philanthropic giving the *shilla* foundation (*shilla* is an Arabic term for a closely knit group of friends who provide mutual support).[35] This model may expand over time to include a large number of wealthy contributors. The most sustained example is the twenty-year-old Welfare Association, which was founded by a group of Palestinian businessmen. Newer but rapidly growing examples include the Egyptian Food Bank and Ruwwad in Jordan.

A related type of philanthropy is the 'community foundation,' which usually has a geographic area or population subgroup as the target of service. Community foundations are still relatively rare in the region, but they provide opportunities for many small contributors to cumulate their donations in order to more effectively benefit the community.

In terms of their modalities of operation, two types of foundations were noted by our researchers: those that channel financial resources to other groups in civil society, or 'grant-making foundations,' and those that choose to conduct their own in-house programs, or 'operating foundations.' Hybrids of the two are also emerging, as well as the tendency for some grant-making foundations to shift over time to more in-house programming. This reduces the flow of resources to CSOs, causing some tension, and blurs the line between philanthropic and other kinds of CSOs.

Philanthropy and Corporate Social Responsibility

A number of publications and recent conferences in the Arab region have attempted to distinguish philanthropy from corporate social responsibility.[36] The argument runs that philanthropy as a field should be defined as 'good deeds' and monetary contributions for public causes, whereas *CSR relates to the strategic decisions of corporate leaders to orient their businesses toward fair labor practices, protection of natural resources, and solutions to major social problems that expand the economy and therefore improve long-term business prospects.* An example of this dichotomy is that philanthropy would offer food or services to the poor while CSR would improve the products or disposable income available to the poorest consumers through so-called 'pro-poor business strategies.'[37] CSR is presumed to be "good for the bottom line" rather than a transfer of resources from the business.

Making these distinctions has been an important way of helping to educate the business community away from thinking that a few public relations gestures by their marketing departments qualify as good corporate citizenship or CSR. Businesses that conduct high-profile activities, for example, to clean up the environment while continuing business practices or offering products that are ultimately harmful to the environment need to have these contradictions exposed. To the extent that the private sector can be more engaged in the eradication of major social problems rather than in offering 'band-aid' local projects, the dichotomy is useful as an advocacy tool.

In the course of interviews, however, the authors of this report found interesting areas of overlap between classic philanthropic activities and corporate responsibility across the region. Business leaders are often the catalyst for both kinds of activities, and they do not see the two as distinct or contradictory. They might, for example, utilize *zakat* contributions from privately owned business profits to create job-training programs for unemployed poor youth. Company CSR activities might be funded on an annual basis through a mix of budget-line transfers, volunteer time, and private contributions from the firm's executives and employees. These creative mixes are in some cases leveraged through lobbying for redefinitions of appropriate *zakat* giving. Business leaders are at the forefront of these innovations. An example are legal, employment, and psychological counseling programs for refugees. When the traditional *zakat* category of 'wayfarers or pilgrims' is redefined to include refugees, who form a large vulnerable population because of war and ethnic displacement in the Arab region, important social benefits are extended to an excluded and underserved group.

As will be seen below, in practice it is virtually impossible to draw clear lines between nonprofit and business-related aspects of social service and giving. We found great dynamism and innovation at this interface between corporate and private philanthropy.

Philanthropists and Public Life

Business leaders engaged in philanthropy are often active in other arenas of public life. They write opinion essays in the press, act as advisors to government, serve as legislators, and sometimes are active in political parties. This level of public engagement can be met with suspicion in contexts where transparency is absent, or when there are exclusive circles of political power. The overlap of philanthropy, politics, and public advocacy is a reality not only in the Arab world but also elsewhere. In other regions, countries have dealt with this issue through legislation or professional associations that set standards for the ethical conduct of philanthropy.

Civil Society, Public Advocacy, and Corporate Social Responsibility

Some of the most interesting and creative initiatives in Arab philanthropy are being generated at the interface between civil society, public advocacy, and corporate social responsibility. Some of the impetus is coming from multinational companies, but local citizen business leaders are increasingly in the forefront. The business and professional communities are revitalizing philanthropy through the application of management expertise and business analysis to social problems. This is a theme that runs through all of the country chapters of this volume.

The field of 'social investing' is relatively new in the Arab region, involving financial and management investments with an intended financial return, making these not purely philanthropic endeavors. Social investing implies a higher tolerance for risk or willingness to defer profit because of the overriding social objective of the enterprise. While it is still rare, our researchers uncovered interesting examples of this hybrid area, for example in fields such as eco-tourism.

Laws and Public Policy

Policies and the legal context of each country play a vital role in shaping philanthropic communities. The authors found considerable frustration among foundation executives about overregulation or a lack of understanding of their contributions from state actors. This was a major theme of the regional consultation on Arab philanthropy held in Dubai at the launch of the study. Much more documentation and sharing of good practice would be useful. Legal reform is urgently needed to provide clearer incentives for institutionalized giving, asset protection, and noninvasive oversight of the sector.

Lessons can be taken from the divergent policy paths taken in other regions. For example, the slow development of European philanthropy has been linked to higher tax burdens and the presence of strong state structures that provide welfare services and a safety net to citizens. In the United States, by contrast, government has a history of minimal involvement in social welfare but generous tax breaks for charitable giving. In that climate, organized philanthropy has flourished over the past hundred years. Over time, it has played an increasingly important role not only in filling gaps in government welfare programs but also in providing new models for social change.

Conclusion

The new wealth currently being generated on an unprecedented scale in the Arab region can and must be captured for the greater public good. The region cannot afford to allow disparities of income and access to modern life to remain as unequal as they are today or to widen. Environmental degradation threatens the future of all societies, rich and poor. Transnational problems of labor migration and integration must be addressed for economies to continue to prosper. This is an opportune time to be taking stock of the resources, institutions, and actors that are providing leadership in tackling these issues through the philanthropic sector.

Hopefully, one of the outcomes of regional consultations and alliances on philanthropy will be to expand the numbers and quality of organizations engaged in the sector. Another will be standards that are transparent and appropriate to the region, much as International Organization for Standardization (ISO) standards are forthcoming for international CSR. Meanwhile, the business-philanthropy interface is just one example of the boundary areas that are sites of innovation in a rapidly changing time for Arab philanthropy.

We offer the eight country chapters that follow in the hope that they will stimulate dialogue and interest in the issues they raise. The concluding chapter points to areas for future work and suggests collective actions that may enhance the philanthropic sector in the Arab region. The authors intend to make the publication of new information on Arab philanthropy a regular contribution to this dynamic field.

Notes

1. El-Daly, 2006.
2. This definition excludes purely individual or informal giving. It would include, however, institutionalized means of collecting individual contributions if they are utilized beyond the community that collected them. It also attempts to distinguish philanthropy from other associations and activities of civil society. For a useful discussion of these distinctions in Egypt, see El-Daly 2006.
3. Ibid., 53.
4. Emara 2003:34–35.
5. University of Southern California. USC-MSC Compendium of Muslim Texts. Quran, chapter 2, Surat al-Baqara (The Cow) 002:283.
    http://www.usc.edu/dept/MSA/quran/002.qmt.html.
6. Benthall 1999:33–34.
7. El-Daly, 2003:57.
8. Ibid, Quran, chapter 9, Surat al-Tawba (Repentance), 009:60.
    http://www.usc.edu/dept/MSA/quran/009.qmt.html.
9. El-Daly 2007.
10. Benthall 1999:32.
11. *Hadith* ibn al-Hambal 8856, cited in Abdel Halim Omar, *al-Qa'id al-hasan li-tamwil al-'amal al-khayri fi-l-gam'iyat al-ahliya fi-itar al-tamwil shibh al-rasmi.* Unpublished manuscript. 2006a.
12. *Hadith* Abdel ibn al-Majeh 91/1, number 1844, cited in Abdel Halim Omar. 2206
13. Omar, Mohamed Abdel Halim (2004). *Muhadarat tajrubat al-awqaf fi-Gumhuriyat Misr al-'Arabiya.* Unpublished manuscript.
14. Benthall and Bellion-Jourdan 2003.
15. Ibid., 31; Daly 2007.
16. Benthall and Bellion-Jourdan 2003:34.
17. Ibid., 30.
18. Singer 2002.
19. El-Daly 2006.
20. UNDP 2007.
21. United Nations Development Program. (2007). *Business Solutions for Human Development.* Cairo: UNDP.

22. Helpful input at the design stage was provided by Barry Gaberman, former senior vice president of the Ford Foundation, and Mohamed al-Waked, a civil society researcher in Egypt.
23. In Palestine, we were fortunate to identify a local researcher familiar with the CSO landscape. In future rounds of the study, we plan to utilize research teams made up of one local and one regional researcher.
24. Abdel Halim and An-Na'im 2006.25.
26. Benthall and Bellion-Jourdan 2003.
27. Sparre and Petersen 2007.
28. Benthall and Bellion-Jourdan 2003.
29. Abdel Halim and An-Na'im 2006.
30. Daly 2006.
31. Ibid.
32. Khalil 2004.
33. The Indomitable Arab: The Life and Times of Abdulhameed Shoman (1890–1974) Founder of the Arab Bank. London: Third World Centre, 1984, (first edition).
34. Bayat 2007.
35. Ibrahim, 2006. "Strengthening Philanthropy and Civic Engagement in the Arab World: A Mission for the John D. Gerhart Center." Working paper number 1, 2006. The John D. Gerhart Center for Philanthropy and Civic Engagement.
36. CSR Summit in Dubai; UNDP 2007.
37. Prahalad 2006.

References

Abdel Halim, Asma Mohamed, and Abdullahi Ahmed An-Na'im. 2006. "Rights-based Approach to Philanthropy for Social Justice in Islamic Societies," John D. Gerhart Center for Philanthropy and Civic Engagement working paper.

Omar, Mohamed Abdel Halim. 2006. Nizam al-waqf al-islami wa-l-nuzum al-mushabiha fi-l-'alam al-gharbi [endowment—foundation—trust]. Unpublished manuscript.

Bayat, Asef. 2007. *Making Islam Democratic: Social Movements and the Post-Islamist Turn.* Stanford: Stanford University Press.

Benthall, Jonathan. 1999. "Financial Worship: The Quranic Injunction to Almsgiving," *Journal of the Royal Anthropological Institute* 5 (1): 27–43.

Benthall, Jonathan, and Jerome Bellion-Jourdan. 2003. *The Charitable Crescent: Politics of Aid in the Muslim World.* London: I.B. Tauris.

El-Daly, Marwa. 2003. "Private Philanthropy in Egypt: Institutionalized Private Philanthropy as a Mechanism for Sustainable Community Development." MA thesis, American University in Cairo.

El-Daly, Marwa. 2006. *Philanthropy in Egypt: A Comprehensive Study on Local Philanthropy in Egypt and Potentials of Directing Giving and Volunteering Towards Development.* Cairo: Center for Development Studies.

Emara, Nancy Fathy. 2003. "Islam: A Guide for the Perplexed: Study and Evaluation of an Attempt of Application: Alleviating Poverty in Tafahna al-Ashraf." MA thesis, American University in Cairo.

Ibrahim, Barbara Lethem. 2006. "Strengthening Philanthropy and Civic Engagement in the Arab World: A Mission for the John D. Gerhart Center." Working paper number 1. The John D. Gerhart Center for Philanthropy and Civic Engagement.

Khalil, Abdullah. 2004. *A Comparative Guide on Laws Relating to the Establishment of an Arab Fund (Endowment or Cash Deposit) to Extend Financial Support for Social Justice Programs in the Arab Region.* Cairo: Ford Foundation.

Prahalad, C.K. 2006. *The Fortune at the Bottom of the Pyramid: Eradicating Poverty through Profits.* Philadelphia: Wharton School Publishing.

Singer, Amy. 2002. *Constructing Ottoman Beneficence: An Imperial Soup Kitchen in Jerusalem.* Albany: State University of New York Press.

Sparre, Sara Lei, and Marie Juul Petersen. 2007. *Islam and Civil Society: Case Studies from Jordan and Egypt.* Copenhagen: Danish Institute for International Studies.

United Nations Development Programme. 2007. *Business Solutions for Human Development.* Cairo: UNDP.

1

The Arab Republic of Egypt

Mona Atia

Overview

Egypt's historic role as an intellectual center of the Arabic-speaking and Muslim world, its deep-rooted traditions of giving, and the longstanding presence of development organizations in the country make it an important location in which to examine philanthropic trends. As the most populous Arab state, many social trends begin in Egypt, and given its historical position as the Arab world's media provider, it is often considered a benchmark for trends in the region.

As an Arab republic with an approximately 90 percent Muslim population, as well as a sizable Coptic minority, the country grapples with the role of religion in governance. Religious associations are the bedrock of civil society in Egypt and religious motivations play a central role today in the expansion of philanthropic ventures. Secular civil organizations date from the beginning of the twentieth century and have emerged as important building blocks of civil society. The large body of research on civil society in Egypt speaks to various forms of organizations, their successes, and the obstacles they face, as well as to the importance of tensions between Islamic traditions and a secular civil society. The philanthropic sector is a clear example of how these tensions play out but also complement one another. Strategic philanthropy is therefore critical to the long-term improvement of the human condition.

Currently, the philanthropic sector is experiencing a boom. The strong historical legacy and cultural-religious practices of *zakat*, *sadaqa*, and tithes continue to motivate giving. Increasingly, organizations are influenced by international development approaches that emphasize the importance of sustainability. The country has experienced a great deal of change in response to both a religious revival and emerging expressions of social responsibility in the private business sector.

Country Background

Egypt at a Glance

Country size	997,739 sq. km.
Population	71.35 million
GDP (2006) USD	107.9 billion
Agriculture	15%
Industry	36%
Services	50%
GDP per capita (2006) USD	1,489
Unemployment rate (2004)	10%
HDI ranking	111/177; 0.659
Religious groups	Muslim 90%, Coptic 9%, other Christian 1%
1 Egyptian pound (EGP)	USD 0.18

Modern History

The post-colonial period of the late 1950s and 1960s was marked by the expansion of the welfare state to include nationalized universal free education, job guarantees and security for high school and college graduates, healthcare, social housing, rent control, and food subsidies. Major institutions were nationalized in the name of socialism, including banks, insurance companies, basic heavy industries, and public works. In the philanthropic sector, control of *awqaf* property, which had been privately administered for centuries, was placed under the Ministry of Endowments *(Awqaf)* and the Endowment Commission (Hay'at al-Awqaf al-Misriya). The custom of establishing *awqaf* for public purposes had fallen out of favor by the mid-twentieth century, and, after nationalization, the practice nearly disappeared, with no other mechanism for private endowments taking its place. In the early 1960s, the swelling of the public sector accounted for 40 percent of GDP, but by the mid-1960s, Egypt's economy was hit by severe inflation, declining productivity, and depleted national savings as a result of state overspending.[1]

Economic liberalization began in 1968 and continued via the Open Door Policy throughout the 1970s. This policy increased foreign trade and investment, established free-trade zones, encouraged the development of the private sector, and shifted the focus from redistribution to an efficiency and growth-oriented model. At the same time, state systems of education and healthcare became underfunded and overburdened, informal housing and squatter settlements proliferated, and parallel private industries of healthcare and education catered to the growing upper class.

In 1992, Egypt instituted a structural adjustment policy that promoted privatization, extended market logic into social affairs, eliminated many state provisions of social services, reduced the state's role in social service and encouraged the proliferation of civil society organizations (CSOs).[2] Since then, Egypt has embraced neoliberal policies, the immediate effects of which have been increased consumerism, income polarization, growth of the informal economy, and a decline in public infrastructure.[3] Shrinking public services have led low-income Egyptians to increasingly rely on CSOs for social services previously provided by the government.[4] Religiously inspired organizations have grown much more rapidly than those with secular orientations, yet secular organizations receive the majority of international aid. The increase in social services provided by civil society organizations is part of a wider revival of popular religious interest and commitment to social work. This revival can be observed in both Muslim and Christian communities in Egypt.

The Economy

Economic activity, including services and government investment, is concentrated in the north of the country and in major cities like Cairo and Alexandria. Lack of opportunity outside these areas has created substantial rural-urban migration, with the economies of the cities unable to keep pace. The effects of socialist economic policies still reverberate within the economy; the public sector as of 2005/2006 accounted for one-third of gross domestic product. Tourism is Egypt's most important economic sector, employing directly and indirectly some 2.2 million people. The sector's performance, however, tends to fluctuate sharply with national and international political events, such as the bombings in Sinai and the fallout from 9/11. Foreign investment has been plagued by the vagaries of the value of

The Political Scene

Type of Government

Egypt is a republic with a partially democratic governing system based on a constitution passed in 1971. The president serves for a renewable term of six years. The current president is Hosni Mubarak, who was recently elected for a fifth six-year term. The most recent election allowed for contending candidates, but Mubarak garnered 90 percent of the votes, according to post-election statistics. Article 76 of the Constitution (May 2005) requires that prospective presidential candidates either be on the executive board of a political party controlling at least 5 percent of the seats in both houses of Parliament or secure the support of 250 members of parliament and municipal councils.

National Legislature

The People's Assembly (Majlis al-Sha'b or lower house) has 444 directly elected members and 10 additional members nominated by the president, all serving five-year terms. The President has powers to dissolve the Assembly. The Consultative Council (Majlis al-Shura or upper house) has 264 members of whom 176 are directly elected and 88 appointed.

National Government

The Council of Ministers is the highest administrative and executive body managing the state's affairs. The Cabinet is headed by Prime Minister Ahmed Nazif. The president is responsible for appointing and dismissing ministers.

Legal System

The legal system is based on both Islamic law and civil law that draws its origins from the French legal system. Judicial authority is quasi-independent, with judges having some degree of political clout. The government is able to invoke Emergency Law which is able to circumvent potential judicial rulings.

the Egyptian pound, which has achieved some stability in the past few years. The petroleum sector receives a large share of foreign investment, while liberalized privatization measures are now drawing foreign direct investment into industries such as telecommunications, banking, and tourism. Yet, foreign investment figures still lag behind those of more 'successful developing' countries.[5]

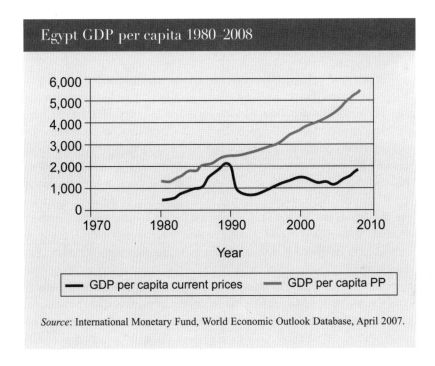

Egypt GDP per capita 1980–2008

GDP per capita current prices — GDP per capita PP

Source: International Monetary Fund, World Economic Outlook Database, April 2007.

GDP per capita has increased but fails to reflect accurately the income disparities that exist within the country. The Gini coefficient, which measures distribution of wealth, is 0.332, pointing to an unequal distribution of both wealth and the benefits of economic growth. Although average GDP per capita was USD 1,488.61 in 2005–06 the richest 20 percent of the population accounts for almost 44 percent of income and consumption, while the poorest 20 percent accounts for approximately 9 percent of income and consumption. Economic growth averaged 4.8 percent between 1998 and 2006 yet appears to benefit primarily the wealthy minority.

Philanthropy in Focus
The Culture of Giving

Egypt has a long history of religiously motivated contributions of individual wealth, with deep roots in both the Muslim and Christian traditions. These include the Muslim giving of *zakat*, which is required of all believers, and voluntary giving, *sadaqa*, which includes the form of *sadaqa jariya*, perpetual giving, which itself includes *waqf*. Christians give in the form of *'ushr*, or tithe, which is traditionally 10 percent of wealth, and are active in volunteerism. A survey conducted by the Center for Development Studies found little difference between Muslim and Christian attitudes toward giving.[6]

Attitudes are changing, however, about the targets of individual philanthropy in Egypt. For at least a decade, groups that include international donors, community activists, and the Egyptian Ministry of Social Solidarity have encouraged CSOs to be more developmental in their activities rather than to operate as charities. Thus, many of Egypt's twenty-two thousand CSOs are moving away from a charity model that relies largely on handouts and direct social service provision and towards a development model that emphasizes sustainability, skill upgrading, and microfinance for the disadvantaged. In a survey conducted by the Center for Development Studies, Marwa Daly found that philanthropy to create jobs was the most valued form of giving and seen especially as the responsibility of the private sector.[7]

In the last few years, successful businessmen or their families, many of whom made their money during the recent era of privatization, have begun to institutionalize their giving through the initiation of foundations *(mu'assasat)*. When asked about their giving, these business owners persistently refer to the social obligation of *takaful*, or social solidarity.[8] Business owners express *takaful* as a religiously inspired proclivity to give back to society and see their *mu'assasat* as part of fulfilling their social responsibility to Egyptian society. In addition, they may benefit financially from this type of philanthropy, as Egyptian law gives fiscal incentives that allow individuals and corporations to deduct donations (up to 10 percent) from their income before calculating taxes.[9]

While these changes are slowly happening, corporate social responsibility (CSR) as an ethos in the private sector is becoming increasingly influential, with strong support coming from multinationals and United Nations agencies. Socially responsible business practices are driven by a variety of motives, including improving public image, minimizing detrimental environmental impact, and improving the attractiveness of employment. This growing movement to involve private business in 'good citizenship' and sustainable forms of economic and social development will add momentum to the shift towards development and institutionalized forms of philanthropy.

While CSR is influencing the ways in which Egyptian businessmen and young people go about their giving, charity remains a strong component of philanthropy. Given its strong roots in religion and the growing needs of a society in transition away from state welfare, charitable giving to the most disadvantaged groups in society will continue to form a strong element of Egyptian philanthropy in the foreseeable future.

The Legal Environment for Philanthropy

The legacy of restrictions on endowments and confiscation of private property has created a major obstacle to institutional giving in Egypt. The *waqf* institution, in particular, has lost its prominence in Egypt over the past forty years as a result of the government's overhaul of the *waqf* system, the enactment of new laws regulating *awqaf*, and the levying of taxes and fees on *awqaf*.[10]

In 1946, under Law 48, a number of legal changes occurred that transformed the governance of *awqaf*. The law set out rules regarding the conditions for the establishment, distribution, supervision, preservation, and dissolution of *waqf*. In subsequent years, numerous revisions were made that continue to impede attempts to revive the *waqf* system in Egypt: Law 180 of 1952 cancelled the family *waqf*; Law 247 of 1953 vested the ministry with the power to modify *waqf* expenditure and supervision; Law 51 of 1958 gave government control of agricultural lands that were *awqaf*; Law 122 of the same year gave the government jurisdiction over expired *waqf*; Law 44 of 1962 moved supervision of buildings and land *waqf* to local governorates; and Law 80 of 1971 established the Egyptian Endowment Authority.

As a result of these legal steps, new *awqaf* have ceased to be established and existing *waqf* revenue has declined (although financial information is difficult to obtain). The family *waqf* is still prohibited by law and, today, many organizations that would plausibly have been established as *waqf* are set up as *mu'assasat*.

There have been calls for a *waqf* comeback in Egypt,[11] modeled after the successful revival of *waqf* in Iran,[12] Turkey,[13] and across the Arab Gulf states of Kuwait, Saudi Arabia, Qatar, and the United Arab Emirates (UAE).

The persistence of government control over *waqf* in Egypt remains a major obstacle. Waqfeyat al-Maadi, discussed below, is a good example of one attempt in Egypt to revive *waqf* as a relevant and sustainable model for funding development projects. The rise of *mu'assasat* is an important response to the decline of *waqf*. It is also a result of legislative restrictions on the operations of private associations and occasional government interventions in their affairs.

Private associations in Egypt are governed by Law 84 of 2002. The main features of the law are: regulations regarding the registration process and tax exempt status; a requirement that organizations notify the ministry of any fundraising efforts and obtain advance approval from the ministry for funds from abroad; and the right of government authorities to investigate board member backgrounds and the financial records of the organization and to abolish organizations that violate restrictions. The law forbids military or political activities, acts that threaten national unity, disrupt public order, or breach ethics, and activities that discriminate among citizens.

Regulations of the law allow organizations to register as either an association *(gam'iya)* or a foundation *(mu'assasat)*. The main differences between the two are that the law requires associations to have ten founding board members while foundations only need three. Foundations are based on the allocation of a fund rather than the presence of a set of members, and regulations regarding annual meetings and general procedures are simpler for foundations. Since the inclusion of foundations as an acceptable form of organization, nearly four hundred foundations have registered with the Ministry of Social Solidarity.

mu'assasat, then, have become the predominant form of institutionalized philanthropic giving in Egypt. Some of these foundations operate as membership associations, but others, such as the Sawiris Foundation, which is described below, are beginning to act in ways that resemble modern foundations. In that regard, the new legislation has been supportive of a shift from informal charity to the development of an institutionalized philanthropic sector.

Institutionalized Philanthropy

Developing a typology of philanthropic institutions in Egypt is a difficult and highly contentious task that continues to spark debate among scholars of Egyptian civil society.[14] For the purposes of this chapter, six 'types' of philanthropic institutions in Egypt have been identified, namely operating foundations, grant-making foundations, religious charities, community foundations, private sector partnership or *shilla* foundations, and corporate grant-making. A seventh type, venture philanthropy, is now emerging. While this is a useful typology for identifying diverse organizations, in reality many organizations have features of more than one type. Classification could be geographically distinct or operationally distinct, but what is clear is that multiple stakeholders are increasingly cooperating to address either a specific cause or a specific area. An explanation of each general type and its organizational structure, roles, and obstacles to success are outlined below, followed by illustrative examples from the Egyptian philanthropic sector.

Operating Foundations

Operating foundations are established with an initial sum of funds to be channeled toward a particular cause. The foundation is directly involved in the provision of services or activities. Funding may come from one family, or contributions may be accepted.

Al-Noor Foundation

Al-Noor is an operating foundation with linkages to the Maghrabi Medical Group. Al-Noor's mission is to alleviate blindness and visual disease and promote healthy eyesight. The foundation is a leader in its field, performing clinical work and service delivery that addresses community needs in ophthalmology. The organization participates in action research, community service, and subsidized services. Its specific objectives are to collect reliable and situational analysis; provide accurate data on eye disease; provide high-level eye-care services to the communities it serves; operate as a model for high-volume, quality, sustainable eye-care services; provide knowledge of eye-care issues to the public; and serve as a national policy advocate.

Al-Noor began engaging in charity work in the mid-1990s and was officially established as a nongovernmental organization (NGO) in 1997. The organization works in close collaboration with the Maghrabi Medical Group, a private sector entity that provides services at market prices. Al-Noor provides the same services at subsidized prices for those who qualify. The administration is the same for both entities, they are serviced by the same staff and same facilities, and their buildings are connected by a bridge.

The donations to establish the organization came from Dr. Akef al-Maghrabi in his capacity as the chief executive officer of the Maghrabi Group Corporation. Currently, the foundation is self-sustaining, with revenues slightly greater than operational costs. In 2005, its projects became self-sustaining. During the start-up phase, al-Noor was successful in leveraging additional funding. The foundation received support from the Kilimanjaro Center and the Canadian International Development Agency (CIDA) during 1999–2002 under the International Trachoma Initiative. The foundation also was funded by USAID, the NGO Service Center, the Ebsar Center for the visually impaired, Osman ibn al-Osman, and the Egyptian NGO Support Center (al-Markaz al-Misri li-Da'm al-Gam'iyat al-Ahliya).

The foundation, which has twelve permanent staff members, is very much a specialized NGO, both structurally and capacity-wise. The foundation believes in networks and evolution of services and activities. Some of its CSO partners include al-Tanweer in Minya, Asdiqa al-amrad in Fayoum, Haya' al-quptaya in Minya, Salama mousa, Gamiyat al-saeed, and Caritas. Although it is an operating foundation, al-Noor is interested in grant-making and would like to share its technical training and capacity building regarding other primary eye-care issues, as well as gender issues.

Grant-Making Foundations

A number of foundations in Egypt make grants to other CSOs working in their areas of focus. Administrators set selection criteria, and processes for applying for support vary based on individual institutional cultures. These organizations often provide support beyond funding, including strategic advice, technological support, consulting services, and feedback.

The Sawiris Foundation

The Sawiris Foundation is thought of as Egypt's first modern family grant-making foundation. Established in April 2001, its goal is to support social development through job creation. The foundation offers grants to intermediary organizations engaged in job training. Cultural and educational work is a secondary goal. The foundation is 'market driven,' tailoring its projects around jobs demanded in the marketplace. The Sawiris Foundation has over forty projects, ranging from healthcare, vocational training, and microfinance/credit, to education and professional development, scholarships, and literacy awards. Its largest projects are in the healthcare sector.

The Sawiris family has been involved in giving for decades. Yousreya Sawiris, an active national advocate on behalf of the poor, played a pivotal role in institutionalizing the family's work. Dr. Ibrahim Shehata, former executive director of the World Bank, helped establish the foundation's bylaws and procedures. The Sawiris Foundation was the first foundation in Egypt to be based on the dedication of corporate shares to endow the foundation. Because of objections from the Ministry of Social Solidarity, however, stemming from the variable value of stocks, the shares were liquidated. The foundation now has a cash endowment. Its board consists of eleven members and an executive committee that meets twice a year.

The foundation's operating procedures are well documented and its model for measuring performance is based on deliverables. Grantees are selected competitively. All the organizations the foundation supports must be registered for a minimum of three years and have the capacity to implement projects successfully and to serve as an intermediary between the foundation, other donors, and the trainees. The foundation emphasizes sustainability, replication and expansion, mainstreaming innovative solutions, and social entrepreneurship.

In addition to funding, the Sawiris Foundation provides its grantees with support in monitoring and supervision, capacity building, technical assistance, and troubleshooting. The foundation is committed to establishing long-term partnerships with different types of institutions, including local CSOs, universities, international organizations, ministries, and local governorates.

Religious Charities

Religious charities are typically registered as associations under Law 84 of 2002. Undoubtedly, some operate without registration, and are therefore difficult to document. Financed largely through individual donations, some organizations also receive governmental support or grants from foundations. Their activities tend to center around supporting orphans and female-headed households and subsidizing medical care for the needy. As part of the shift towards development, many organizations are attempting to include more sustainable projects, such as skills training, but the bulk of their support is in the form of food, clothing, medicine, and care for the poor and disadvantaged.

Al-Orman

The organization began in 1985 and was formalized in 1993 under Ahmed al-Abbany, Dr. Khaled al-Kouri, and Dr. Magdy Badran. Al-Orman is one of the largest and most well-known charities in Egypt, with sixteen chapters across sixteen governorates, covering fifteen thousand projects in Upper Egypt alone. The organization has traditionally focused on orphan care, but it has expanded to include support for cancer victims, microenterprise, *qard hasan* (interest-free loans), and vocational training.

At the end of 2006, al-Orman began developing a philanthropic initiative that involves forty businessmen in eight villages, utilizing a community/joint foundation model in an attempt to have each businessman completely cover the needs of a particular village. Behind the project is a desire to mobilize private sector expertise and provide funding, planning, and supervision from the private sector to help each village improve its standard of living. This project is still in the preliminary phase, but work has begun in the eight villages. The businessmen provide the ideas and donations but are not involved at all in the administration. Al-Orman maintains close relations with the businessmen and the villages, including a monthly strategy meeting for the businessmen. The organization is working in the areas of skill building and upgrading, including training for carpet weavers, potters, and other artisans. The businessmen are financially responsible for a village from beginning to end, covering food procurement, healthcare, literacy, medical treatment, and infrastructure building.

So far, al-Orman has spent EGP 2,965,000 in private sector funding across the eight villages. The projects include four literacy programs, improved production of milk and cheese products, school improvement programs, sewing projects for girl orphans, and medical buses that take patients from their villages to hospitals for medical treatment. The goal is to work in a hundred villages over the next eight to ten years with an overall cost of EGP 150–200 million in private sector funding.

Community Foundations
Community foundations are initiated by multiple donors who pool their financial resources together for a specific purpose, often focused on a particular place. Similar in form to Egypt's community development associations (CDAs) in terms of their focus on a defined geographic area, community foundations attempt to foster solidarity and civic participation within a community by addressing social needs. Community foundations potentially can play a vital role in urban regeneration or rural development.

Al-Maadi Community Foundation (Waqfeyat al-Maadi)
Waqfeyat al-Maadi was established in 2007 with the aim of reviving and modernizing the *waqf* concept as a means of creating a sustainable system for channeling and mobilizing local resources toward development. The foundation was set up by a group of residents of Maadi, a Cairo suburb that houses some of the capital's wealthiest residents. Squatter settlements have sprung up on the outskirts of the suburb. Their inhabitants are mostly employed in the informal sector and barely able to make ends meet. The foundation serves the seven districts of Maadi, as well as several of the settlements.

The work of al-Maadi Community Foundation revolves around four main axes: introducing and promoting the *waqf* model of development as a local mechanism for sustainable development, including implementing nationwide awareness campaigns about *waqf* concepts and modern applications; providing social services in Maadi and its outskirts, either directly or through grants to CSOs; providing facilitation, coordination, and capacity-building services to CSOs and socially responsible businesses; and promoting research and development, and creating access to scientific, practical resources using interactive online technologies (through the development of the *waqfeya* portal) and the existing physical learning resource center on philanthropy, Diwan al-Waqfeya.

The foundation is supported by an endowment to fund its development programs, forge partnerships with CSR initiatives, and collaborate with schools and ministries. In addition to being a foundation, it is an advocacy organization, lobbying and supporting public education for policy change and citizen involvement in the revival of *waqf*.

Private Sector Partnership or *Shilla* Foundations

Shilla, or partnership, foundations are based on a group of individuals committed to a particular cause or vision who pool their financial resources and generally play an active role in the foundation, serving as board members or administrators. These foundations arise largely from the efforts of businessmen whose social or religious convictions stimulate their desire to engage in social work. They apply their private sector expertise to a social issue, and their approach tends to be characterized by a focus on strategic planning and sustainability.

The Egyptian Food Bank (Bank al-Ta'am)

The Egyptian Food Bank began as an initiative of a group of business partners and rapidly grew into a broader community partnership. Because of the essential role of executives from the corporation, Olympic Group, such as Niazi Sallam and Wael Olama, the bank is often associated with that corporate entity. Until B-Tech donated a building, the bank was operating out of the Olympic Group's headquarters in Nasr City in Cairo.

The overall aim of the Egyptian Food Bank is to ensure a more equitable distribution of food among all Egyptians. The foundation started off as an initiative to pack food for the needy during the month of Ramadan, but the "bank" model is being expanded to include vocational training, housing, clothing, and medical care.

The foundation has a staff of fifteen professionals who work under the directorship of Moaz al-Shohdy and whose salaries are paid by sponsorship from businessmen. During the month of Ramadan, several hundred volunteers regularly participate in the packing of food bags, and ninety smaller organizations countrywide help to distribute the bags. Campaign and marketing expenses are covered by other sponsoring companies. Schools, such as Cairo International College and the American International School, are integrating service learning into their curriculum, partly through training students to pack food for the Food Bank.[15]

Additional activities are being taken on by affiliated businesspeople who would like to work together to address broader social issues. They share a centralized information technology unit, a central database for information on partner organizations, equipment, staff, and other infrastructure. Each rents a space on the foundation's new premises and works via organizations spread across more than twenty governorates.

In 2007, the Egyptian Food Bank partnered with United Bank on a coupon campaign for the *Eid al-Adha* lamb sacrifice. One thousand animals were slaughtered in the governorate of Ismailiya, and numerous organizational partners were utilized to create a broad distribution network that benefited from economies of scale. Their target for Ramadan 2008 is to produce ten thousand cartons of food (each carton feeds five people for a month at a cost of roughly EGP 150). New projects include plans to introduce school feeding and soliciting contributions for the cartons through supermarket shoppers.

On the organizational level, Food Bank staff and volunteers are training CSOs in social marketing skills and fundraising. They also are building a social network and expanding their relationships with other businessmen. The board is focusing on institutionalizing its management processes and developing its infrastructure, including expanding its shared database.

Corporate Grant Making

Corporate grants are usually channeled through a unit within a company or a legally registered entity associated with the corporation. In this study, we chose to focus on corporate entities that have actually set up a separate legal entity for giving, thereby demonstrating long-term commitment. These entities contribute to social or environmental causes through in-kind contributions, sponsorship of activities, or grants. The corporation sets aside funds of some kind for this purpose (e.g., a set percentage of profits, shares of the company, or an annual budgetary allocation). Multinational corporations have been the key players in the CSR movement worldwide, although many Egyptian business owners have been involved in similar activities without referring to them as CSR or setting up a distinct business unit to manage their giving.

EFG-Hermes Foundation

The mission of EFG-Hermes Foundation is to help people and institutions overcome the financial, educational, and health-related challenges facing society. The foundation supports innovative and sustainable programs that increase the opportunities for those most in need to make a positive change in their local communities. Established at the end of 2006, the foundation is still in its early stages; however, the corporation has been involved in charity and social responsibility for some time now. The foundation's sole source of funding is the EFG-Hermes Holding Company. Funds are geared toward projects that support sustainable development, and the organization hopes to help those groups that are most in need, encourage social entrepreneurship, and encourage partnerships among various sectors of society. The future plans of the foundation include specializing in poverty alleviation, including a focus on housing, water, sanitation, and income generation.

The EFG-Hermes Foundation has initiated several projects, including a full scholarship program for students pursuing studies that support the foundation's mission. The foundation has allocated EGP 3 million to the United for Children Project: Keeping Children Out of the Streets Initiative. Implemented in partnership with UNICEF, the project seeks to help prevent children from living on the street, while protecting those who are already there. The project also supports the building of a permanent facility in Mokattam for the Young Street Mothers' Shelter, which is the first of its kind in Egypt. An additional EGP 3 million has been set aside to support the Egyptian Paralympics (special needs Olympics) and EGP 450,000 is going towards a paper and graphics center that will engage underprivileged youth in the art of recycled paper making and the graphic arts. The foundation has allocated EGP 250,000 to a Youth Sustainability and Viability Fund aimed at building Egyptian youth civil society by supporting emerging NGOs. In the future, the fund will act as a liaison between youth NGOs and corporate sector specialists.

The foundation also supports two projects in Minya Governorate. The first is being implemented at a cost of EGP 2 million over a three-year period through the Habitat Project and a partnership between the Nazlet Hussein Housing Project and the Better Life Association for Comprehensive Development (BLACD). It involves the provision of loans by BLACD to needy families to construct or rebuild their homes. The second, a water and latrine facilities initiative also implemented in association with BLACD, aims to install water taps and latrines in three thousand homes. The foundation has allocated EGP 500,000 to the project.

Finally, the foundation is working with the Egyptian NGO Nahdet El Mahrousa on a Hepatitis C and blood-borne viruses awareness campaign and combat project at Kasr al-Aini Hospital. It will provide medical equipment and training for nurses and patients in prevention, as well as implement a national television awareness campaign at a cost of EGP 2,092,000 over two years.

Venture Philanthropy

Venture philanthropy has received a great deal of attention in the twenty-first century. A new wave of philanthropic ventures is emerging that borrows from the practice of venture capitalists, seeking to provide funding, technical expertise, and strategic thinking to promising social enterprises with the expectation of results and accountability. Venture Philanthropy Partners (VPP), a philanthropic investment organization, defines venture philanthropy as "the process of adapting strategic investment management practices to the nonprofit sector to build organizations able to generate high social rates of return on their investments."[16] Alfanar Community Foundation is an example of this emerging trend.

Alfanar Community Foundation

Previously known as the Arab Learning Initiative, Alfanar (The Lighthouse) was established by Tarek Ben Halim in the United Kingdom in 2004 and in Egypt in 2005. Alfanar is a nongovernmental, nonprofit venture philanthropy fund that supports innovative civil society organizations in the Arab region with the aim of promoting social change. One of the foundation's long-term goals is to support grassroots organizations in the Arab region that demonstrate an ability to become partially or completely financially sustainable and, as a result, less dependent on donors and more capable of responding to the direct needs of their communities.

Alfanar has adopted a venture philanthropy approach in the sense that it acts as a channel between innovative and promising ideas and available resources from within the region. The organization is pooling financial resources from Arab philanthropists, multinational corporations, and international organizations that have an interest in the region. Alfanar has received funds from the Westminster Foundation for Democracy and Shell. As yet, however, no endowment has been set up.

Alfanar provides grants to organizations seeking to address deep-rooted problems of inequality in a variety of sectors, including, but not limited to, education, health, capacity building, women's empowerment, and human rights. It places a heavy focus on the sustainability of the funded projects. Accordingly, Alfanar adopts a 'hands-on' approach that involves building the capacity of grantee CSOs in the hope that these organizations will move beyond dependency on donor funding. Although it is heavily supported by members of the private sector, Alfanar is an independent organization that is not affiliated to any government or private enterprise.

Alfanar plans to expand throughout the region over the next few years, starting with Morocco in 2008. It has funded six programs in Egypt, one of which is in partnership with the Minya-based Wadi al-Nil Association, an offshoot of the Better Life Foundation. In 2005–2006, Wadi al-Nil set up a revolving credit program to extend loans to quarry owners to enable them to upgrade their machinery, introduce on-site safety measures, and provide workers with protective gear. A feasibility study showed that the planned upgrade would not only create a safer and healthier working environment for the workers but also increase production and, hence, the profitability of the quarry. As the loans are repaid, credit will be extended for the upgrade of other quarries, ensuring the continuation of the cycle and sustainability of the project. Twelve loans have been disbursed to date, with an 85 percent success rate, and another ten loans were scheduled for disbursement in 2007.

Alfanar has four trustees: Tarek Ben Halim, Laila Iskander, Julia Middleton, and Lubna S. Olayan. The foundation has four staff members, three of whom are based in Cairo. The fourth is a trustee and founding member. Alfanar also has a UK-based consultant who works on specific projects. The foundation is hiring a senior-level managing director who will be based in the UK and oversee the expansion of Alfanar into other areas of the region. No project evaluations or impact assessments have yet been conducted, but a monitoring system will be developed for the projects being funded. Currently, regular progress reports are required, and weekly visits are conducted to project sites.

Conclusion

Private philanthropic giving in Egypt is estimated at no less than EGP 5.5 billion annually,[17] and Egyptian philanthropy is experiencing a period of vigorous transformation. The revival of religious benevolence, adaptive government attitudes toward private sector social ventures, expanding national and regional interest in social responsibility, and a conviction that charity needs to be supplemented with sustainable institutions that support development initiatives are just a few of the factors driving institutional philanthropy in Egypt.

Many obstacles remain, however. A lack of trust stemming from the historical legacy of government confiscation of family, community, and other endowments has left many hesitant to participate in institutionalized giving. Egyptians continue to prefer informal channels of giving to institutional forms, largely as a result of a cultural and religious conviction that philanthropy is best given discreetly and without public knowledge. Wariness regarding the motivations behind CSR ventures inhibits the growth of such initiatives. The sector still lacks trusted entities for certifying and developing capacity for philanthropic ventures and ensuring transparency. Self-regulation and a means of providing legitimacy to organizations could help create greater trust. A network of foundations would improve knowledge sharing and thereby strengthen the sector. Finally, public education and an emphasis on best practices could serve to inspire others to emulate these pioneering foundation leaders.

The institutionalization of philanthropy in Egypt will require a serious commitment by the Egyptian government, especially through training and capacity building for the units that oversee *mu'asassat* affairs. This is an emerging area in which a number of government leaders are taking interest. The sector's position should improve over time if government, CSOs, the private sector, and, ultimately, individual donors collaborate to overcome the obstacles. Organizations such as those profiled above signal a healthy diversity and expansion. The Gerhart Center will continue to document and support the development of Egypt's philanthropic sector.

Notes

1. Bayat 2006.
2. Zetter and Hamza 2004.
3. Bayat 2006: 135.
4. Abdelrahman 2005; Clark 2004; Bayat 2003.
5. Data taken from the International Monetary Fund's World Economic Outlook Database, April 2007. Estimates start after 2005.
6. El-Daly, 2007:141.
7. El-Daly, 2006
8. *Takaful* translates as "social solidarity" but today is used in Islamic banking and finance in the sense of Islamic insurance.
9. ICNL 2006. Information about the NGO laws in Egypt and their implementation (2005) retrieved 5/11/2008 from http://www.icnl.org/knowledge/library/showrecords.php?country=Egypt.

10. Omar, Mohamed Abdel Halim. Nizam al-waqf al-islami wa-l-nuzom al-mushabiha fi-l-'alam al-gharbi [endowment—foundation—trust]. Unpublished manuscript.
11. Douara 2007.
12. Documented by Fariba Adelkhah.
13. Documented by Murat Cizakca.
14. See, for example, the work of Amani Kandil, Sara Bin-Nafissa, Maha Abdelrahman, Asef Bayat, Denis Sullivan, and Diane Singerman for different categorizations of the third sector in Egypt.
15. Service learning is a faculty-initiated process by which students are involved in community engagement with explicit learning objects that contribute to their academic understanding, civic development, and personal growth.
16. See Community Wealth Ventures. 2001. *Venture Philanthropy 2001: The Changing Landscape* Washington, D.C.: Venture Philanthropy Partners.
17. El-Daly 2007.

References

Abdelrahman, Maha. 2004. *Civil Society Exposed: The Politics of NGOs in Egypt.* London: I.B. Tauris.
Bayat, Asef. 2002. "Activism and Social Development in the Middle East." *International Journal of Middle East Studies* 34 (1): 1–28.
Bayat, Asef. 2006. "The Political Economy of Social Policy in Egypt." In Massoud Karshenas and Valentine M. Moghadam, ed., *Social Policy in the Middle East: Economic, Political and Gender Dynamics.* Houndmills: Palgrave.
Clark, Janine A. 2004. *Islam, Charity, and Activism: Middle-class Networks and Social Welfare in Egypt, Jordan, and Yemen.* Indianapolis: Indiana University Press.
Community Wealth Ventures. 2001. *Venture Philanthropy 2001: The Changing Landscape.* Washington, D.C.: Venture Philanthropy Partners.
El-Daly, Marwa. 2006. *Philanthropy in Egypt: A Comprehensive Study on Local Philanthropy in Egypt and Potentials of Directing Giving and Volunteering Towards Development.* First edition. Cairo: Center for Development Studies.
Douara, D. 2007. "Philanthropy and Development Conference Presents New Research, Calls for Waqf Revival," *Daily Star Egypt.*
Economist Intelligence Unit. 2007. "Country Profile: Egypt."
Fiani and Partners. 2006. "Egypt Financial Data."
International Center for Not-for-Profit Law (ICNL). 2006. "Information About the NGO Laws in Egypt and Their Implementation 2005." http://www.icnl.org/knowledge/library.
Omar, Mohamed Abdel Halim. 2004. "A Lecture on the Egyptian Awqaf Administrations' Experiences." Presented in Tatarstan, 14 June (Arabic).
United Nations Development Programme. 2005. *Egypt Human Development Report: Choosing Our Future: Towards a New Social Contract.* Cairo: UNDP/Ministry of Planning and Local Development.
United Nations Development Programme. 2006. *Egypt Human Development Report.* Cairo: UNDP. http://www.icnl.org/knowledge/library, retrieved 2008.

Weisman, Steven R. 2005. "Meeting of Muslim Nations Ends in Discord," *New York Times*. 13 November.

Wilson, Rodney. 2006. "Islam and Business," *Thunderbird International Business Review* 48 (1): 109–23.

Zetter, Roger, and Mohamed Hamza, ed. 2004. *Market Economy and Urban Change: Impacts in the Developing World*. London: Earthscan.

2

The Hashemite Kingdom of Jordan

Dina H. Sherif

Overview

The Hashemite Kingdom of Jordan is situated in a regional hotspot, surrounded by Syria to the north, Iraq to the northeast, Saudi Arabia to the east and south, and the West Bank and Israel to the west. This geopolitical position makes the country vulnerable from a security perspective. Jordan has accommodated thousands of Palestinian and Iraqi refugees over the years, a factor that has impacted all aspects of its public life, from politics to the economy to the nature of philanthropic giving.

Unlike many of its neighbors, Jordan is lacking in natural resources. Nevertheless, the country continues to grow and develop. During the reign of His Majesty King Hussein, a conscious effort was made to invest in human resources as the basic wealth of the kingdom. This has continued under Their Majesties King Abdullah II Bin Al Hussein and Queen Rania Al Abdullah, with strong investment in education, social programs, and job creation. Recent economic growth has created an expanded sector of successful entrepreneurs, as well as a growing professional class. Simultaneously, consistent efforts have been made on behalf of the royal family, particularly HM Queen Rania, to encourage the private sector and wealthy individuals to give back to their surrounding communities.

Jordanian culture is founded on tribal and religious-based principles of generosity and giving. While giving was mostly charitable in the past, the modernization of the country coupled with attempts by its citizens to become more competitive in the global arena have led to a transformation in the overall culture of giving. Businesses and wealthy individuals are directing increasing attention to the long-term impact that their contributions will have. As a result, giving has gradually become more institutionalized and strategic.

Country Background

Jordan at a Glance[1]	
Country size	92,300 sq. km.
Population (2006)	5.63 million
National	*93%*
Non-national	*7%*
GDP (2006)	USD 14.3 billion
GDP PPP (2006)	USD 31.2 billion
Services	*68%*
Manufacturing	*19%*
Construction	*5%*
Electricity, gas and water	*3%*
GDP per capita (2006)	USD 2,544
GDP per capita PPP (2006)	USD 5,209
HDI ranking	86/177
Religious groups	Muslim (Sunni) 92%, Christian 6%, Other 2%
1 Jordanian dinar (JOD)	USD 1.41

Modern History

Modern-day Jordan, initially known as Transjordan, was created after the dissolution of the Ottoman Empire in the wake of the Second World War. The country has undergone several border changes and demographic shifts, the greatest of which was a massive influx of Palestinian refugees following the creation of the state of Israel in 1948, and another wave of Palestinian refugees in the 1967 war. Today, an estimated 40 percent of the country's population is of Palestinian descent. Since the beginning of the war in Iraq in 2003, another massive influx of refugees, this time from Iraq, has driven up prices and intensified existing shortages of employment and housing.

The Political Scene

The Hashemite ruling family traces its legitimacy to the descendants of the Prophet Muhammad. Although the 1952 Jordanian constitution effectively left legislation in the hands of an elected parliament, the political turmoil resulting from the 1967 war led to nearly two decades of imposed martial law. During the 1980s, an economic crisis emerged on the heels of high levels of debt and inflation, compromising the ability of the state to provide basic goods and services. Riots in 1989 fueled by the removal of subsidies led to liberalized political policies as a means to mitigate economic hardship. Martial law was lifted in 1991.

The Political Scene

Type of Government
The government is based on a constitutional monarchy. The constitution, which was issued in 1952, provides for a directly elected parliament. Executive authority is vested in the monarch, King Abdullah, and a Council of Ministers headed by a prime minister, currently Nader Thahabi.

National Legislature
The legislature consists of a bicameral National Assembly. The Senate, known as Majlis al-Umma or Majlis al-A'yan (House of Notables) has 40 members appointed by the monarch. The Chamber of Deputies, known as Majlis al-Nuwwab (House of Representatives), is comprised of 110 members elected by popular vote.

Legal System
The legal system is based on Islamic and French codes, with judicial review of legislative acts occurring in a special High Tribunal. The constitution provides for three categories of courts: civil courts, religious courts, and special courts.

National elections were last held at the end of 2007. Opposition groups such as the Islamic Action Front (IAF), the political arm of the Muslim Brotherhood in Jordan, have agreed to ease efforts to mobilize public opinion against Jordan's pro-United States alignment in return for economic progress, limited freedom of expression, and the right to political participation.[2]

The issue of political participation has been contentious since a 2007 law was passed that weakened smaller parties and lent support to fewer but stronger ones. The law promises annual government funding, the establishment of individual media outlets without prior permission, and a reduction in the number of founding members required from five hundred to two hundred and fifty. Political parties fall under the jurisdiction of the Ministry of the Interior. They are not allowed to obtain funds from professional associations, charities, or religious groups.[3]

The Economy

Classified as a low- to middle-income country by international standards, Jordan boasts one of the highest per capita disposable incomes among emerging nations in the sub-region. Despite its location in the crossfire of several regional political conflicts over the last fifty years, the kingdom's ability to maintain social and political stability within its borders has translated into a relatively stable economy. This economic stability stems in part from the country's high levels of unilateral transfers in the form of workers' remittances and donor grants. While the internal political atmosphere may encourage growth, external political turmoil, such as the increasing number of refugees turning to Jordan, has complicated the country's efforts at sustainable growth and contributed to some of Jordan's major social, political, and economic challenges.

Jordan suffers from insufficient supplies of water, oil, and other natural resources. Because of the ongoing war in Iraq—traditionally the kingdom's main oil supplier—the Jordanian government has had to remove subsidies on oil prices and increase the sales tax base, as well as turn to other Gulf nations for petroleum resources. Jordan's export market, similarly dependent on the Iraqi economy, has been affected by the war but has recovered somewhat through contributions to the Iraq recovery effort. Lack of water continues to present a serious challenge to Jordan's future economic growth; increasing the water supply and better management and conservation are highest policy priorities.

Despite a mild recession in 2003, the Jordanian economy continues to perform steadily. Net flows of foreign direct investment reached USD 801 million in 2000, but then decreased to USD 620.3 million in 2004 because of the country's proximity to the Iraqi war zone.[4]

Recently, Jordan has seen an increase in Arab investments, with companies like the United Arab Emirates-based Emaar investing heavily in construction. In addition, the government has been trying actively to promote free trade by establishing 'free zones' like the Aqaba Special Economic Zone, which was established in 2007 using Dubai's free zones as a model. Considering all the outside forces affecting the economy, Jordan has managed to achieve positive growth in its gross domestic product per capita.

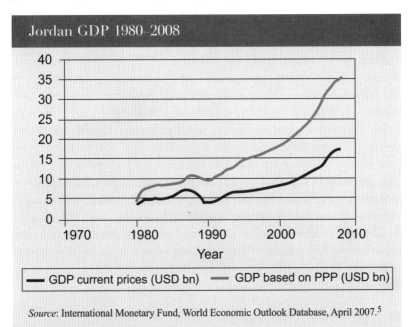

Source: International Monetary Fund, World Economic Outlook Database, April 2007.[5]

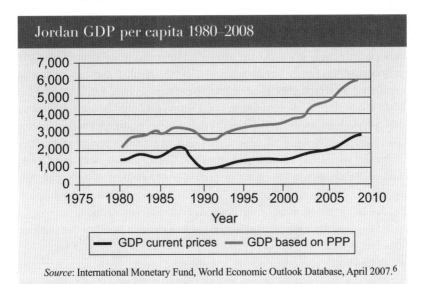

Source: International Monetary Fund, World Economic Outlook Database, April 2007.[6]

Since assuming the throne in 1999, HM King Abdullah has enacted sweeping economic reforms in an effort to improve living standards and alleviate poverty, unemployment, and inflation. In 2002, Jordan completed its most recent International Monetary Fund (IMF) program and continues to follow IMF guidelines on monetary policy with substantial headway in the area of privatization. Liberalized trade measures secured Jordan membership in the World Trade Organization (WTO) in 2000, a free-trade accord with the United States in 2001, and an association agreement with the European Union in 2001. Its other efforts include improvements to commercial laws, reforming financial and capital markets, greater support for small and medium-sized businesses, and strengthening the information and communications technology sector. These measures have helped improve productivity and have created more opportunities for foreign investment. Yet, Jordan still faces major economic challenges, such as reducing its dependence on foreign grants, reducing the budget deficit, and attracting more investment to promote job creation.

The national vision involves galvanizing the young population of Jordan, transforming the kingdom into a modern knowledge-based economy, enhancing human capital, eliminating poverty, and modernizing the country's economic, institutional, and political infrastructure.

Philanthropy in Focus
The Culture of Giving

Philanthropy and social causes receive exceptional attention from the royal family in Jordan. According to Her Royal Highness Princess Haya Bint Al Hussein, giving is a way of life strongly integrated into the upbringing of members of the Hashemite family, most of whom adopt their own cause in adulthood to which they systematically contribute time and energy. They often see their role as one of catalyzing action and mobilizing funds rather than serving primarily as a financial donor. This tradition evolved during the reign of HM King Hussein Bin Talal, when the siblings established important social and cultural programs and Their Majesties the late Queen Alia and Queen Noor Al Hussein each actively dedicated their time and energy to the development of Jordan. For example, Queen Noor spearheaded the establishment of the Noor Al Hussein Foundation.

HM Queen Rania has introduced a new approach that involves engaging the private sector as a strategic partner for social change. Her programs build upon the country's tradition of social work and charitable activities, while encouraging more systemic and sustainable development.

According to HM Queen Rania, who views the investment of time as equally important to the investment of money, philanthropy should be "ingrained" into the culture and taught as part of the basic socialization of all youth.[7]

An important aspect of Jordan's culture of giving is the system of associations widely known as royal nongovernmental organizations (RNGOs). The royal family traditionally has seen one of its roles as providing models for institutionalized social welfare, where individual members of the Hashemite family have lent their name and involvement to associations in support of culture, healthcare, education, and general social development. RNGOs in Jordan have made attempts recently to move beyond the model of operating NGOs surviving on grants from the international donor community. These organizations are gradually transforming into entrepreneurial, asset-bearing, and grant-giving institutions. RNGOs encountered throughout the research for this study, such as the Jordan River Foundation (JRF) and the Noor Al Hussein Foundation, described below, have negotiated endowment funds from bilateral donors. In the case of JRF, for example, the funds are supplemented by contributions from the corporate sector and from individual philanthropists.

Increased liberalization of the economy has resulted in increased wealth for the business and entrepreneurial class, an overall rise in local small and medium-sized enterprises, and a process of graduation for some companies into large-scale businesses. While the increasing gap between rich and poor could be criticized, the growth and affluence of the Jordanian private sector has been accompanied by higher levels of commitment to social responsibility. Just as the government has supported private sector growth, it also has pushed for private sector involvement in the resolution of basic social problems.

Until recently, private sector involvement in social issues took the form of giving that was, by and large, charitable in nature. Typically, the corporate sector became 'grant givers' in response to worthy requests from the surrounding community. Although unquestionably laudable, such attempts could be labeled more reactive than proactive. A company would receive a grant proposal from an NGO and issue a check in response. While the private sector was responsive to the financial needs of members of civil society, corporate social responsibility (CSR) was not formally integrated as a corporate policy per se.

Recently, members of the private sector have begun to see themselves not only as providers of financial resources but also as partners in the development process, offering skills and business acumen in addition to funds. Likewise, some wealthy individuals are less likely to give only to charitable causes, preferring to invest in development projects that are longer term and more sustainable.[8] Because of this, Jordan is experiencing an increase in private foundations, in the provision of expertise in addition to money, and in the establishment of public-private partnerships that have as their target public policy reform.

On the whole, the culture of giving in Jordan, like its geopolitical status, is complex and in transition. While more traditional forms of charity continue to exist, clear evidence has emerged that giving in Jordan is becoming more strategic and geared toward societal change.

The Legal Environment for Philanthropy

All forms of group work and collective action in Jordan must be registered with a ministry, which is charged with reporting and inspecting collective activities within its administrative purview.[9] According to Law 33 of 1966, charitable associations fall under the supervision of the Ministry of Social Affairs, while social and professional associations come under the supervision of the Minister of Interior. The procedures and bylaws of both secular and religious associations must be approved in advance by the relevant administrative authority, which may accept or reject the application for incorporation. An association that is not religiously affiliated must obtain prior permission from the designated administrative authority to receive and distribute funds and/or grants. The designated authority has the right to dissolve any association.

Religious organizations and congregations must obtain prior permission from the corresponding minister to make any amendment to their services. The minister of the interior has the authority to dissolve these organizations, which in fact has happened in the past. Generally, religious organizations must follow the same guidelines as nonreligious associations, but they enjoy more freedom in receiving and distributing funds, offering grants, and giving aid to the poor and needy. Charitable associations, social, ordinary, and religious organizations, and congregations are governed by the Donation Raising Act of 1957 and Social Aid Wills Act 14 of 1959. New regulations are currently being drafted.

According to Income Tax Law 57 of 1985, as amended, donations offered to ordinary and charitable associations and social organizations enjoy limited tax exemption. These provisions do not seem to be widely understood and currently do not act as a significant incentive for giving.

Foreign associations are allowed to operate, but they abide by the same rules and regulations as native associations within the Jordanian Associations Act.[10]

Institutionalized Philanthropy

The overall institutionalized culture of giving in Jordan can be divided broadly into four main categories: 1) family foundations built on the independent wealth of a family or family business; 2) community foundations built on the pooling of wide-scale resources from the community; 3) RNGOs with a philanthropic arm; and 4) corporate-led philanthropy. We also are seeing the emergence of a fifth type, namely *shilla*-based foundations, which are built on the pooling together of financial resources by a number of individuals.

Family Foundations[11]

Many of Jordan's philanthropic institutions are endowed in the name of a family or a family member. These foundations might offer grants and technical assistance to organizations in Jordan or in the region in support of a particular cause to which they are dedicated. They also might initiate and manage their own programs, either singly or in partnership with other entities. The examples provided below are of grant-making foundations.

The Abdul Hameed Shoman Foundation

The Abdul Hameed Shoman Foundation (AHSF) was founded in 1978 by Abdul Maguid Shoman, son of Abdul Hameed Shoman, the founder of the Arab Bank. It is one of the oldest modern institutionalized philanthropies in the Arab region and the oldest in Jordan. The foundation is financially supported by the Arab Bank, which allocates 3 percent of its annual profits to the running of the foundation and its activities. While the foundation was established to honor the legacy of an outstanding Arab entrepreneur, the corporate profits providing sustained annual funding also places it in the category of corporate foundation.

The mission of AHSF is to support and enhance scientific research and Arab humanistic creativity, build bridges of dialogue and cultural communication, and collect and disseminate general knowledge in conformity with the grand vision of the late Abdul Hameed Shoman, who believed that "money is useless without knowledge and information."[12] The foundation's objectives include developing Arab scientific research with a focus on natural, basic, applied, and technological science and building the capacity of

Arab scientists to become experts and scholars in their fields, in addition to developing the capabilities of Arab intellectuals, educators, and creative thinkers at large. Some of the foundation's activities include:

- Supporting Jordanian universities and their scientific institutions in conducting research
- Contributing to various conferences and scientific seminars in Jordan and the Arab world
- Providing annual monetary contributions to scientific institutions, associations, and assemblies in Jordan and the Arab region
- Giving annual awards to Arab scientists who have demonstrated excellence in their field
- Giving annual awards to inspirational science teachers in primary and secondary schools in Jordan
- Establishing libraries throughout Jordan
- Offering a weekly lecture series on key issues related to the preservation of Arab culture and the promotion of science and technology

AHSF is a clear example of philanthropy that is focused, sustained, and institutionalized. The foundation has had clear impact in areas such as promoting and supporting research (specifically among Arab youth) and in promoting dialogue on important issues facing the region. Having been in operation for three decades, the foundation would benefit from an assessment of its impact on the fields of science and culture in order to encapsulate and highlight the fruits of its labor. In addition, foundations like AHSF would benefit from networking with others in the same field in order to exchange best practices and think more strategically about collaboratively addressing core problems.

Eliah Nuqul Foundation

Eliah Nuqul, the founder of the Jordan-based Nuqul Group, established his company from the bottom up in 1952. The company currently is being run by his first-generation descendants, who recently established the Eliah Nuqul Foundation with the aim of giving back to society in a manner that would lead to long-term and effective social change. As with the Abdul Hameed Shoman Foundation, Ghassan Nuqul named the foundation after his father to preserve and honor the family name, and the Nuqul Group, like the Arab Bank, will allocate 1 percent of its annual profits to the foundation.

The foundation, which is in the process of being legally registered, will focus on the education and healthcare sectors. The Nuqul family has decided to begin its activities in Jordan and slowly expand to the Arab region. Unlike many other initiatives in the region, the Eliah Nuqul Foundation will not be an operating foundation but rather will adopt a 'venture philanthropy' approach. Its goal is to add value to new and already existing initiatives as an involved partner by providing financing coupled with intensive management and other technical support, as needed.[13]

Community Foundations

Community foundations are initiated by multiple donors who pool their financial resources together for a finite purpose. This type of philanthropy attempts to foster solidarity and civic participation within a community by addressing specific needs.[14] The King Hussein Foundation and Tkiyet Um Ali are two relevant examples of community foundations in Jordan.

The King Hussein Cancer Foundation

The King Hussein Cancer Foundation (KHCF) was launched in 1997 by royal decree with the mission of combating cancer in Jordan and the Middle East. The foundation acts as a financial umbrella for the King Hussein Cancer Center, the foundation's medical arm and the only specialized cancer center in the Middle East that treats both adult and pediatric cases.

The foundation is run by a board of trustees composed of prominent members of the community and chaired by Her Royal Highness Princess Ghida Talal. The director of the foundation is Her Royal Highness Princess Dina Mired. The Cancer Center is guided by an international advisory board of nineteen healthcare practitioners and specialists from Europe and North America. The center also has forged partnerships and agreements with the National Cancer Institute of the United States (NCI) and St. Jude Children's Research Hospital (located in Nashville, Tennessee) to help guide their work and provide required expertise. The Cancer Center's main activities are:

- Comprehensive Cancer Care Services: In addition to medical treatment, the center provides services that cater to the physical, emotional, social, and environmental needs of patients, including therapy programs, survivor groups, physical rehabilitation, and the services of a specialized nutritionist.
- Education, training, and public awareness: The center offers fellowships and training programs in all fields of cancer specialization, and

has its own medical library. A hospital-based registry collects information about patients treated in the center with the aim of eventually setting up a database of patient demographics. The center also conducts awareness-raising campaigns throughout Jordan on prevention/control of cancer, as well as its early detection. It operates a toll-free hotline for those with questions on cancer prevention, detection, or treatment.

• Clinical research: Through its partnerships with international institutions, the center aims to carry out research on the more effective treatment of cancer patients. Resources have not yet been heavily invested in this initiative, but it is a priority for the foundation.

KHCF's main source of funding is contributions from the general public and the private sector. The foundation encourages donations from the public through its *zakat* fund and other fundraising mechanisms, such as coin collection boxes placed throughout the country and cell phone (SMS) campaigns. According to HRH Princess Dina Mired, the foundation has been successful in its fundraising campaigns not only because it is the only organization in Jordan that raises funds solely for cancer but also because the Jordanian community has come to realize that "everyone is poor in the face of cancer,"[15] and that KHCF can and has made a difference to those faced with the disease. The foundation hopes to extend its activities beyond Jordan if it is financially sustainable.[16] Senior managers realize that they cannot rely solely on community-based fundraising to achieve long-term sustainability and that the foundation will need an endowment fund to support it and, by default, the Cancer Center.

While KHCF is widely classified as an RNGO in Jordan, it actually functions as a large-scale community foundation, where multiple donors and individuals from the local community pool their resources together in support of a delimited cause—in this case, cancer treatment. For the purposes of this study, KHCF serves as a model of how royal patronage can leverage broader community involvement, and how such foundations can strategically contribute to a cause in a way that leads to long-term social impact and change.

Tkiyet Um Ali

The first initiative of its kind in Jordan, and comparable, on many levels, to the Egyptian Food Bank (Bank al-Ta'am) initiative, Tkiyet Um Ali was established by HRH Princess Haya Bint Al Hussein with a mission "to feed and sustain underprivileged citizens who would otherwise go without, through the collection of food and funds from local and regional contributions." In addition, Tkiyet Um Ali guides needy individuals and families to supportive social relief programs that offer more sustainable assistance, with the ultimate aim of allowing them to become "happier and more productive members of a society that proves it cares."[17] HRH Princess Haya established the *tkiyet* to fulfill a lifelong ambition of her mother, HM the late Queen Alia al-Hussein, to eradicate hunger problems in Jordan.[18] According to HRH Princess Haya, one of the biggest victories achieved by Tkiyet Um Ali thus far has been for "Jordanian people to acknowledge that there is indeed a hunger problem in Jordan that needs to be systematically addressed."[19] The *tkiyet* is named after HM the late Queen Alia, who had tried to draw attention to the issue long before her death.

The concept of the *tkiyet* is inspired by an Islamic concept of providing for the poor. Dating back to the eleventh century, it began as an adjunct to the mosque, where the Sufi mystics devoted themselves to the contemplation of God, forsaking all worldly possessions. Over the centuries, some of the most prominent families in the Arab and Ottoman world maintained *tkiyet*s, underlining the inherent closeness between the adoration of God and the extension of charity to the needy.[20]

The physical infrastructure of the *tkiyet* is much like that of the soup kitchens found across the United States. It contains meeting places, eating quarters, kitchen facilities, and shower areas, in addition to warehouse and storage areas. In order to take the initiative of the *tkiyet* beyond charity and towards social change and development, Tkiyet Um Ali does not stop at feeding the hungry; it houses counseling offices that document and follow up the hunger cases they encounter and help each citizen find long-term solutions to poverty and hunger. Tkiyet Um Ali has established several long-term partnerships with other local NGOs dedicated to enhancing the long-term livelihood of Jordanian citizens.

As with the KHCF, many would categorize Tkiyet Um Ali as an RNGO. For the purposes of this study, the *tkiyet* exemplifies the institutionalization of individual private philanthropy. HRH Princess Haya donated USD 3 million to the organization: USD 1 million in the form of an endowment fund to cover operating costs and USD 2 million as seed money for the organization's activities. The fund has grown over time and now also qualifies as a community foundation. The *tkiyet* continues to grow and expand based on widespread contributions from the Jordanian community and private sector.

RNGOs with a Philanthropic Arm

A number of RNGOs have made the transition from grant-seeking institutions to providing financial support to other organizations. Awareness regarding the importance of achieving financial sustainability by establishing endowment funds and increasing private sector involvement has pushed a number of organizations to slowly become asset bearing and grant giving, which has enabled them to have a higher impact on their surrounding communities.

The Jordan River Foundation

The JRF was established in 1995 and is registered as a nonprofit, nongovernmental organization. Chaired by HM Queen Rania Al Abdullah, it was launched with a vision to promote, in partnership with stakeholders, the development of a dynamic Jordanian society by initiating and supporting sustainable social, economic, and cultural programs that empower communities and individuals based on their needs and priorities. JRF's two main areas of concentration are: 1) protecting the rights and needs of children; and 2) empowering individuals and communities. According to HM Queen Rania, today, JRF "is providing thousands of people with the tools to make the most of their own potential—from women reviving traditional weaving skills to young men learning management and administration skills at beekeeping projects in the south of Jordan."[21] Some of JRF's key activities and programs include:

- Prevention and training activities for local and rural communities through the Queen Rania Family and Child Center (QRFCC)
- Development of training manuals and programs related to child protection, serving as a model for the Arab region
- The Community Empowerment Program (CEP), which provides local community members with economic opportunities to improve the livelihoods of their family members and communities
- Income-generating initiatives such as handicrafts, ecotourism, agri culture, animal husbandry, water management, and dairy production
- The Jordan River Children Program (JRCP), which involves strengthening the family unit through enhancing positive child-parent relationships and promoting positive family dynamics
- The Child Safety Program (CSP), which creates awareness, prevention, and intervention services for tackling child abuse.

Like the King Hussein Cancer Foundation, JRF currently has an endowment fund of USD 3 million. Made up essentially of USAID-allocated funds that were transferred by the government to the foundation, the endowment fund is being expanded through donations from the corporate sector and individual philanthropists. JRF is currently giving out small grants to other NGOs in Jordan and has been working with organizations regionally to transfer the expertise it has acquired. Recently, JRF became a member of the newly established Arab Foundations Forum (AFF), a regional network of asset- bearing and grant-giving philanthropic institutions.

The King Hussein and Noor Al Hussein Foundations

The King Hussein Foundation (KHF) is a nonprofit, nongovernmental organization that serves as an enduring commitment to King Hussein's humanitarian vision and legacy. KHF seeks to foster peace, sustainable development, and cross-cultural understanding through programs that promote education and leadership, sustainable community development, peace, and democracy.

The Noor Al Hussein Foundation (NHF), which falls under the umbrella of the King Hussein Foundation, was established in 1985 to help improve the overall quality of life of Jordanians by responding to their diverse socioeconomic needs; introducing innovative, dynamic, and sustainable development models; and setting national and regional standards of excellence. The principal areas of NHF activity are community development, women empowerment, microfinance, family health, and culture and arts. Affiliated programs for both organizations include:

- Education and leadership programs
- Community development programs
- Microfinance and income-generating programs
- Family health programs
- Culture and arts programs

Like JRF, KHF/NHF also has established an endowment fund of JOD 5 million. According to Hana Shahin, the director of NHF, the foundation is putting effort into becoming financially sustainable and is slowly moving in the direction of giving grants to other local organizations. In order to become completely financially sustainable, the foundations will, of course, need to expand their endowment.

Corporate Philanthropy

Corporate philanthropy and CSR are gaining in popularity in Jordan, and we can expect rapid growth in these areas in the coming months and years. As with other countries in the Arab region, CSR is still in its early stages of implementation in Jordan. Corporate philanthropy, where companies donate their assets or volunteer time for worthy projects, is more prevalent. Examples include the Nuqul Group, Zain (previously known as Fastlink), and Aramex.

Nuqul Group

Nuqul Group's corporate philanthropy strategy is to maintain the group's support of local communities in the areas of education, healthcare, and socioeconomic development in general by assisting associations that target those in need in a sustainable and systematic way. The Nuqul Group supported the 2004 Ministry of Social Development national campaign to provide food to impoverished families in the month of Ramadan in the southern, northern, and central areas of the kingdom. The group also has provided in-kind assistance and financial support to a school and village in Zarqa (northern Amman). During 2006–2007, it supported a campaign implemented by Tkiyet Um Ali under the supervision and guidance of the Ministry of Education to feed schoolchildren in impoverished areas of the country.

Nuqul Group is a classic example of how the private sector in Jordan is moving from charity to philanthropy. It gradually has begun to give more attention to social investments that lead to long-term social change. This shift was clearly reflected in the group's 2007 CSR strategy, which dedicated corporate giving to the integrated sustainable upgrade of al-Koura village in northern Jordan. This initiative is being implemented in partnership with the Jordan Hashemite Fund for Human Development (JOHUD), which is chaired by Her Royal Highness Princess Basma Bin Talal.

Zain (Fastlink)

Zain, which previously was known as Fastlink, is a mobile telecommunications company that is a leading 'social investor' in Jordan. The company's social investment/CSR strategies are based on perceived community needs and implemented in collaboration with the public and in partnership with well-established NGOs. As a company, it has strategically invested its funds, staff time, and expertise in sectors such as education, healthcare, and income generation. Zain has supported initiatives such as the Jordan Education Initiative and the recently launched Jordan Children's Museum. According to

Director of Communications Suzanne Afaneh, Zain's giving is proactive rather than reactive, which enables it to give attention to the impact of its giving. The company has one of the highest levels of employee volunteerism in Jordan, as well as employee financial contribution to company-supported initiatives. According to Afaneh, one of the things its employees are most proud of is the impact the company has on Jordan's social development.

Aramex

Aramex is one of the world's leading total transportation and logistics solution providers. The company offers an excellent example of corporate philanthropy transitioning into broader CSR. Aramex has committed to allocating 1 percent of its pre-tax profits to its global corporate philanthropy initiatives, including those in Jordan. In 2006, Aramex released its first corporate sustainability report—the first of its kind in the Arab world—in a forum entitled "Changing Today, Protecting Tomorrow."

Community empowerment and sustainable community development are at the heart of Aramex's corporate philanthropy strategy, as is reflected in the vital role the company has played in the establishment and support of Ruwwad (described below). While Aramex's efforts are planned with the entire community in mind, the company has concentrated on underprivileged areas where unmet needs exist. Aramex is concerned with the division between economically developed and developing nations, and the marginalization of the underprivileged across all countries and cities where the company operates, which, ultimately, directly impacts its business. It is with this in mind that Aramex focuses on the following key areas:

- Youth development, with a focus on youth empowerment;
- Sustainable community development, with a focus on marginalized communities; and
- Emergency and disaster relief, as well as responding rapidly to devastating natural and human disasters.

In addition to the abovementioned activities, Aramex has been a long-time supporter of sports in Jordan, sponsoring a professional basketball team and major sports tournaments. As part of an initiative to turn Amman into a child-friendly city, Aramex has supported a project to create new sports playgrounds or develop existing ones in underprivileged urban communities. Aramex is broadening its efforts in the region and now in the process of socially investing its money in urban poor areas in Cairo, Egypt. It also plans to invest in other poor countries in the region.

Shilla-based Philanthropy

Shilla-based philanthropy, where a group of individuals committed to a particular cause or vision pool their resources in support of that cause, is new in Jordan. Ruwwad is the first example of its kind to be institutionalized in the country. It is funded solely by local individuals and companies from the private sector and is strategic in its approach.

One attractive aspect of this model of philanthropy is that it provides a forum through which like-minded individuals and companies who may not have the inclination or the resources to spearhead an initiative on their own can pool their resources together. Ruwwad is a good example of how the private and public sectors can partner to resolve social problems in an efficient and effective manner.

Ruwwad

Spearheaded by Aramex in 2006, Ruwwad is registered as a nonprofit company with an operational office based in Jabal Natheef, the organization's first target area.[22]

Aramex has committed a minimum of USD 200,000 for five years beginning in 2006, which gives the company a 20-percent stake in Ruwwad.

The idea behind the creation of Ruwwad is to adopt a poor and marginalized area that is densely populated and work closely with the local community to define and solve its problems. Ruwwad provides the resources, support, and training required to holistically develop a targeted community, while at the same time involving local community members in every step of the process. As an organization, Ruwwad operates on values of empowerment, responsibility, and inclusiveness. Participation in Ruwwad is open to members of various ethnic and religious backgrounds. Ruwwad believes in establishing a partnership with the community in order to provide a platform for change and development. The company works with community members to identify their needs and the solutions and tools required to solve the problems they face. The implementation process is the result of this partnership.

Through its projects, Ruwwad is introducing innovative teaching methods in education and providing support to local schools through renovations, teacher training, and extracurricular activities for students. Ruwwad also offers 250 scholarships to students from Jabal Natheef and neighboring communities, and organizes training programs, employment opportunities, internships, opportunities for volunteerism, and support for social and business entrepreneurship. In addition to its focus on education, Ruwwad helps community members renovate their houses and living spaces; raises awareness of community needs and legal rights; assists the elderly in overcoming bureaucratic obstacles related to healthcare; and supports community members in developing income-generating projects.

Ruwwad's Web site provides a channel for cash or in-kind contributions from businesses and individuals in Jordan's private sector. Ruwwad's policy is to accept only private local money. According to Fadi Ghandour, chief executive officer of Aramex and chairman of Ruwwad's board, he and his colleagues "just want to give back to their surrounding communities."[23] They also believe that it is their duty as citizens and as part of this community to strategically invest in the most important resource Jordan has—its people. Since its inception, Ruwwad's efforts have led to measurable improvements in the community of Jabal Natheef, not only because of the sustained involvement of its private sector founders but also because Ruwwad has actively partnered with government, lobbying to provide the community with necessary public services, such as a post office, a police station, and a health center.

While Ruwwad does not have an endowment, all its board members are committed to allocating annual funds to the organization to ensure its financial sustainability. At the time of this study, an endowment fund was being explored. Spurring that discussion is the desire to find ways of duplicating the Ruwwad model elsewhere in the Arab region.

Conclusion

Although Jordan is not a wealthy country by world standards, the philanthropic sector in the country is thriving and the private sector is fully engaged. Private philanthropic giving in Jordan has grown into a multi-million-dollar industry, one that is undergoing a vigorous transformation. The institutionalization of philanthropy in Jordan is rapidly increasing, with many philanthropists thinking in terms of long-term social change as opposed to charitable giving. Even with the positive change in Jordan's philanthropic landscape, says HM Queen Rania, "there is still much to be done if we want to increase the return on social investments. We need to scale up existing initiatives . . . work in new communities . . . encourage other private sector companies and individual philanthropists to come on board . . . and we must strengthen the management of NGOs, and insist that they report openly on their performance and impact, showcasing their setbacks and successes."[24]

The further institutionalization of philanthropy in Jordan will require dedicated commitment not only by the private sector and wealthy individuals but also by government and civil society. Jordan's philanthropic scene has room for expansion, but the sector will only continue to grow if all stakeholders work together collaboratively and transparently.

Notes

1. Gross domestic product and population figures taken from International Monetary Fund (IMF) data and the Economist Intelligence Unit's country profile of Jordan. GDP estimates begin after 2005, based on existing IMF data. The human development index (HDI) is derived from United Nations development reports and is a measure of life expectancy, literacy education, and standard of living. GDP purchasing power parity is denoted by 'PPP' to reflect the weight of GDP in relation to the purchasing power of other countries. The population and religion breakdown is from NationMaster.com and from Jordan's Department of Statistics 2004 population and housing census.
2. Freedom House 2007.
3. Economist Intelligence Unit 2007:13.
4. Based on World Bank data.
5. Estimates start after 2005.
6. Estimates start after 2005.
7. Personal interview with HM Queen Rania Al Abdullah, Amman, December 3, 2007.
8. As mentioned earlier, this shift occurred as a result of increased support from the royal family for the private sector to be a 'partner' in development, as well as a need on the part of the private sector to see clear results emerging from its giving. The Nuqul Group, which traditionally has been very reactive in its giving, is a clear example. Recently, it has chosen to partner with the Jordan Hashemite Fund for Human Development (JOHUD) to further develop a poor settlement in Jordan.
9. Wiktorowicz 2000: 49.
10. Khalil 2004:15–16.
11. It is important to note that the family foundations described here also can be categorized as corporate foundations because they are financially supported by funds coming from the family business. For the purposes of the study, these foundations have been listed as family foundations because they were established by a family in the name of a family member with a family legacy in mind.
12. Personal interview with Thabet al-Taher, managing director of the Abdul Hameed Shoman Foundation, Amman, March 2007.
13. All of the information here was derived from a personal interview with Ghassan E. Nuqul, vice chairman of the Nuqul Group, Amman, March 2007.
14. Definition derived from Egypt chapter by Mona Atia
15. Personal interview with HH Princess Dina Mired, director of the King Hussein Cancer Foundation, Amman, Jordan, November 2007.

16. It should be noted that, like a number of RNGOs, KHCF has a temporary endowment fund in the form of a cash transfer from USAID. This amount of money is allocated to the foundation for five years, and the foundation is able to make use of the interest coming out of the fund to support its activities and cover its operating costs.
17. Mission statement taken from the official Web site of HRH Princess Haya Bint Al Hussein, http://www.princesshaya.net.
18. Personal interview with HRH Princess Haya Bint Al Hussein, Dubai, UAE, October 2007.
19. Ibid.
20. For more details, refer to http://www.princesshaya.net.
21. Personal interview with HM Queen Rania Al Abdullah, Amman December 3, 2007.
22. Ruwwad is registered as a nonprofit company, as opposed to a foundation or NGO, so it is not constrained by the rules and regulations of the Ministry of Social Affairs. The legal framework governing organizations that are not affiliated to the royal family does not allow flexibility in regard to the allocation and dissemination of private sector wealth. A number of philanthropists in Jordan who are thinking about establishing foundations or who have established a foundation, such as the Nuqul family, are following the same path of registering as a nonprofit organization.
23. Personal interview with Fadi Ghandour, CEO of Aramex, Amman, Jordan, March 2007.
24. Personal interview with HM Queen Rania Al Abdullah, Amman, Jordan, December 3, 2007.

References

Economist Intelligence Unit. 2007. "Country Report: Jordan."
Freedom House. 2007. "Freedom in the World: Jordan."
Khalil, Abdullah. 2004. *A Comparative Guide on Laws Relating to the Establishment of an Arab Fund (Endowment or Cash Deposit) to Extend Financial Support for Social Justice Programs in the Arab Region*. Cairo: Ford Foundation.
United Nations Development Programme. 2004. *Jordan Human Development Report*. Amman: UNDP.
United States Agency for International Development. "Jordan," http://www.usaid.gov/locations/asia_near_east/countries/jordan/jordan.html.
United States State Department. 2008. "Background Note: Jordan." http://www.state.gov/r/pa/ei/bgn/3464.htm
Wiktorowicz, Quintan. 2000. "Civil Society as Social Control: State Power in Jordan," *Comparative Politics* 33 (1): 43–61.
World Bank. "Jordan," http://web.worldbank.org/WBSITE/EXTERNAL/COUNTRIES/MENAEXT/JORDANEXTN/0,,menuPK:315136~pagePK:141159~piPK:141110~theSitePK:315130,00.html.
World Bank. "Jordan: Data Profile," http://devdata.worldbank.org/external/CPProfile.asp?PTUYPE=CP&CCODE=JOR.

3

The Kingdom of
Saudi Arabia

Karim Shalaby

Overview

Responsibility for services to the public has been a contested honor among the tribes of Mecca as far back as history can record. Providing for the pilgrims to Mecca was a coveted honor, even before the advent of Islam. Philanthropic giving has thus always been part of the culture of the Arab Peninsula, and Islam organized and structured aspects of that giving. In the process, giving was placed in the context of a larger individual responsibility toward society. The region and culture that is now the Kingdom of Saudi Arabia initiated of many of the institutional forms of 'giving management' now familiar to the area.

The merging of tribal populations into the greater population of Saudi Arabia in 1932 and the wealth that resulted from the discovery of huge oil reserves after 1938 have translated into an increased capacity for giving both within the kingdom and internationally. While the better part of individual philanthropic giving has remained anonymous, it has also become manifest through local and international philanthropic institutions. The bonds that tie individuals and institutions go deep; one might even go so far as to say that they are stronger than those between individuals and the state. Much of individual and institutional giving is directed toward charity and to supporting the provision of basic needs of the poor.

The revival of institutionalized philanthropy in the kingdom has been taking place quietly, with new forms emerging and defining the future to come. In the process, philanthropic institutions have begun to integrate strategic approaches and modern financial and cultural applications while holding fast

to traditions and religious foundations. Philanthropic wealth is being channeled to an array of fields, and the sector's engagement with government and
private businesses is breaking new ground for philanthropy in the region. It
also is creating pressure for more enabling legal environments and demands
on cultural norms for higher levels of participation and civic engagement.

Country Background

Saudi Arabia at a Glance[1]	
Country size	2,149,690 sq. km.
Population (2006)	23.7 million
National	*80%*
Non-national	*20%*
GDP (2006)	USD 348.6 billion
GDP PPP (2006)	USD 396.7 billion
Oil and gas	*48%*
Services and other	*34%*
Manufacturing	*10%*
Construction	*5%*
Agriculture, forestry and fishing	*3%*
GDP per capita (2006)	USD 14,719
GDP per capita PPP (2006)	USD 16,744
HDI ranking	76/177
Religious groups	Muslim 100% *(Sunni 95%, Shia 5%)*
1 Saudi Arabia Riyal (SAR)	USD 0.25

Modern History

Saudi Arabia was unified in 1932 under King Abdul Aziz Al-Saud. The
kingdom functions as a monarchy governed by Islamic law, ruling in accordance with a conservative school of Sunni Islam known as Wahabism.
Decision-making power is centralized, but the monarchy has a tradition of
consulting with elite members of Saudi society. The current ruler is King
Abdullah Bin Abdul Aziz Al-Saud, who officially assumed the throne after
the death of his father, the late King Fahd.

The Political Scene

Saudi Arabia has been ruled by the royal family since unification. Pressure from within the country to incorporate greater elements of decentralization led to the codification of what is known as the Basic Law and the Law of the Provinces, which essentially solidified into law what had been common practice in the political system. The Basic Law stipulates that the government derives its authority from the Quran and the *Sunna* of the Prophet, the ultimate sources of reference for this law and the other laws of the state. The Law of the Provinces consolidated the existing duties of provincial governors and introduced procedures for the establishment of provincial councils.

In August 2005, the former finance minister Prince Talal Bin Abdul Aziz called for additional powers for the Majlis al-Shura (consultative council), which was indicative of a growing trend within the royal family and, more broadly, in Saudi society to support political reform. Because of the highly

The Political Scene

Type of Government

Monarchy led by King Abdullah Bin Abd al-Aziz Al Saud, who officially assumed the throne after the death of his father, the late King Fahd. The King appoints a Crown Prince to help him with his duties. The King governs with the help of the Council of Ministers, made up of 22 government ministries.

National Legislature

The legislative branch consists of a Consultative Council known as the Majlis al-Shura. It was established in the early 1990s due to increased pressure towards a limited program of political reform. The council has evolved into a membership of 150, with the king holding the post of prime minister. Nevertheless, the council continues to maintain limited power. The acting chairman is appointed by the king every four years.

Legal System

Shari'a law governs the legal system, although some secular codes have been introduced. The judiciary lacks independence from the monarchy, which functions as the highest court of appeal and appoints all judges, albeit subject to the recommendation of the Supreme Judicial Council.

centralized political apparatus, no political parties or political pressure groups are overtly active within the kingdom. Some groups and individual activists who advocate greater political opening exist, but many of them operate outside the country.

Despite the slow pace of political reform, the increasing flow of oil revenues has kept the Saudi 'social contract' intact. Through a policy dating back to the 1960s, the royal family has sustained tacit acceptance from Saudi citizens in exchange for a relatively even distribution of oil wealth. The distribution of wealth among royals and non-royals has led to a 'binary' economy, whereby activities relating to oil, finance, industry, and commerce are handled by non-royals. Merchants in the commercial sector benefit from a liberal economic policy that encourages trade and commerce over manufacturing, which creates a climate for political accommodation. Activities relating to the military, the interior, and agriculture remain within the purview of the royal family. Income is redistributed through contracts and investments.

The Economy

The country experienced a period of high economic growth in the 1970s, with an average annual growth of 15 percent in the first half of the decade and of 8 percent in the second half. The economy suffered a recession from the early to mid-1980s as a result of oil prices bottoming out. In the late 1980s to early 1990s, it saw another period of high growth, at 7 percent, which was followed by successive years of low growth hovering around 1 to 2 percent.[2] The country still is highly dependent on oil revenue, despite attempts to diversify to other sectors. Higher oil prices since 2000 have allowed the country to stave off structural reform. Substantial holdings of foreign assets are required to provide long-term investment income when oil production inevitably declines. Since the oil sector is not labor intensive, a good deal of public revenue is directed to public sector salaries.

Diversification of the economy is recognized as a necessary step to neutralizing the effects of volatile oil prices and to stabilizing the economy. The gross domestic product has not maintained steady growth, and per capita income has seen an overall decline since the high growth period of the 1970s. Per capita income has varied widely, peaking in 1981 at just under USD 19,000 (based on current prices) and then decreasing in the late 1980s and early 1990s only to rally again in the first part of the current decade.[3] Private sources of wealth tend to be invested outside the country. Associated figures are in excess of USD 650 billion (some estimates are as high as USD 1 trillion),[4] which has weakened domestic investment.

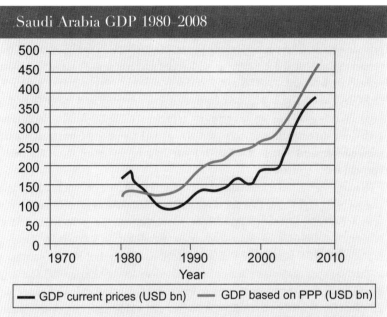

Source: International Monetary Fund, World Economic Outlook Database, April 2007.[5]

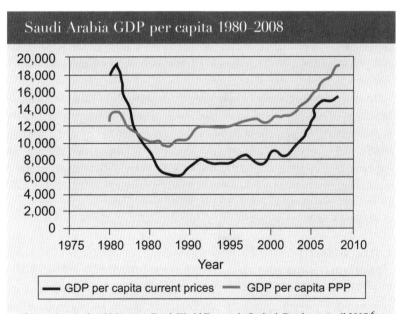

Source: International Monetary Fund, World Economic Outlook Database, April 2007.[6]

Central to the government's reform policies is the liberalization of laws on foreign direct investment to attract more investment and shore up the private sector. The country plans to establish six 'economic cities' in different regions of the country in which the government is seeking private sector investment. The Saudi Arabian General Investment Authority (SAGIA), the body in charge of attracting, approving, and facilitating foreign investment, has an investment target of USD 80 billion in foreign and joint investment projects, but the actual number of projects implemented remains unclear.[7] Tax reform has resulted in more attractive corporate tax structures.

Saudi Arabia has experienced a population explosion coupled with an excess of foreign labor that the economy is unable to absorb efficiently. Figures for unemployment range from 13 percent to 25 percent for Saudi citizens.[8] A long-term plan known as Saudiization (sa'wada) aims to replace up to 75 percent of foreigners with nationals, but Saudis command higher salaries and often are not interested in lower-skill jobs.[9] The government is torn between fighting the tide that encourages cheaper and efficient foreign labor to make companies and industries competitive on the world markets and creating employment opportunities for its own citizens.

A series of development plans have emphasized improvements in human capital formation and diversification. In the early 1990s, the emphasis was on education and replacement of foreign labor. In the mid- to late 1990s, the focus shifted to privatization and the role of the private sector in the transition to Saudiization. The theme of the current development plan is integration into the global economy.

Development indicators show significant advances. Literacy rates for Saudis aged ten years and older rose from around 64 percent in 1974 to approximately 80 percent in 2000.[10] The literacy profile of youth for both males and females is almost 100 percent. In the same period, life expectancy has gone from around 54 to 71 years. School enrollment of youth aged six to twenty-two went from approximately 40 percent in 1975 to around 86 percent in 2000. Major challenges remain to integrate school graduates into the economy.

Philanthropy in Focus
The Culture of Giving

The culture of giving in Saudi Arabia is public and pervasive. It is not reserved for private spaces. A newcomer is struck by the notices and posters put up by charity organizations on the exit doors of airports and other public spaces. Before recent regulation changes, it would not be uncommon to find seven to ten donation boxes for different charitable organizations in local mosques.

The layperson's knowledge of *shari'a* technicalities related to individual obligations to give is noteworthy. Multiple terms are used to denote different types of giving. They are *khums, waqf, sadaqat, bir*, and many forms of *zakat* for different types of activity, ranging from *zakat* on knowledge to *zakat* on wealth and commercial activity. These and other terms identifying varieties of giving are used in everyday language.

Giving is a welcome duty and a competitively solicited practice. How else would one explain the distribution of meat on the street, offers to give away free scent bottles, and other seemingly haphazard forms of in-kind giving? Generosity extends to hospitality to people as well as to ideas. Speakers from abroad are hosted in private homes to enrich discussion, and the meetings are open to anyone.

Some informants have explained this ingrained culture of generosity by the presence of the holy cities of Mecca and Medina. Proximity to Mecca and Medina implies continuous hospitality to foreign guests. This may well set a standard and an example in other areas of life. Others have said it stems from the fact that the culture has benefited from continuity, as the Kingdom of Saudi Arabia has never been occupied. Some complain of the foreign beggar gangs that have set up operations in the country. More and more say that it is no different from any neighboring country—giving is simply a religious responsibility. The fact that generosity is a highly valued quality in Bedouin culture also may be part of the explanation.

Giving in Saudi Arabia may be widely motivated by religion, but it is guided by mission. Each channel of collection is associated with a specific mission and most are backed by endowments that sustain that goal. For the most part, these missions are associated with traditional charity or basic needs. They include helping the poor, the sick, orphans, and widows, and other categories as enjoined by the Quran. An emerging trend is for missions to be strategically oriented and to contribute to the sustainable development of society.

The country's 'National Dialogue' sessions are a recognized force of change accredited with the mobilization and revival of a sense of national responsibility. Publicly aired on television, these sessions bring together scholars and intellectuals to discuss a wide range of subjects addressing national concerns. Each meeting focuses on a particular subject, and the ensuing discussions are "guided by tolerance and diversity."[11] Not all discussions held so far have led to institutional change, but even so, they have oriented the public toward important issues and ways of addressing challenges at a strategic level.[12] Individual, corporate, and institutional philanthropic initiatives of a strategic nature have been guided by these sessions.[13]

Saudi Arabia is experiencing a renaissance of institutionalized giving. More foundations and associations are being established, and at a much faster rate than before. Approximately 65 percent of the country's associations were registered after 2000. Fifty-five percent of these associations were registered in the last five years alone. This same swell in numbers is mirrored in the establishment and registration of philanthropic foundations.

A few of the country's associations and foundations venture to deal with a wider array of aspects of social change, but the majority focus on providing supportive medical services or are general-purpose *bir* (benevolent) associations. Organizational missions built around environmental issues, human rights, and smoking abatement are examples of associations branching out to more diverse approaches to social change.

The Legal Environment for Philanthropy

The Ministry of Social Affairs' National Authority for Associations and Civil Organizations is responsible for organizing and developing the civil society sector, facilitating the tasks of associations and civil society organizations (CSOs), and easing any potential hardships. The authority supervises and evaluates the activities of associations. A national fund exists within the authority to provide financial support to organizations.

The official governing legal reference for CSOs is the regulations of charitable associations and foundations, issued on 23 January 1990, the bylaws of charitable associations and foundations, issued on 2 July 1992, and the model internal rules and regulations of charitable associations and foundations, issued on 26 November 1992. The law requires that an association have at least twenty founding members of Saudi origin who have not been convicted of a crime against honor or decency. Associations can be dissolved by the authority if they do not meet certain requirements stipulated in the draft regulations.

According to the law, associations can derive their income from the designated national fund; monies from *zakat*, donations, grants, and *waqf*; membership fees; returns on their activities; and investments derived from internal activities. Associations are not allowed to accept foreign funds. An association must have a board of directors, and the authority must be notified of the nominees for membership to the board. The authority may assign a person to attend the election process in order to ensure that rules of procedure are respected.[14]

Ultimately, the authority has a considerable amount of control over the decision making and operation of all associations and foundations. This control is equivalent to veto power, which may apply to decisions ranging from approvals to receive visitors to program development and approval of board members. The choice to exercise these controls is solely at the discretion of the authority officials at the regional and central levels. While interventions may not occur frequently or even at all, the mere possibility of the exercise of these control rights maintains within the majority of associations and foundations a high level of conformity with government policy and official expectations. The consequences can be destructive, as reported by several philanthropists.

Institutionalized Philanthropy

Philanthropy in Saudi Arabia can be channeled through five forms of philanthropic institutions:

- Corporate philanthropic organizations
- Royally decreed associations
- Associations and foundations of the Ministry of Social Affairs
- Associations and foundations under other ministries
- International philanthropic institutions

Corporate Giving

Companies and corporations in Saudi Arabia act in ways similar to individuals when it comes to giving. The strong connection between companies and communities has led to an active culture of corporate giving. While giving is partly dictated by *zakat* in proportion to the profits generated from commercial activity, it is not limited to that. Corporate giving, as a recent study reveals, occurs mostly in response to requests and is directed largely toward charity.[15] Evidence has emerged, however, of a growing trend among larger corporations to direct giving toward more strategic philanthropy and the institutionalization of financial and operational mechanisms of giving.

Corporate social responsibility (CSR) is evident in the pride companies and corporations are taking in employing nationals. This comes in response to the government's policy of Saudiization, which has been in place for over a decade and has gradually been gaining momentum. It also coincides with the graduation of a generation of nationals that have benefited from Saudi

Arabia's investments in education and are prepared to respond to the needs of the labor market. Employment is only one aspect of CSR. Companies are combining this with capacity-building programs that are not limited to national hires.

Corporations simultaneously may be involved in charitable activities, CSR initiatives, and strategically oriented philanthropic programs. All three forms of giving are seen as complementary in Saudi Arabia. The distribution and allocation of funds among the three change in accordance with the perceived needs of society. Currently, the trend is toward corporate contribution to sustainable development, as opposed to meeting basic needs.

Philanthropic activities that have been ongoing for years are taking on institutionalized forms, whether as corporate foundations or simply as departments within corporations. The motivations behind the choice of institutional set-up are multiple. One is to maintain financial independence and management without compromising transparency. Corporations are becoming increasingly transparent in their operations, both as part of their commitment to CSR and because of the need to live up to international standards and to communicate with their client base. In the process, companies are increasingly applying some of the same principles of strategic management to their social investments as those applied to corporate investments.

The institutionalization of corporate philanthropy in the kingdom also is a result of the growth of funds allocated to corporate giving, and it coincides with the succession of second-generation corporate owners (the sons and daughters of founders). These two factors, combined with the growth of civil society, both in the number of organizations and in the volume of funds, are driving corporations to structure their efforts around areas of specialization where they can effectively contribute. This trend is being accompanied by the gradual separation of the individual owners' philanthropic efforts from those of their corporations.

Companies and corporations remain important platforms that allow individuals and families some flexibility in carrying out or managing the financial aspects of their philanthropic work outside the traditional legal framework of associations and foundations. This is an accommodation to and haven from some of the restrictions and risks that philanthropic work entails under the current legal and administrative systems.

Dallah Albarakah

Dallah Albarakah (DB), one of the large corporations and regional conglomerates in Saudi Arabia, recently established a department of social responsibility to serve the corporation's commitment to sustainable development and effective social change. The department is funded through designated DB proceeds that are separate from the company's *zakat* and *sadaqa* giving.

The department will provide grants to CSOs whose ventures are consistent with DB's mission and values, as well as its social program. The department also will develop an incubator capacity to support individuals with ideas and initiatives in the field of sustainable social development through strategic planning, institutionalization, and financing. At the same time, the department will guide existing DB initiatives and programs toward making a more strategic and sustained contribution to society. As part of the company's CSR activities, a small-loans project for male and female entrepreneurs has been initiated in partnership with a local nongovernmental organization with the aim of alleviating poverty.

Abdul Lateef Jameel Community Services Programs

Established in 2003, the Abdul Lateef Jameel Community Services Programs started by offering vocational training and capacity building to youth and recent graduates to prepare them for the job market. The program has expanded to include four main components, which created 12,292 jobs in 2006.

The first, a vocational training component, is made up of six separate nonprofit vocational training schools targeting Saudi men and women. The majority of graduates find employment at Abdul Lateef Jameel (ALJ) Corporation, and those who do not are usually employed by other national companies. One of the programs, the Toyota Program for Technical Education, which is a joint ALJ and Toyota Motor Corporation initiative implemented in collaboration with the Public Organization for Technical and Vocational Training, was launched two years ago and now is being applied in forty-seven countries.

The second component promotes job creation through the direct financing of small projects implemented by Saudi men or women. It also offers facilities to help Saudis buy cars to start up or expand transport-service businesses.

The third component, the ALJ Fund for Administrative and Leadership Development, offers scholarships to outstanding students for the pursuit of further education in management sciences. It also will promote the development of improved teaching skills among Saudi teachers, both men and women.

The fourth component, Health and Social Services, focuses on orphanages and homes for the elderly, and supports Red Crescent emergency services by providing equipment and training for emergency personnel and contributing to their salaries. A specialized center for rehabilitation provides healthcare both in the center and at patients' homes and manufactures upper limb prostheses. Under the umbrella of its social services component, ALJ programs support other organizations in the field, whether through direct financing or through the donation of buildings and centers.

Civil Society Organizations Established by Royal Decree

CSOs whose philanthropic initiatives are not well suited to the existing institutional setting and novel ideas that are inconsistent with existing programs can be established by royal decree. Their case is adopted by champions and presented in one of the many forums with access to the king. Forums and other similar intermediary groups under the auspices of a 'champion' offer havens for philanthropic initiatives directed at innovative social change. These initiatives are discussed in a tolerant environment that allows them to see the light of day without being stifled or becoming outdated because of bureaucracy, red tape, and resistance to change. Eventually, they are established under the king's sponsorship.

After the case is considered, a document of internal rules and regulations is drawn up and approved by the king's office. Once decreed, the document becomes, in effect, the bylaws of conduct and operation of the established entity. The newly formed entity is directly accountable to the royal office. The king usually provides financial support to the initiative, but he does not necessarily cover all the organization's financial needs. The credibility bestowed by the king encourages the community to contribute.

The National Society for Human Rights

The National Society for Human Rights (NSHR) was established by royal decree in 2004 at the request of forty-one community members. NSHR aims to protect human rights, cooperate with international organizations working in this field, and oppose injustice, dogmatism, violence, torture, and intolerance. The society was granted a generous endowment by HM King Fahd, which covers the society's salaries and running costs (mainly publication costs). The financing of the representative office and five NSHR centers now open in different parts of the kingdom came from donations and grants.

One of the primary aims of NSHR is to raise awareness of the public—local and foreign, male and female—of its rights and to correct related misconceptions. In the words of Jawhara Bin Mohamed Alanjary, NSHR's executive director, "without being aware of their rights, how can individuals ask to be redeemed?"[16]

NSHR achieves its aims through publications, workshops, conferences, and discussion forums. It spearheads discussions on social change in local and national forums such as the 'National Dialogue' sessions. These venues offer opportunities not only for awareness raising but also sometimes for change in laws and procedures.

Through its centers, NSHR acts as a facilitator for people who need advice and legal representation. The centers provide guidance and information on the competent authority to approach. The center also puts people in touch with lawyers, encouraging the latter to charge nominal fees or provide free services to those who cannot afford representation. There has been no shortage, to date, of lawyers willing to take on such cases.

NSHR is careful not to bypass the governance system or abuse its connection to the king. The society's long-term strategy for bringing about desired change is to work with the establishment and provide guidance in strengthening its role.

The many letters of gratitude NSHR has received from wives, maids, foreign workers, and others attest to the role the society plays in people's lives. NSHR has chosen to focus on the daily concerns of the population and is addressing a real need. A major challenge will be to reach out to geographically isolated populations dispersed in different parts of the kingdom.

Associations and Foundations of the Ministry of Social Affairs

Of the hundreds, perhaps thousands,[17] of CSOs in the Kingdom of Saudi Arabia, four hundred and twenty benevolent associations and forty-two individual benevolent foundations are registered under the Ministry of Social Affairs, more than double the number registered five years ago. The CSOs are governed by the law on benevolent associations and foundations issued in 1989. Foundations may be established by as few as one individual, while associations require an initial establishing board of at least twenty members. Foundations can accept donations and bequeathed assets and funds, but are not to engage in fundraising activities. They are not eligible for financial support offered by the ministry to its registered associations.

Depending on their activities and geographic coverage, registered associations can receive financial support from the ministry ranging from SAR 50,000 to SAR 5 million. Other benefits include land for their offices, technical support paid by the ministry, reduced utility rates, and, occasionally, in-kind donations (such as dates for distribution). Associations have received an estimated SAR 2 billion in direct financial support and donations in recent years.[18] Bank transfers are the accepted channel for giving money to nonprofit organizations, and donation boxes in mosques are now banned as part of new controls to monitor the flow and use of funds. Associations maintain an acceptable and appreciated level of transparency with donors and beneficiaries and do not hesitate to communicate and publicize their activities. They recognize that trust is a valuable asset for fundraising and for the establishment of lasting relations.

Subject to the ministry's consent, associations and foundations are entitled to invest funds in excess of their needs in profit-making activities, provided these reserves are double the amount of their last expenditure budget. The emerging trend among regional associations is to invest in real estate in major cities such as Jeddah and Riyadh. These investments are designated endowments to support their operations, partly in response to the ministry's attempts to wean established CSOs off its support.

Another rising trend has been for associations and foundations to expand their activities beyond charitable giving to include the establishment of technical schools, provision of support to productive families, and the financing of social projects. The ministry has taken a relaxed view of the fact that many of these activities fall outside the organizations' original goals and objectives, looking upon the trend as a positive one. Indeed, the ministry is going as far as to initiate a program to revise these organizations' defined objectives and to support them in setting a strategic plan for their future involvement in sustainable social development.

Restrictions placed by the Ministry of Social Affairs on the flow of information from organizations registered with it to any local or foreign organization make it difficult to obtain official information on this sector of institutional philanthropy. Hence, no examples are provided here. Unofficial interviews and information gathering revealed a general trend among associations registered with the ministry to be involved in predominantly charitable activities focusing on children, the sick, and poverty reduction, mainly through the provision of grants and in-kind support. Some associations are moving towards small-loan programs supported by marketing services to help families living in impoverished conditions earn a livelihood.

Associations and Foundations under Other Ministries

In addition to the Ministry of Social Affairs, all other ministries can register nonprofit organizations working in their areas of specialization. Operations under other ministries are reported to be less restricted than under the Ministry of Social Affairs. Organizations are given more latitude in defining their goals and in decision-making, and they benefit from greater leniency in the management of funds.

No known census exists of the total number of organizations registered under other ministries. These associations and foundations render services that are usually complementary to their respective ministry's activities. At times, they lead the way into new and uncharted domains that later may become integrated into their ministry's plan and work. One recently established CSO focuses on raising awareness of autism and providing support to individuals and families coping with this disorder. Another CSO has been set up recently to work in the field of HIV/AIDS.

The Help Center

The Help Center is a nonprofit organization registered under the Ministry of Health. Founded in 1985 through an endowment by the Ahmed Juffali Foundation, the Help Center stands unparalleled in the quality of service offered to children who are mentally and physically challenged. It works with children from birth, as well as with their parents and, in some cases, their employers, to help them overcome learning constraints and lead an independent life and integrate into society.

Located in one of the prime real estate areas of Jeddah, the Help Center does not take in boarders but is more of a day school. The center's 350 children, and their parents benefit from the services of almost ninety trained and qualified staff members and from the center's state-of-the-art equipment and space.

The endowment is managed separately from the Health Center's operations, and the annual budget covers the activities set out in the center's annual plan. The center does not rely exclusively on the endowment funds, encouraging the community to contribute and get involved, which is in line with its philosophy of helping society to invest in itself. Parents are required to pay fees ranging from SAR 150 to SAR 16,000, depending on their income. Only 2 percent of the parents pay full fees. These fees represent only a fraction of the cost per child and do not go toward tuition. Instead, all fees and other contributions are placed in a Children's Account to cover the additional expenses of the needier children, such as surgery, medication, special equipment, and transportation.

The Health Center has contributed to changing societal perceptions of children with mental disabilities in Saudi Arabia. Prior to its establishment, the mentally challenged were kept out of sight by their parents, and the government did not see the value of an initiative of the kind. This is less so today. Through workshops, exposure, and partnership building, government attitudes have changed and officials have come to recognize the importance of the program and to lend it their support. Parents are actively participating in the training and reinforcing it, helping their children become independent participants in society.

The Health Center students brought home nine medals in the last Special Olympics, mostly in swimming, and of its sixty-two graduates, twenty-five currently hold regular jobs. The knowledge base, experience, and training expertise the center has accumulated over the past twenty-three years is now being sought by and exported to other countries in the region.

International Philanthropic Institutions

Saudi Arabia is one of the countries in the Arab region that are strongly oriented toward philanthropic investment abroad. While the country provides humanitarian and relief aid in response to disasters, its international philanthropic efforts are also strategic in nature, focusing on sustainable development. A whole range of institutional set-ups can be identified, from government-funded programs under bilateral cooperation agreements, to individual or family foundations operating at the international level, to individual and corporate donations to international organizations such as the United Nations and through universities.

Some of the foundations operate at the international level while others run local programs with a presence in other countries, sometimes spanning the globe. Organizationally and legally, these institutions are not necessarily structured as one entity. They are registered abroad but are known to have their roots in Saudi Arabia. Although the funds for their programs are sometimes raised through individual contributions, for the most part, the foundations rely on joint funding by other multinational or local organizations. Alternatively, funding is secured through sizable endowments.

Foundations of this kind have come under scrutiny in the post-9/11 clamp-down on the international flow of funds. Some have battled out their cases in court and managed to clear their names, receiving sizable compensation.

Coexist Foundation

Coexist Foundation was established by Mohamed Abdul Lateef Jameel in London in 2006 to promote better understanding among Jews, Christians, and Muslims through education, dialogue, and research. The foundation began its first project, 'A billion Muslims . . . Can you hear us?,' as a ten-year nonprofit partnership with the Gallup Organization to help disseminate the findings of the independent World Poll on Muslim opinions around the world. The foundation also was one of the lead sponsors of an international exhibit called 'Sacred Scriptures,' which was organized by the British Library to show the shared heritage of the Jewish, Christian, and Islamic faiths.

Al-Mansouria Foundation

Established in Paris by Princess Jawaher Bint Majed Bin Abdul Aziz Al Saud, al-Mansouria Foundation supports creativity in Saudi Arabia and builds bridges between Saudi artists and the general public. The foundation organizes exhibitions and produces publications, and its studio in Paris offers Saudi and Arab artists opportunities for self-expression.

The King Faisal Foundation

The late King Faisal is credited with establishing the current educational system in Saudi Arabia in the early 1950s, and the King Faisal Foundation was established by his heirs in his honor in 1976. Based in Riyadh, the foundation offers research and scholarship prizes, as well as grants to community development projects that bring long-term benefits to the community.

One of the foundation's major achievements is the King Faisal Center for Research and Islamic Studies, a beacon for researchers and knowledge seekers in the field of Islamic studies from around the globe. The center promotes research and knowledge building through a seminal library in Islamic studies, lectures and seminars, and periodicals. Scholarships are offered to outstanding Muslim students of all nationalities.

The foundation also has set up several nonprofit educational entities to offer quality education, including:

- King Faisal School, a leader in quality education that sets standards for an education system that marries traditional values with modern knowledge acquisition. The school initiated a civics course that later was institutionalized in the national education system.
- Al-Faisal University, which began receiving students in 2008.
- Prince Sultan College, the first college in Saudi Arabia to establish and build capacity for tourism services.

• Effat National College, Saudi Arabia's first women's college, which is fast expanding in number of students as well as in areas of specialization and courses. The college receives students from all over the world. It was initiated by Her Highness Princess Effat Bin Mohamed al-Thunnayyan, wife of the late King Faisal, and later was donated to the foundation.

All of these entities are nonprofit operations. The King Faisal Foundation is endowed with real estate investments that are landmarks in Riyadh, as well as financial and commercial investments that are managed to facilitate the foundation's growth and development.

Conclusion

A full picture of philanthropy in the Kingdom of Saudi Arabia requires a more complete study of the multifaceted nature of the sector. This brief overview touches on some of the institutionalized forms of philanthropic investment in Jeddah and Riyadh. Other aspects of philanthropy in the country may remain undocumented, given the preference of many philanthropists for anonymity.

A recent page in *Okaz* newspaper, dedicated to the issue of civic engagement, addresses some of the sector's needs and achievements. For the most part, however, discourse on philanthropy is noticeably absent in the Saudi media. Coverage tends to be limited to sporadic articles and recognition of exceptional donations. Secondary sources also are rare, given the widespread nature of activity in the field.

Philanthropy is publicly manifest in the vibrant fundraising that takes place at all levels of the population, and in the positive response it receives. A relationship of intrinsic trust exists between philanthropic institutions and the public, as evidenced by the flow of SAR 2 billion in donations to only one institutional modality, associations linked to the Ministry of Social Affairs. One weak side of the trust triangle is between the philanthropic organizations and government regulators. This aspect of institutionalized philanthropy requires considerable development to foster a more enabling environment for philanthropic and charitable organizations to expand their role and contribution to development of society in Saudi Arabia.

Despite the privacy of philanthropic institutions, their undertakings, endowments, and offices reveal a deeply imbedded sense of responsibility to lead by example and the pride they take in their activities. One is struck by their insistence on perfection at all levels. The pursuit of excellence and obsession with detail is visible in the quality of the real estate developments that house their offices or constitute their endowments. The practice of endowing philanthropic organizations, be they charitable or strategic in focus, is well established in Saudi Arabia, providing a sustainable financing mechanism that is suited to modern financial and commercial practices.

Philanthropy in its many guises has been a leading force for innovation in social change in the Kingdom of Saudi Arabia. Philanthropic institutions have acted as an implementing arm for civic contributions to social development, complementing the services offered by the government and filling the gaps or venturing into innovative approaches. They have managed to do so despite a highly regulatory environment in terms of administrative limitations and official restrictions.

Individuals, associations, and foundations have worked within and around these limitations by employing their own creativity to circumvent and tackle obstacles to their philanthropic work. These have ranged from simply operating under an alternative legal system, namely operating outside the country, to forging alliances with government officials and building partnerships with the government. One can only imagine what this sector could contribute to the development of society in Saudi Arabia and beyond, if it operated in a more enabling legal and administrative environment, given the growing momentum of social and political constructs for change.

Today's generation of highly skilled and eager graduates, who benefited from the previous decade's investment in education, is assuming leadership and executive roles. They are poised to support and further the implementation of new initiatives. The growing sense of national pride epitomized in the momentum of Saudiization, the inward flow of philanthropic funds imposed by the post-9/11 whiplash and the attention the events brought to internal problems, and the heightened sense of social responsibility and ensuing cultural awareness brought about by the 'National Dialogue' sessions, especially in the business community, all have the makings of change in Saudi Arabia.

Notes

1. Population and gross domestic product (GDP) figures taken from IMF data. GDP estimates start after 2004, based on existing data. The human development index (HDI) is derived from United Nations development reports and is the measure of life expectancy, literacy education, and standard of living. GDP purchasing power parity is denoted by 'PPP' to reflect the weight of GDP in relation

to the purchasing power of other countries. The breakdown of religious and population groups is taken from NationMaster.com.
2. Ministry of Economy and Planning. Kingdom of Saudi Arabia, http://www.planning.gov/sa/i-mop/home/
3. International Monetary Fund World Economic Outlook Database. April 2, 2007. Saudi Arabia: Gross Domestic Product per capita, current prices (USD). http://www.imf.org.
4. Niblock 2006:128.
5. Estimates start after 2004.
6. Estimates start after 2004.
7. Economic Intelligence Unit 2006.
8. United States Central Intelligence Agency World Fact Book.
9. Saudi Arabia Human Development Report 2003. 12:146
10. Saudi Arabia Human Development Report 2003. 9:146
11. Salah al-Din, Mohamed. 6 August 2007. "Distinguished Project by a Unique Organization." Almadinah.
12. Personal interview with Jawhara Bin Mohamed Alanjary, Riyadh, November 10, 2007.
13. Salah al-Din, Mohamed. 6 August 2007. "Distinguished Project by a Unique Organization." Almadinah.
14. Information on the legal environment is taken from International Center for Not-for-Profit Law. Saudi Arabia Draft Regulation of Associations and Civil Organizations 2006.
15. Tamkeen and IIIEE 2007.
16. Personal interview with Jawhara Bin Mohamed Alanjary, NSHR executive director, Riyadh, November 10, 2007.
17. No single survey of all nonprofit organizations exists.
18. Personal interview with Jawhara Bin Mohamed Alanjary, NSHR executive director, Jeddah, November 10, 2007

References
Economist Intelligence Unit. 2006. "Country Profile: Saudi Arabia."
Economist Intelligence Unit. 2006. "Country Report: Saudi Arabia."
Freedom House. 2007. "Country Report: Saudi Arabia."
International Center for Not-for-Profit Law. 2006. "Draft Regulations of Associations and Civil Organizations."
"Interview with Manager of the Social Responsibility Department in the Dallah Albarakah, Dr. Nadia Baeshan," *Dallah Albarakah Newsletter* 44 (July 2007), 44–45.
Jones, Toby. 2003. "Seeking a 'Social Contract' for Saudi Arabia." *Middle East Report* 228:42–48.
Kechichian, Joseph A. 2001. *Succession in Saudi Arabia*. New York: Palgrave.
El-Khazen, Jihad. 2007. "Ayoon wa azan (Should They be Given a Chance)," *al-Hayat*, 18 March.
Ministry of Economy and Planning, Kingdom of Saudi Arabia. http://www.planning.gov.sa.

Mohamed, Salah al-Din. 2007. "Distinguished Project by a Unique Organization." *Almadinah*, 6 August .

Niblock, Tim. 2006. *Saudi Arabia: Power, Legitimacy and Survival*. London: Routledge.

Seznec, Jean-François. 2002. "Stirrings in Saudi Arabia," *Journal of Democracy* 13 (4): 33–40.

Tamkeen Development and Management Consulting, Saudi Arabia, and the International Institute for Industrial Environmental Economics, Sweden. 2007. "Saudi Companies and Social Responsibility: Challenges and Ways Forward," February.

United Nations Development Programme. 2003. *Saudi Arabia Human Development Report*. UNDP. http://www.pogar.org/publications/other/undp/hdr/2003/saudi-arabia-e.pdf

4

Palestine: West Bank and Gaza Strip

Hadeel Qazzaz

Overview

Palestine has a rich history of institutionalized philanthropy. Like other Arab societies, it shares the Islamic values of personal giving as well as a rich Christian culture of giving. In addition to compassion for those in need, philanthropy in Palestine has developed to provide social services in the absence of a functioning state, to preserve Palestinian culture, and to protect the holy places of both faiths. As Palestine is a country under occupation and suffering from uprooting and violence, philanthropy there also has evolved as a means of 'steadfastness' to support Palestinians remaining in their homeland.

Philanthropic giving stems from deeply held beliefs that it is blessed to offer material beneficence to fellow human beings.[1] The impulse to institutionalize giving may spring from a mix of motives that are religious, nationalistic, or humanitarian, but it has an added dimension of desire for sustainability.

Country Background
Socioeconomic and Political Environment

The Occupied Palestinian Territories (OPT) are geographically divided into two distinct areas: the West Bank and the Gaza Strip. The population of the West Bank, including Jerusalem, is 2,385,000, and the population of the Gaza Strip is 1,376,000.[2] East Jerusalem fell under the jurisdiction of Israeli domestic law and was annexed by Israel in 1980.

The Palestine Liberation Organization (PLO) represents the Palestinian people. Between 1992 and 1993, the PLO negotiated and signed the Oslo Accords with Israel. The accords granted Palestinians the right to self-governance in some areas of the West Bank through the creation of the Palestinian National Authority (PNA). The PNA is now the executive body of the PLO, with authority over Palestinians living in the territories. The Oslo agreements limit the power of the PNA to passing primary legislation.

As a result of elections in Gaza in 2005 that were not recognized by the international community, political instability intensified there. In 2007, Hamas forcibly took control from the PNA. This led to international boycotts, Israeli border closures, the collapse of public services, and further deterioration of already dire economic conditions. The poverty rate in the Gaza Strip is estimated at approximately 70 percent.[3] Average income figures for 2004 show that 65 percent of the overall population of the Gaza Strip live in poverty and that 54 percent live in extreme poverty.[4]

Freedom of Expression and Association

Palestinian society has benefited in the past from a relatively liberal atmosphere and freedom to express political and social opinions. Prolonged occupation and internal divisions, however, have created a degree of self-censorship. Following Hamas' takeover of the Gaza strip, President Mahmoud Abbas declared a state of emergency. Both Hamas in the Gaza strip and Fatah in the West Bank currently are violating some basic rights related to freedom of expression and freedom of association.[5] Nonetheless, the extensive development of civil society organizations (CSOs) in the area is striking, as is the activism of significant portions of the population at all age levels. This may be attributed to the stark conditions of life under occupation and the long periods during which private associations have had to make up for the lack of Palestinian public services.

Civil Society and the Public Authorities

As with other Arab countries, there is no functioning 'social contract' or set of rights and responsibilities between citizens and the state. Throughout the short history of the PNA, allegations of corruption and mismanagement have increased. This situation was little better, however, when the territories were administered by Jordan or Egypt, or, after 1967, by Israel. Under occupation, basic services were underdeveloped. Education, healthcare, and social services were outdated and had not been expanded to meet increased demand. Palestinians substituted for this vacuum by establishing a network of CSOs, which were registered as nonprofit companies during the occupation, and a number of private professional practices, such as private schools, clinics, and law offices. Following the establishment of the PNA, private investors were encouraged to engage in service delivery. More private schools and hospitals were established, but this had the effect of widening the gap between the rich and poor.

Public–Private Partnerships

Until the establishment of the PNA, public–private partnership did not exist. The Palestinian economy had not developed a vigorous private sector because of the various restrictions on marketing and investment during occupation. In addition, private entrepreneurs tended to avoid sectors of work or open connections with the PLO as long as it was a banned organization. After 1994, many Palestinian private businesses opened or were reestablished in Palestinian-controlled areas, including new companies in the fields of telecommunications, electricity, and construction. These firms have contributed to a range of community development projects. Their efforts tend to be somewhat isolated and lack a cumulative impact on the society, however.

Socioeconomic Indicators

In March 2007, the value of gross domestic product (GDP) was USD 982 million. GDP per capita was USD 269, down almost 9 percent from the corresponding period in 2006.[6] Palestine was ranked 100 out of 177 countries on the human development index. Economically, Palestine has been considered in the middle development category, although at this time Gaza is sinking into severe poverty. The Palestinian economy is service driven rather than production driven. Table 1 summarizes some of the main economic indicators in recent years.

Table 1: Economic Indicators (1999–2006)				
Indicator	1999	2002	2004	2006
GDP (million USD)	5095.0	4169.3	4131.3	4150.6
GDP/per capita (USD)	1617.2	1203.4	1217.8	1141.4
Unemployment (%)	11.9	31.3	26.8	23.6
Debt (million USD)	286.6	950.0	1009.9	1824
Foreign Aid (million USD)	523.9	966.1	925.0	750.3
Percentage of poor	21.0	60.0	61.0	(no official data)

Source: MAS, March 2007 and July 2007

Income Distribution

The Palestinian National Poverty Report for 2005 estimates that approximately three out of five Palestinians live under the income poverty line, while a third of the Palestinian population lives under the consumption poverty line.[7] The report also indicates continued gaps in poverty rates between the West Bank and the Gaza Strip, with poverty in Gaza being twice as high as in the West Bank. Poverty rates in refugee camps are the highest, with real expenditure poverty rates close to 32 percent, compared with almost 25 percent in rural areas and around 25 percent in urban areas. Income poverty rates are approximately 59 percent, compared with 54 percent and around 52 percent in rural and urban areas, respectively.

Foreign Funding and Multinationals

Significant donor funding to Palestinians started long before the Oslo agreements. Funding in the West Bank and the Gaza Strip was aimed at improving living conditions and paving the way for a peace agreement. Prior to Oslo, donors disbursed funding directly through Palestinian CSOs and local committees, not through an official body. While Western funding was significant, it was much less than that provided by regional and Islamic sources. Khalil Nakhleh estimates that from 1977 to 1992, Palestinian, Arab, and Islamic sources contributed approximately USD 564 million to Palestine. From 1975 to 1987, the United States government contributed nearly USD 77 million in aid to Palestinians. Donor funding through the PNA started immediately after the signing of the Oslo Accords. This was to have provided capacity-building support to the new authority. According to the 2004 Palestine Human Development Report, the overall commitment of donors to the Palestinian people from 1994 until 2003 was USD 6,708 million, of which USD 6,553 million was actually disbursed.

Given the underdeveloped nature of institutions in Palestine, donor funding is focused across many sectors. According to reports by the Ministry of Planning covering 1994–2005, 41 percent of donor funding went to social sectors, followed by the institution-building (21 percent), infrastructure (20 percent), and production sectors (10 percent).

Economic Policy and Activity

Economic surveys for 2006 show that the gross fixed capital formation amounted to USD 88.6 million. This value was distributed as follows: industrial activities received 25 percent, internal trade activities 14 percent, services 25 percent, and transport, storage, and communication activities

35 percent. While the PNA has declared its support for a free market economy, Israeli control over borders, tax revenues, and resources renders the territories dependent on external donor funding. Markets cannot operate normally. Since 1993, the PNA has submitted a development plan to the annual international donors' meeting, consisting in earlier years of a shopping list for basic needs. Since 2005, the planning process has become more structured, with a clearer vision and set of priorities presented in the Palestinian National Development Plan for 2005–2007. Nonetheless, conditions placed on some donor contributions have impeded locally conceived development projects.

Literacy

Illiteracy rates have declined in recent years to a low of 7 percent among those aged fifteen years and older, compared to 16 percent in 1995. Illiteracy in urban areas is 5 percent, in rural areas it is 9 percent, and in refugee camps it is 7 percent. Illiteracy is considerably higher among women at 10 percent, compared with 3 percent among men.

Population Distribution and Migration

According to the 2004 Palestine Human Development Report, 56 percent of Palestinians live in urban areas, 29 percent live in rural areas, and 15 percent live in refugee camps. Palestinians were subject to two waves of large-scale migration during the 1948 and 1967 wars. As a result, more Palestinians live in the diaspora than currently live in the occupied territories. A significant number have succeeded as professionals and private business owners. This creates a large pool of potential diaspora philanthropists. It is estimated that there were more than 7 million Palestinian refugees and displaced persons at the beginning of 2003.[8]

Philanthropy in Focus
The Culture of Giving

The strong tradition of philanthropy in Palestine stems primarily from four main factors that have created a culture of giving and social solidarity:

- The strong religious motive for philanthropy, both in Islam and Christianity: Palestine houses holy sites for three major faiths and is a meeting point for world religions, so it historically has been a place where good deeds and charitable offerings are well established. Church and *waqf* establishments in the old city of Jerusalem date from before the time of the Crusades, as do Jewish schools and

seminaries. The first modern-era schools in Palestine were mission-
ary Christian schools based on volunteerism and philanthropic
contributions from abroad. Islamic schools in major cities followed,
in addition to many religious organizations set up to provide support
to poor families, award scholarships for Palestinian students to study
abroad, and provide housing for the poor.

- The historical strength of *waqf* institutions: As an Ottoman province,
Palestine was a site of active *waqf* establishment, mainly to protect
the religious sites and assist the poor. In the first quarter of the last
century, 5 to 7 percent of Palestinian land was considered *waqf*,
including tens of villages. Some sources estimate that 15 percent of
village land and 7 percent of town land was held in *waqf* status.
While there is less activity in the formation of new *awqaf* today,
existing institutions remain strong in Palestine, controlling assets that
serve poor families and operate schools and orphanages.[9]

- Displacement and war: The uprooting of Palestinians from their original homes led to two major waves of population movement to the
West Bank and the Gaza Strip. Most of those who became long-term
refugees were poor and had lost livelihoods in addition to property.
Many local charitable organizations and work committees were
established to provide support for these refugees, with women often
in founding and leadership positions. An example is the well-known
social welfare organization, In'ash El-Usra, which was established
by Samiha Khalil in 1965.

- Extended occupation and lack of self-rule: Since 1967, occupation has
restricted economic opportunity and contributed to large-scale migration out of the territories. Increasingly, youth have become
discouraged about their personal and collective futures. This led to
popular uprisings in 1987 and 2000, with resultant loss of property
and life and further economic setbacks. In response, new forms of
philanthropy have arisen that have enabled diaspora Palestinians, who
had always sent individual contributions back to the territories, to
channel their giving through foundations and solidarity associations.
Other Arab and Muslim philanthropists have supported these efforts,
as well as universities, CSOs, and enterprises well beyond the territories. Support is distributed over social welfare, cultural preservation,

scholarships, and vocational training, as well as an array of other developmental activities.

• A confluence of these four factors has created a unique array of institutional forms of philanthropy and a modern sector that is more highly developed than in some parts of the Arab region. Wealthy Palestinian businessmen with bases in Jordan, the Gulf, and Europe created some of the earliest grant-making foundations. Many other organizations draw their support from individual donors living around the world. Recently, one of the first Arab community foundations was established in the West Bank.

Sources of Philanthropic Giving

Three main sources of philanthropic giving exist in Palestine that are of an indigenous nature. The first is the local philanthropy of individual Palestinians living in the OPT. These people channel funds through established charitable organizations and CSOs spread across the West Bank and the Gaza Strip. Poor people, and more recently the 'new poor,' or employees of the PNA who did not receive their salaries, queue in front of these organizations to get some financial help, food parcels, clothing, or students fees.

The second source is Palestinians living in diaspora who either support the existing network of Palestinian nongovernmental organizations (NGOs) or establish their own agencies (typically registered as a charity abroad with an office or operations in the West Bank and the Gaza Strip). These institutions are important because of the scale of funds involved and because they often have a developmental rather than charitable orientation in their programs. Sari Hanafi identified the blurred relationship between donations and investments of Palestinian diaspora, as some philanthropic giving also contributes to the creation of economic assets and income-generating activities.[10]

Part of this second source of Palestinian philanthropic giving is Arab citizens of Israel who have established foundations and organizations to support Palestinians in the territories. One example of this, from a religious perspective, is the Islamic foundations established to support poor families and needy communities or to lead campaigns for the protection of al-Aqsa mosque.

The third source of giving is Arab or Muslim philanthropy, which may be channeled through local or international CSOs working in Palestine.

One characteristic of the philanthropic sector in Palestine is the extent to which old institutional structures of giving coexist with modern philanthropic institutions. There are differences in the scope and objectives of giving and the structures of the organizations. For example, religious *zakat* committees are very active and well institutionalized. Some of them have evolved a mode of work that is less charitable than developmental in nature, such as the Nablus Zakat Committee described below. *Waqf* institutions still exist in Palestine, but they now are operated under the supervision of the Ministry of Religious Affairs. Charitable organizations also exit, but they often run on lower budgets and more in-kind contributions from the community.

At the same time, new and modern philanthropic organizations are becoming active. The new model of wealthy families and persons establishing their own foundations is becoming more common. Examples are the Abdel-Mohsen Qattan Foundation, Faisal Hussein Foundation, and the older, more extensive Welfare Association.

The coexistence of different modalities of philanthropy can be explained partly by the severity of needs in the society, partly as a result of political developments. For example, the founding of the Welfare Association occurred when the PLO was forced to leave Lebanon in 1982. Wealthy Palestinian businesspeople felt the need to support Palestinian refugees, especially in camps in Lebanon and the occupied territories. Following the first Intifada in 1987 and the second Intifada in 2000, philanthropy experienced growth as a result of heightened community needs.

Motives for Giving Among Individuals

There are two major motives for giving. The first is religious giving driven by Islamic values and duties (*sadaqa* and *zakat*). This motive is increasing as a stated reason for giving and reflects the growing influence of Islam and Islamic popular movements in the area. This kind of giving is mainly in the form of cash donations. Giving in kind also occurs, but less often. The second motive is nationalistic, based on solidarity with those affected by the occupation or a sense of belonging to the Palestinian cause. This giving largely takes the form of in-kind donations and volunteering of time and effort.

A study conducted a decade ago shows that 24 percent of the representative sample was regularly giving money as a sustainable act all through the year.[11] An additional 16 percent gave money occasionally on religious occasions or feasts.

Channels of Giving

In general, because of the political situation and ongoing crisis, Palestinians are actively engaged in social affairs and community services. Gestures of solidarity and support through NGOs or to directly affected family members are frequent. The strong network of charitable organizations facilitates Palestinian philanthropy. Many individuals pay regularly and have for years to certain organizations and NGOs. The aim is not always charity. In some cases, money is given for infrastructure projects (roads, schools, or clinics) or to rebuild destroyed houses.

Some individuals contribute to relief assistance by channeling their donations through Islamic charity organizations in the Gulf, Europe, and the United States, and through charity coalitions like the Islamic Charity Association, the Islamic Compound, and al-Salah Islamic Society.

Other individuals channel their contributions through non-Islamic NGOs active in the West Bank and the Gaza Strip. In 2005, these organizations offered monetary assistance ranging between JOD 20 to JOD 50 to seventeen thousand families, as well as relief aid in the form of food parcels, house renovations, and craft training for poor women.[12]

In recent years, public opinion polls showed less trust in 'modern' NGOs because of allegations of corruption and following a Western agenda. The respondents distinguish, however, between NGOs that depend on foreign funding and philanthropic institutions such as *zakat* committees and the Red Crescent.

An opinion poll conducted by the Development Studies Program at Birzeit University indicates that respondents tend to have trust in *zakat* committees (58 percent) and NGOs and charity organizations (47 percent).[13] A census of NGOs conducted in 2007 found that 62 percent of NGOs receive some local funding (donations and grants), which is an indication that the culture of giving is thriving. However, the 2007 figure is lower than that in 2000, when 72 percent of NGOs received local funding.[14]

A Palestine Economic Policy Research Institute (MAS) study in 1997 identified 13 percent of family giving channeled to *zakat* committees, 29 percent to charities, 23 percent to families and individuals suffering from a crisis, 22 percent to families from the same town or village, 18 percent to neighbors, and 9 percent to friends.[15] Like Egyptians, Palestinians prefer to give directly, especially to relatives and family members. However, there are many who prefer to give (especially *zakat* money) to religious organizations such as *zakat* committees or the al-Salah or al-Falah organizations in the Gaza Strip. There is also an increasing trend to give money for needy students by paying their fees directly to universities, or to support the families who are affected by occupation, such as the families of prisoners or those killed, families whose homes were demolished, or where the breadwinner has a disabling injury.

The Legal Environment for Philanthropy

According to Law 1 of 2002, the Palestinian Ministry of the Interior is responsible for overseeing NGOs, foundations, and charitable endowments. The ministry has the authority to register organizations and to dissolve those that do not comply with the law. Each NGO or charitable organization has to apply for a license. The Ministry of Social Affairs reviews the programs and activities of charitable organizations but does not have the power to close them or prevent any of their activities.

Despite the existence of an NGO monitoring department within the Ministry of the Interior, the ministry lacks the professional capacity to fulfill this role completely or to implement decisions. Since the last parliamentary elections and the formation of the Hamas government, NGOs and charitable organizations have, unfortunately, become a political tool. Hamas Prime Minister Ismail Hanieh froze registration of new NGOs, claiming that they were being used by the Fatah movement for the rechanneling of funds. Following Hamas' takeover of the Gaza Strip in June 2007, the Fatah-controlled government in the West Bank closed down 103 NGOs and organizations, most of them charitable organizations close to Hamas.

Law 1 of 2000, which governs nongovernmental and charitable organizations in the West Bank, requires an organization to have a board (administrative committee) of at least seven members, a general assembly, bylaws that state the aim and objectives of the NGOs, and a specific bank account with names of signatories. The organization is required to hold regular general assembly and board meetings, maintain a proper narrative and financial documentation of its activities, and submit annual reports. Board elections should be held at least once every two years.

To apply for registration, an organization should have at least seven founding members, as well as bylaws. The process of registration is lengthy and requires multiple security clearances and checks on individual members, objectives, and suggested activities. Up to the present, the process is linked to factional and political requirements. Some NGOs find it easier to register than others because of the political connections of its founders. The registration process reportedly is not consistent for all applicants.

There is a unified registration law for all NGOs with clearly defined bylaws. The recent experience of the PNA makes it difficult sometimes to apply the law consistently to all NGOs. However, some attempts to have consistent application of the law are being made.

According to Income Tax Law 17 of 2004, donations to *zakat* funds, charities, or nonprofit organizations are deductible from taxable profit. The amount should not exceed 20 percent of pretax profit. The income tax law, the charity and nongovernmental organizations law, and the penal code are the main laws that govern the different types of philanthropic organizations in Palestine. Official institutions lack the ability to guarantee full implementation of the law.

Institutionalized Philanthropy
Philanthropic Organizations

NGOs and charity organizations offer basic assistance to the poor, such as educational, nutritional, and health services. According to the NGOs census conducted in 2007, 1,495 NGOs are working in the West Bank and the Gaza Strip, with 69 percent in the West Bank and 32 percent in the Gaza Strip. The same study shows that 16,882 paid employees are working in 573 NGOs (an average of twenty employees per NGO), 19 percent of whom work in relief and charity organizations.[16] According to the study, more than half of these NGOs are engaged in charity and philanthropy, including 17 percent whose main field is charity and philanthropy and 39 percent that have a charity and philanthropy component in their work. Most of the NGOs in Palestine are either national or community-based, but a few individual- or family-based foundations exist. Even individual-based foundations have a proper board of directors and are governed by a system that can be monitored by the Ministry of the Interior.

It is difficult to estimate the overall amount of money invested by philanthropic organizations in Palestine because of the different types of organizations and registrations. In addition, no centralized record of this money is available. For a variety of reasons, different institutions tend to underestimate or, in some cases, overestimate their budgets. The Ministry of the Interior does not keep records of audited financial statements and narrative reports of the institutions, although it has begun collecting data. The 2007 MAS census of NGOs estimates the NGOs received USD 223,607,358 in 2006, 19 percent of which went to charity and philanthropic activities.[17]

Networks

Networks of Palestinian NGOs serve as forums for information exchange and coordination of positions among NGOs and charitable organizations. At least five well-established networks of Palestinian NGOs are in operation. The most prominent is the Palestinian NGOs Network (PNGO), which has 91 member NGOs. Charitable organizations and philanthropic institutions are members in the General Union of Charitable Societies, which has 450 members. There is also a special union for Jerusalem charitable organizations and one for Gaza charities, in addition to the Council for Nongovernmental Organizations in the West Bank and Gaza Strip. A specialized network for grant-making foundations in Palestine has yet to be established.

Corporate Philanthropy

Corporate philanthropy is still new to Palestine. Few local companies have regular philanthropic activities. Likewise, little is done by international companies. In the last two years, however, activities have been initiated by Intel, which is establishing computer clubs for youth and centers of excellence in universities. Most corporate giving concentrates on educational activities, especially for youth and children. Some also fund culture and art, which offers high visibility.

Mapping Institutionalized Philanthropy in Palestine

Like other countries covered in this report, Palestine has at least five or six distinct forms of giving. These include community and family foundations, corporate philanthropy, direct organized individual giving or group giving, and individual giving through an existing network of local and international philanthropic organizations.

Community Foundations

There are two types of community foundations in Palestine. The first focuses on a specific geographical area or local community in the West Bank or the Gaza Strip. Examples include the Society of In'ash El-Usra, Friends of Birzeit Foundation, and Dalia Association. The second type draws on the affiliation and loyalty that a family holds for its original village in historical Palestine. A typical example is al-Lod Charitable Society.

The Society of In'ash Usra

The Society of In'ash El-Usra was founded in 1965 by a group of committed volunteers headed by the late Samiha Khalil with the aim of empowering Palestinian women and serving various sectors of the community. In the aftermath of the 1967 war and throughout the Israeli occupation, the society has played a vital role in dealing with the severe economic, social, and political hardships emanating from the occupation. In'ash El-Usra is a prominent address for individual philanthropists and nonreligious donations. At the same time, it is an address for thousands of orphans and widows who seek help. The charity has managed to establish and run an orphanage and a vocational training center that teaches women sewing, hairdressing, and food economy.

Al-Bireh Association, Palestine

The association, which was founded in 2003 by a group of al-Bireh children and original residents, supports the work of al-Bireh local community in the fields of health and education. It also donates money for individuals in need and connects al-Bireh with people all over the world. The association has accumulated a wealth of knowledge on effective strategies for addressing the needs of children and youth, from innovative means of applying technology to enhance young people's learning to holistic approaches to equipping young people with valuable life skills. The association's activities focus on four issues:

- Education: The association seeks to improve the quality of education and increase learning opportunities for young people both in and out of school through expanded access to information technology, innovative school reform, and instructional support for teachers.
- Employability: It seeks to improve young people's employment, entrepreneurial, and personal skills as a way of building their capacity for and engaging them in productive work.
- Leadership and Engagement: The association aims to inspire, support, and promote youth engagement and the role of young people as leaders of positive social change as a way to foster a lifelong commitment to active citizenship.
- Health Education and Awareness: It works to prepare children and youth to lead healthy lives by providing them with the knowledge and personal skills needed to make informed and healthy choices.

Friends of Birzeit Foundation

Friends of Birzeit Foundation was established in 1993 to support Birzeit University morally and financially. Members are businessmen, professionals, and wealthy Palestinians who live in the West Bank. The foundation is run solely by volunteers and students and, accordingly, does not have any administrative costs. Its main activities are the provision of scholarships, food vouchers, books, and clothes to students in need. Other activities include planting trees in the university, building computer labs, and establishing a system for the donation of expensive university books. Some businesspeople channel their funds through the organization. The carrier mail company, Aramex, for example, supports five scholarships through the foundation.

The organization's membership has dropped from one hundred and twenty active general assembly members prior to the year 2000 to fifty active members, largely as a result of the economic situation.

Dalia Association

A new Palestinian community foundation was recently founded by members of the Palestinian community from the West Bank, East Jerusalem, the Gaza Strip, Israel, and the diaspora. The founding board, which is diverse in terms of religion, gender, age, and politics, is committed to mobilizing, investing, and distributing resources according to local Palestinian priorities using community-based decision making. Its aim is to:

- Link people who have resources, expertise, ideas, contacts, equipment, and other assets with community activists who need those resources to serve their communities
- Fund hopeful, inspirational, and sustainable civil society initiatives, including community efforts that just need a small grant to supplement their local resources. A permanent endowment is being built over time to ensure sustainable income for current and future generations
- Involve people of all kinds in expanding traditions of philanthropy, volunteerism, and working together to strengthen the Palestinian social fabric
- Advocate for an international aid system that respects and responds to local priorities

Al-Lod Charitable Society

Founded in Nablus in 1995, al-Lod Charitable Society originally was a charity that served people from the occupied city of al-Lod. It has expanded to serve the Palestinian community in general. The society has managed to raise funds to expand its activities to include democratization processes, women's empowerment, refugee rights, and other issues. It is now an active NGO serving local communities in the north of the West Bank.

Family Foundations

Family foundations are private foundations where donations are derived from personal assets and management stays at least partially among family members. Some of the prominent examples in Palestine are described below.

Abdel-Mohsen Qattan Foundation

The Abdel-Mohsen Qattan Foundation was established in 1993 and registered in the United Kingdom. In 1998, the foundation set up a branch in Ramallah. The foundation has a board of family members and executive staff and a well-qualified staff of sixty-nine employees. Its main goal is to improve the quality of education and culture in Palestine and the Arab world.

One of the foundation's main achievements has been the establishment of a center for children in the Gaza Strip. The center offers courses for children and organizes cultural and art shows. It boasts a library with more than ninety-five thousand items, and also has a mobile library.

The foundation offers annual prizes in the field of culture and art (especially for young artists and journalists), funds creative art projects, and awards special scholarships for studies in education and art. The foundation also has a well-developed program that focuses on teacher training in quality education and improving the level of educational research in Palestine.

Almost 90 percent of the foundation's annual budget of USD 2.5 million comes from the Qattan Trust Fund. The foundation's publication is an additional source of self-financing. In 2004, the foundation received a grant from the European Union to implement an audiovisual project in Palestine to promote Palestinian film and television production. Currently, around 10 percent of the foundation's budget comes from funding sources such as the Swedish Anna Lindh Fund that do not place conditions on their support.

The foundation is a member of the Art and Culture Network, the Association of International Development Agencies in Palestine (AIDA), and the Arab Foundations Forum.

The Scientific Foundation of Hisham Adeeb Hijjawi

The Scientific Foundation of Hisham Adeeb Hijjawi (SFOHAH) is an independent, nonprofit, nongovernmental organization established by the late Hisham Hijjawi in 1981, with registration in Vaduz, Liechtenstein. Its objective is to support technical and applied science education in order to enhance technology transfer and absorption and thus develop a suitable industrial base for better human welfare. The foundation provides grants and support derived from its investment portfolio, endowed by Hisham Hijjawi.

A board of directors sets the policy for the foundation's grant making and operations. An advisory board made up of public figures advises on SFOHAH's general strategies. The foundation has a liaison office in Amman that follows up on its projects and programs in Jordan and Palestine.

SFOHAH's core programs include an annual award for three research projects in the applied sciences. The foundation supports existing colleges and universities, making annual contributions for the supply of computers and labs both in Jordan and Palestine, and for the support of scientific workshops, conferences, and so forth.

The foundation's main initiative is the establishment of a technical college in Palestine. SFOHAH donated USD 1.5 million to the project and is raising the additional financial requirement of around USD 10 million. The college will be owned and administered by al-Najah National University.

Hani Qaddumi Scholarship Foundation

The Hani Qaddumi Scholarship Foundation (HQSF) aims to assist young Palestinians who have the intellectual capacity but lack the financial means to acquire superior professional and managerial skills through quality education. It ultimately seeks to enable them to participate in the development of their country and society.

The heirs of the late Hani Qaddumi created the foundation in his memory in 2001. They were driven by their father's strong belief, and their own, that a distinguished education offers a unique opportunity to enrich one's personal life and greatly affect one's career through interaction with different cultures, the formation of lasting friendships, and the acquisition of new educational horizons.

HQSF allows young Palestinian men and women to compete annually for a number of endowment grants in a range of specializations, with an emphasis on engineering, information technology, and business administration. The grants are awarded to selected individuals on the basis of academic excellence, professional qualifications, and financial need.

Faisal Husseini Foundation

The Faisal Husseini Foundation aims to preserve the cultural character of the city of Jerusalem, maintain the Palestinian identity of its residents, and develop the services of its institutions. Through its various projects and commitment, the foundation supports Palestinian institutions in East Jerusalem that provide services in healthcare, education, and youth development.

Corporate Philanthropy

Palestinians did not have self-rule until 1993. Before then, the private sector was weak and corporate giving was therefore neither systematic nor institutionalized. Palestinian private businesses in the OPT, however, always have provided support discreetly to needy families and Palestinian schools and universities. This trend expanded following the establishment of the PNA. Telecommunication companies, which had monopoly contracts, felt compelled to adopt policies of corporate social responsibility. Their philanthropy took the form of grants and contributions for community development projects, especially in the field of education and youth.

In 2006, a telecommunication group that includes Jawal, Paltel, Palmedia, and Wasel launched its first social responsibility report, announcing the formation of the first social responsibility fund in Palestine.[18] The report claims to be the first Arab report that focuses on private sector social responsibility (defined as social grant making). The declared objective of the fund is to support the community with social services that bring no financial gains to the companies involved. Individual Palestinians and NGOs can apply in writing to the fund for projects in the fields of education, healthcare, and social affairs. In 2005, the fund donated JOD 1.2 million to projects in these fields, with 32 percent going to culture and art and 31 percent to education. A larger share of the funds (60 percent) went to projects in the West Bank, while 40 percent was spent on projects in the Gaza Strip. Most of the funds (41 percent) were channeled through NGOs, while 31 percent were channeled through governmental organizations and 14.3 percent through universities.

Other companies, such as Safad, al-Quds Pharmaceutical Company, and Birzeit Pharmaceutical Company also donate to the community, although their contributions tend to be smaller. Intel is establishing computer clubs for youth and centers of excellence in universities. The national beverage company, Marawi, is focusing on services for youth and children, including a children's library in Beit Jala Hospital, as part of a program to set up children's libraries all over the West Bank and the Gaza Strip. In September 2007, the company announced a three-year project called 'Layna al-Ghad' (Tomorrow is Ours), which will support fifteen Palestinian schools with computer labs and more than 150 computers.

Al-Quds Pharmaceutical Company

Al-Quds Pharmaceutical Company is an example of both individual and institutional philanthropy. The company awards ten full university scholarships a year. It also gives small contributions to more than thirty charities all over the West Bank and the Gaza Strip, most of which run orphanages or clinics. In addition to financial contributions, the company makes in-kind contributions in the form of medicine for remote clinics, among others.

The foundation's chairman, Mohamed Masrouji, and a number of others established the al-Mustaqbal schools and a hospital in Bethlehem almost a decade ago. These projects focus on providing affordable quality health and education services. While the projects are designed to operate for profit, the donors were aware from the start that they would be costly and unlikely to generate profit. The donors continue to provide the schools with partial financial support as part of their corporate social responsibility.

Transforming Philanthropy: Organized Individual Giving

Palestine has many forms of philanthropic giving initiated by a group of individuals who do not create a formal foundation but have maintained their giving over time. Some are moving away from charitable activities like food aid to give their money for developmental causes. A good example of this type of giving is Children of Ramallah, which is based in the United States. Members meet regularly and collect money for projects in the Ramallah al-Beireh area in the West Bank. They send a delegation once a year to visit sites and decide on priorities for developing the two small cities. Such donations have contributed to large projects, such as the building of a major community center and the development of a botanical garden in al-Beireh. The center is rented out to the local community, which provides revenue for the al-Beireh municipality to perform its tasks. Children of Ramallah has donated to charities in Ramallah, to the only sports center in town (First Ramallah Group), and directly to the Ramallah municipality, which has used the money to improve the road and other services.

A notable example of its activities occurred during the international boycott of the Hamas government from March 2006 to January 2007. Following the teachers' strike, which was called because teachers had not received their salaries, a group of Beir Nabala children in the United States donated two months of salaries to more than fifty teachers working in three schools to enable them to go back to work. The amount collected exceeded USD 28,000, which is more than the three schools needed. The remaining funds were distributed to three schools in a nearby village. Similar donations occurred in the Mekhmas and Beit Exa villages, usually from the children of the village in the diaspora.

Under the same category fall donations of individuals who do not have a well-established or institutionalized organization but have regular funding patterns associated with a commitment to a particular idea. The prominent Palestinian businessman, Hasib Sabagh, for example, funds an annual summer camp for Palestinian children from all over the world to introduce them to historical Palestine and to establish a strong bond among Palestinians from across the globe. In the last two years, the summer camp has been held near destroyed Palestinian villages.

A Network that Facilitates Philanthropy

The strong network of charitable organizations facilitates Arab and Palestinian philanthropy. Many individuals contribute regularly to certain organizations and NGOs. Some of them have been doing so for a long time. These donations do not always go toward charity. In some cases, the funds go toward infrastructure projects, including roads, schools, and clinics; in others, they are used to rebuild destroyed houses. Islamic organizations like al-Salah Islamic Society, non-Islamic organizations, *zakat* committees, grant-making organizations like the Welfare Association, and intermediary organizations like the Palestine International Institution are some of the entities through which Arab and Palestinian individuals channel their philanthropic giving.

Al-Salah Islamic Society

Established in 1978, al-Salah Islamic Society is a charity institution whose mission is to participate in building the Palestinian community by improving the conditions of children and relieving their suffering in all aspects of life. In 2003, the society assisted a thousand families and gave away 76,750 food baskets. Currently, the society is extending assistance to 5,113 orphans in Gaza. The society also has supervised the building and renovation of houses in the aftermath of Israeli attacks.

Zakat Committees

Zakat may not be considered a form of philanthropy, as it is a requirement in Islam. These individual contributions are intended to help the poor and needy and rarely are directed toward building capacity and sustainable development. In the case of Palestine, however, *zakat* has been institutionalized through *zakat* committees that direct long-term financing and expertise toward self-sustainable community development projects that provide long-term social benefits. The Nablus Zakat Committee, for example, established the first dairy factory in the West Bank (as-Safa Dairy Products), and the Tulkarem Zakat Committee established the only hospital in town.

Zakat committees offer humanitarian aid in the West Bank and Gaza. The *Zakat* Fund at the Ministry of Waqfs and Religious Affairs in Palestine lists eighty-one committees operating in the Palestinian territories, sixty-seven of which operate in the West Bank. These committees offer assistance to a large number of orphans and needy families. Their activities are diverse, ranging from monthly donations to orphans and needy families, to assistance to students in schools and universities, to medical services for thousands of patients in health units and hospitals. *Zakat* committees affiliated to the Ministry of Waqfs assist more than eighteen thousand orphans through the disbursement of symbolic amounts of money ranging between JOD 20 to JOD 25.[19]

Examples of these committees include al-Quds Zakat Committee, Nablus Zakat Committee, Gaza Zakat Committee, and Burqa Zakat Committee.

Welfare Association

The Welfare Association can be considered, without hesitation, the most important association in the field of philanthropy in Palestine. Gathering prominent Palestinian businesspeople and intellectuals, the association is a philanthropic and independent voluntary foundation established in 1983. It has earned a solid reputation as a serious organization that is leading Palestinian development. From the start, the association adopted the principle of self-sustainability, setting up an endowment that is supervised by an investment committee and looked after by professional portfolio managers. The revenue covers the association's recurring costs. This ensures that annual dues and donations are directed wholly toward funding grants related to Welfare Association programs and projects.[20]

Since 1984, the Welfare Association has been acting as an intermediary NGO, managing the grants of private donors in and outside Palestine. Between 1983 and 1996, the association disbursed twelve hundred grants to over three hundred NGOs in Palestine and abroad. The strong international reputation that the Welfare Association has established has encouraged donor institutions to partner with the association. Funds under management from donors such as the European Union and the Arab Fund for Social and Economic Development (AFSED) are directed toward projects in the OPT, Israel, and Lebanon.

The association is open about its funding and projects—something that is still rare in the field of Arab philanthropy. Between 1983 and 1996, the association funded 1,307 projects totaling USD 90 million (USD 43 million from its own sources and USD 47 million from external sources). This averages out to approximately USD 6.42 million per year, of which around USD 3 million came from the association's funds.

Recently, the Welfare Association, heading a consortium that includes the British Council and the Charities Aid Foundation (CAF), submitted a successful proposal to the World Bank for the establishment of a Project Management Organization (PMO) to manage World Bank assistance to Palestinian NGOs. This project is a major breakthrough when it comes to NGO activity in Palestine.

The association constitutes an important pillar of Palestinian philanthropy, with the ability to help beyond small-aid initiatives. Additionally, because of their financial and intellectual capacities, the members of the Welfare Association have the potential to influence decision-making processes at the national level.

Palestine International Institution

The Palestine International Institution is a newly founded organization based on setting up a two-way channel between communities of Palestinian and Arab origin and friends of the Palestinian people. The organization facilitates the transfer of donations and funds from Arabs and Palestinians abroad to address Palestinian national and developmental priorities. The organization also facilitates the transfer of Palestinian and Arab knowledge, human resources, and expertise in support of the Palestinian cause and works to facilitate experience sharing and investment opportunities in Palestine.

Conclusion

Palestinians have a rich culture of philanthropy that has helped to sustain social and economic well-being through conflict and prolonged occupation. Over Palestine's long history of philanthropic giving, several different trends of organized giving for social good have emerged. Today, most philanthropic institutions in Palestine are registered under Palestinian law, and organizations that are registered abroad usually try to reregister as a branch of a foreign organization working in Palestine. In theory, all these organizations are accountable to the Ministry of the Interior, though oversight in the ministry is as yet not well developed. In general, citizens enjoy a liberal environment when it comes to establishing organizations in Palestine and a rather free and tolerant atmosphere regarding media and freedom of expression. Recent political developments following the Hamas election victory and takeover in Gaza are threatening to undermine these fragile achievements.

Motivations behind philanthropy in Palestine have religious roots, but go well beyond religious obligations today. They extend to a sense of belonging to a national cause and a desire to provide material and moral support to a people under occupation. Philanthropy in Palestine facilitates development, as in other Arab countries, but it also has contributed to maintaining the 'steadfastness' of Palestinians and their connection to their homeland.

Increased poverty and unemployment, allegations of terrorist connections, the international financial boycott, and restrictions on money transfers and bank transactions are all factors that discourage the growth of the sector. These major challenges have not kept the field from evolving in important ways. Corporate involvement, application of successful business practices to giving, and international links are some of the ways that philanthropy in the area is becoming more strategic and effective.

Notes

1. Ibrahim 2005.
2. Palestinian Central Bureau of Statistics. At the moment, a Palestinian census is being implemented that may lead to a slight change in population projections.
3. Palestinian Centre for Human Rights 2006.
4. Palestinian Ministry of Planning National Authority for Combating Poverty and Palestinian Central Bureau of Statistics 2006. This report was prepared by the Pro-poor Participatory Planning Project, implemented by the Ministry of Planning in cooperation with UNDP, with funding from the United Kingdom's Department of Foreign International Development. Data is unofficial.
5. See Reporters Without Borders' 2007 worldwide press freedom index.
6. MAS, March 2007.
7. The average poverty line for the reference family (composed of six members: two adults and four children) in the OPT reached ILS (USD 433) 1,934 in 2004, while the severe poverty line for the same reference family was ILS 1,622 (USD 363).
8. Remittances from family members abroad were always important for supporting Palestinian society in the OPT. Although it is not within the definition of institutionalized philanthropy, this phenomenon would be interesting to study, especially given the fact that some of these remittances support for non-family members, scholarships in universities, orphans, and other causes.
9. Well-known examples of *waqf* are Waqf Tamim al-Dari and Waqf Khalil al-Rahman in Hebron, Waqf Sinan Basha in Yaffa, Waqf Lala Mustafa Basha in the north of Palestine, and Waqf Ahmad Basha al-Jazzar in Akka.
10. Hanafi 2000.
11. MAS 1997.
12. MAS 2005.
13. Development Studies Program Report, No. 17 for 2004. Birzeit University, Ramallah.
14. MAS 2007.
15. Ibid.
16. Ibid.

17. Ibid.
18. http://www.jawwal.ps/press/social%20responsbility%20fund%20report%202005_ar.pdf
   http://www.alriyadh-np.com/2006/06/05/article160559_s.html
19. Palestinian Ministry of Planning National Authority for Combating Poverty
   and Palestinian Central Bureau of Statistics 2006.
20. Hanafi 2000.

References

Abdelhamid, Muhannad. 2005. *Role of the Palestinian Media in Facing Corruption*
   Ramallah: Aman.
Development Studies Center. 2004. *Palestine Human Development Report*. Birzeit:
   Birzeit University.
Economist Intelligence Unit. 2007. "Country Profile: Palestinian Territories."
Hanafi, Sari. 1999. "Palestinian Diaspora Contribution to Investment and Philan-
   thropy in Palestine." Lecture given at the Palestinian Academic Society for the
   Study of International Affairs convention, 10 June.
Ibrahim, Barbara. 2005. "Strengthening Philanthropy and Civic Engagement in the
   Arab World: A Mission for the John D. Gerhart Center." Paper presented at the
   symposium, "Promoting Philanthropy and Civic Engagement in the Arab
   World." American University in Cairo, Egypt, 30 October–1 November.
Nakhleh, Khalil. 2004. *The Myth of Palestinian Development: Political Aid and Sus-
   tainable Deceit*. Ramallah: Muwatin. (In Arabic.)
Palestinian Centre for Human Rights. 2006. *Poverty in the Gaza Strip*. Gaza City:
   Palestinian Centre for Human Rights.
Palestine Economic Policy Research Institute (MAS). 1997. *Social Support Institutions in the West Bank and Gaza Strip*. Ramallah: MAS. (In Arabic.)
————. 2001. *Relationship Between Palestinian Non-governmental Organizations and the Palestinian National Authority and Donors*. Ramallah: MAS.
————. 2005. *Economic & Social Monitor*. Ramallah: MAS.
————. 2007. *Economic & Social Monitor*, March. Ramallah: MAS.
————. 2007. *Mapping Palestinian Non-governmental Organizations in the West
   Bank and the Gaza Strip*. Ramallah: MAS.
Palestinian Ministry of Planning National Authority for Combating Poverty and
   Palestinian Central Bureau of Statistics. March 2006. "Preliminary Draft Palestine Poverty Report 2004."

Web resources
http://www.pcbs.gov.ps, Palestinian Central Bureau of Statistics.
http://www.badil.org, Badil Resource Center for Palestinian Residency and Refugee
   Rights.
http://www.amin.org, Arabic Media Internet Network.
http://www.jawwal.ps/press/social%20responsbility%20fund%20report%202005_a
   r.pdf, Jawwal, a Pal Tel Group Company.
http://www.alquds.com/inside.php?opt=7&id=46028, Palestinian news site.
http://arabic.pnn.ps/index.php?option=com_content&task=view&id=17904&Itemid
   =59, Palestine News Network.

5

The Republic of Lebanon

Fadi Sharaiha
Barbara Lethem Ibrahim

Overview

The origins of Lebanese philanthropy lie in religious institutions of the Ottoman Empire. As in neighboring Palestine and Syria, the once-vibrant traditions of *awqaf*, *zakat*, and *'ushr* survived into the modern age in Lebanon. Contemporary philanthropy, however, is marked by the singular politics of sectarian civil war, Israeli occupation, and external meddling over the past thirty years. In particular, private giving has become inextricably bound to sectarian parties and militias. A small but growing movement attempts to foster nonsectarian civil society groups, believing this to be the only healthy way to rebuild national unity.

A relatively open society reinforced by international trade made Lebanon one of the earliest sites of modern civil society formation. Large flows of migration out of the country coupled with sizable return migration in the last century means that ideas and expertise for civil society organization (CSO) development have been readily available. The native entrepreneurship celebrated by Lebanese was applied to invigorate this sector long before it became fashionable in the era of Bill Gates. The presence of many highly regarded universities and publishing houses contributed to a climate of openness and innovation in the civil society sector.

It therefore is not surprising that as expatriate Lebanese became successful and wealthy, many began supporting social causes at home, and some returned to put their skills to work in promoting social and cultural advancement. The levels of debate around indigenous funding and development

111

today are vigorous and characterized by considerable soul-searching in the CSO community—a result of over three decades of civil strife.

Philanthropic initiatives in Lebanon have been closely associated with sectarian politics, almost from their inception as religious gestures over many centuries, and certainly with the rise of modern foundations today. The fifteen years of civil war that began in 1975 both stimulated private initiatives to rebuild the country and led to a further retreat into sectarianism. Present-day politics remain unstable, prompting a growing number of Lebanese to articulate the need to overcome purely sectarian identities. A few organizations are leading the way toward nonsectarian, professionally managed philanthropy.

Country Background

Lebanon at a Glance[1]	
Country size	10,400 sq. km.
Population (2006)	3.7 million
GDP (2006)	USD 22.6 billion
GDP PPP (2006)	USD 20.3 billion
Services	*75%*
Industry	*20%*
Manufacturing	*12%*
Agriculture	*6%*
GDP per capita (2006)	USD 6,110 (USD)
GDP per capita PPP (2006)	USD 5,457
HDI ranking	79/177
Religious groups	Muslim 60% *(Shia, Sunni, Druze, Isma'ili, Alawite, Nusayri)* Christian 39% *(Maronite Catholic, Greek Orthodox, Melite Catholic, Armenian Orthodox, Syrian Orthodox, Roman Catholic, Chaldean, Assyrian, Copt, Protestant),* other 1%
Lebanese pound (LBP)	USD 0.00066

History

Lebanon is known as a vibrant liberal country in the Middle East with a fractious recent past. The consequences of that past continue to reverberate as the country charts a course toward reconstruction. In order to understand the current political climate, it is imperative to examine Lebanon's modern history.

Once under the jurisdiction of the Ottoman Empire, Lebanon was pieced together to include the area of Mount Lebanon and the coastal cities of Tripoli, Beirut, Sidon, and Tyre, as well as the Beqaa Valley, in the aftermath of the First World War. The country established its independence in 1943, when the acting Maronite Christian president and Sunni Muslim prime minister agreed on a National Pact that divided all government positions among the religious communities with a 6:5 ratio of Christians to Muslims based on a census taken in 1932. Shifts in the demographic balance later became the impetus for a bloody civil war and long-term political problems.

In the years that followed the pact, an increase in the Muslim population in relation to Christians began to threaten the power-sharing accord. In 1970, Palestinians displaced from their land during wars with Israel in 1948 and 1967 took refuge in Lebanon after being expelled from Jordan. This incident served both to complicate existing religious tensions and as the justification for Israeli retaliation and twenty-nine-year occupation of southern Lebanon. Deepening tensions along sectarian lines led to a civil war in 1975 that lasted almost fifteen years. Foreign elements became heavily involved, with France and the West protecting the Christians, Syria and Iran supporting the Shia, and the Sunni Muslim world, particularly Saudi Arabia, backing the Sunnis.

In the 1980s the civil war lost much of its sectarian character. The worst outbreaks of violence began to occur within sectarian communities or between local and foreign forces, oftentimes with shifting alliances. Eventually, the sectarian groups were convinced under the influence of Saudi Arabia to sign the Taif Accords, which altered the constitution, shifting powers from a Christian president to a Sunni Muslim prime minister and granting Muslims more power.

The Taif Accords, signed in 1990, brought about increased Syrian influence in Lebanese affairs. Certain political and civil liberties were allowed to citizens that exceeded those in most other Arab countries in return for tacit Western acceptance of Syrian control.[2] Internally, Lebanese politicians began to side with either the pro- or the anti-Syrian camp. Corruption mounted as the government financed massive deficit spending on reconstruction during the 1990s. By the end of the decade, Lebanon's government debt far exceeded its gross domestic product (GDP) and the economy was in deep recession.[3]

Demographics Today

According to a 2005 International Monetary Fund (IMF) report, population estimates for Lebanon are around 3.58 million, with over two hundred thousand Palestinians living in semi-permanent refugee camps,[4] and some three hundred thousand migrant workers. The Palestinians, many of whom have lived in Lebanon since 1970, are not granted citizenship rights and face many restrictions that reflect the precarious sectarian balance. Because of historically high out-migration streams and a steady flow of repatriation, Lebanon is one of the most transnational of Arab populations. Since 1932, no census has been undertaken for fear of revealing demographic figures that would threaten the current 1:1 ratio power-sharing accord.

The Political Scene

Type of Government

The political system is based on power sharing among religious sectarian groups, 17 of which are officially recognized. The three principle groups, Maronite Christians, Sunni Muslims, and Shia Muslims, hold executive posts. By law, the president must be a Maronite Christian. Traditionally, this position was the most powerful. The president is formally selected every six years by the National Assembly. The president and parliament nominate the prime minister, who is responsible for selecting a cabinet that is subject to parliamentary approval. The speaker of parliament is by law a Shia Muslim. The increasing Shia demographic is demanding proportional shifts in power.

National Legislature

The National Assembly consisting of 128 seats with four-year terms is the only elected structure at the national level. Seats are divided equally between Muslims and Christians.

Legal System

The judiciary consists of civilian courts, military courts, the Judicial Council and Constitutional Council.

In February 2005, after over a decade in politics, Rafik Hariri, a businessman, philanthropist, and former prime minister, was assassinated. This watershed event led to massive street politics and the end of Syria's overt presence in Lebanon, though Syrian influence continues. After twenty-nine years, Syrian troops pulled back to their own borders. Parliamentary elections in May 2005 marked the first post-civil war period free of outside occupation.

The death of Hariri had political reverberations and prompted an ongoing investigation that seeks to implicate pro-Syria actors within the Lebanese government. In the months following Hariri's assassination, his son, Saad Hariri, stepped in to lead what is known as the March 14 Alliance,[5] a coalition of anti-Syria political parties, democrats, and independents with a strong youth base. The opposition consists of Hezbollah and Amal, the two key Shiite parties, and Michel Aoun, who represents the Christian Free Patriotic Movement.

In June 2006, politics on the border of Lebanon blew up once again. A war with Israel broke out, lasting over fifty days and causing billions of dollars in damage to homes, businesses, and infrastructure. This has reversed the momentum of economic gains, causing a second major exodus of high-level manpower and overall serving as a major setback to reconstruction efforts. A long political stalemate was broken in May 2008 by a flare-up of violence between government backers and Hezbollah. Recent accords brokered in Qatar have led to the installation of a new president and an agreement by all sides to allow the Lebanese army to keep the peace.

The media sector in Lebanon has a reputation for liberalism and promoting free speech. Although press freedom has enjoyed a long tradition within the country, at the present time nearly all media outlets are owned by prominent political and commercial elites.[6] Few outlets could be said to operate free of sectarian or political influence.

The Economy

Official economic data has become more reliable since the end of the civil war, but it remains relatively poor. The first part of the decade produced promising increases in economic growth, but this progress was all but reversed by the hostilities with Israel in July and August 2006, which resulted in an estimated USD 3.6 billion in infrastructure damage.[7] GDP growth reversed from an estimated 6 percent forecasted growth for 2006 to a 6 percent contraction.

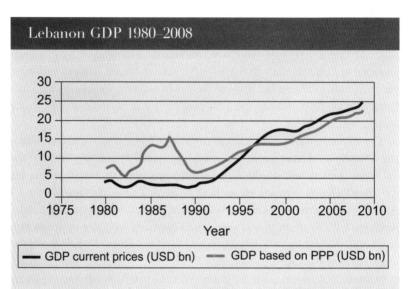

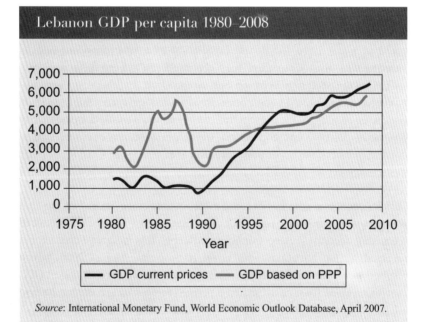

The economy has struggled since the end of the civil war, hampered by political gridlock and ongoing conflicts. Lebanon is mostly a services-based economy, deriving 67 percent of its GDP from that industry.[8] Once serving as a regional banking hub, the country has suffered as a result of the civil war. Although services have been rebuilt to a certain extent, the country now faces tough competition from dynamic and progressive cities in the Gulf. Lebanon had developed a high-end tourism sector that catered to Arab visitors, particularly in the aftermath of 9/11, when Europe and the United States became less attractive destinations. The 2006 war sent those revenues plummeting and created an uncertain future.

The post-war reconstruction effort has depended heavily on the commercial banking sector, as well as on private sector funds. Philanthropic gifts also have played a major role. State spending remains at a high and inefficient level, funding 13 percent of the labor force. Inefficient spending and a massive need to borrow for reconstruction has led Lebanon to have one of the highest debt ratios in the world: around 195 percent of GDP. Debt servicing consistently took 40 percent of total spending and almost 70 percent of revenue on average from 2001 to 2005.

A series of donor conferences have been held in Paris to attract support from existing creditors and foreign allies as a way to mitigate the burgeoning debt crises. The result of these conferences was a series of concessional loans for development projects, long-term restructuring schemes, and a reduction in the average servicing charges of the debt. Little of the money from the Paris donor conferences is in the form of direct grants; rather, it has strings attached to repayment and usage.

Many reform policies have been enacted to jump-start the economy, despite internal and external setbacks. Through a reform instituted by Rafik Hariri, the government legislated a program of deregulation and economic liberalization by slashing custom duties and taxes in an attempt to create a favorable climate for investment. Parliament has passed legislation easing restrictions on foreign real estate ownership and approved a new investment promotion law. Increased revenue also was a result of a government-mandated increase in the value added tax.

Philanthropy in Focus
The Culture of Giving

Lebanese society prides itself on maintaining an open climate for culture and politics, as well as on its entrepreneurial acumen. A widely dispersed and successful diaspora population maintains close ties to the home country, sending back large remittance streams. These have been widely used to build schools, clinics, and mosques or churches, and to support social services, often in an emigrant's village of origin.

Like other countries in the Middle East, religiously motivated giving has a long tradition in Lebanon, with institutions such as *waqf* proliferating in the Ottoman era. While religious origins pervade philanthropy around the region, the years of sectarian civil war and its aftermath have deepened these identities in Lebanon. Like other aspects of civil society, philanthropy almost always has a sectarian character in Lebanon. Both religious and political parties have played a dominant role in the evolution of religious giving. The terminology of sectarian groups and that of political parties comingle because most parties have a religious affiliation. Major sectarian groups have distinct philanthropic arms that direct charity and services to their own constituency, although most would claim that these activities are for all Lebanese citizens.

Each religious sect forms its own safety net around organized religious giving. The collection of donations and provision of social services may become a way of creating group loyalty, or, as is often alleged, a way of winning over converts to a political cause. Hezbollah is recognized for its effective provision of social, medical, and other kinds of support to disadvantaged populations of the rural south and the slums of Beirut. It is not surprising that such giving engenders a kind of loyalty and gratitude, if not outright political support. The mixing of social services and efforts at voter turnout, for example, is a problem faced not only in Lebanon but also elsewhere in the Arab world, such as Jordan and Egypt.

The Lebanese desire to protect democratic institutions has kept elections alive in recent years despite continuing sectarian stand-offs. Ironically, electoral politics both encourage philanthropy and keep it closely tied to sectarianism. Election campaigning is a time of heightened giving, both by candidates and their wealthier supporters. Philanthropic gifts have a short-term impact on the living conditions of less advantaged voters, and they 'buy' support.

The scale of election-related giving is not known, but most Lebanese believe it has increased dramatically in the past decade. In the months and weeks prior to voting, communities tend to be showered with gifts and donations designed to leverage electoral support. In some cases, beneficiaries take control of the transaction, specifying the levels of donations that will result in a given proportion of the community's votes. This was seen in the last parliamentary elections, for example, when a village church renovation project set contribution levels, managed by the mayor, that were tied to a sliding scale of the votes to be delivered by the populace.[9] A promising development in 2008 is the creation of a civil society coalition to improve electoral processes—the Civil Campaign for Election Reform.

In the current atmosphere of political stalemate and economic duress, the Lebanese government lacks the ability to pursue vigorous development. A small but growing group of organizations that identify themselves as specifically nonsectarian believes that unified citizen action is the only way forward for Lebanon. New and existing philanthropic initiatives attempt to bridge the gap between the needs of the population and government services.

The Legal Environment for Philanthropy

The culture of giving in Lebanon is complicated by the tenuous political situation. The Ministry of the Interior plays a strong role in the activities of civil associations, in contravention to rights secured by the Law of Associations. The ministry requires its own registration procedure beyond that stipulated in the law, including the imposition of a template version of bylaws. Nonetheless, the environment for CSOs is recognized as among the least constrained in the region.

Private associations and public interest organizations are governed by the Ottoman Law of 1909, as amended, which differentiates between the two types of organizations. The procedures of incorporation of a private association do not need to be approved by the corresponding administrative authority, meaning the Ministry of the Interior, but notification is required. Associations are free to offer grants and to receive and distribute funds from abroad in the country. If funds are transferred from Lebanon to an entity outside, then it is considered a foreign association and must be framed accordingly in its bylaws.

The existence of public interest organizations is subject to the Council of Ministers under a watchdog body known as the Control Authority. This authority has the right to inspect the public interest organization and to require it to submit a detailed report on annual activities, one on accomplishments, the year-end balance sheet, and how the organization will use its resources to achieve the designated programs in the following year. Organizations in violation of these procedures may be disqualified and face legal consequences before a criminal court. Public interest organizations are not allowed to give cash donations and their general position is relegated to a supporting role. According to Edict 1785 of 1979, donations offered to private associations or organizations receive a limited tax exemption of a maximum of 10 percent of the taxpayer's net profits.

The Ottoman Law stipulates that if an association fails to state its purposes accurately or to provide the government with sufficient information about its activities, it may be banned, its properties can be confiscated and activities suspended, and, ultimately, it can be closed down by the proper authorities. Approval of new amendments must be licensed in advance. Associations may extend grants if this is included in the bylaws, or otherwise must obtain prior approval from the proper authorities.[10]

Foreign associations are allowed in Lebanon, but they must obtain licenses beforehand. They are licensed by a decree from the cabinet and monitored through the Ministry of the Interior.

Institutionalized Philanthropy

Institutionalized philanthropy in Lebanon is similar to that in neighboring countries in its mix of older *waqf* structures, institutions to distribute religiously mandated donations such as *zakat*, and more contemporary forms of grant-making or operating foundations. Many of the operating foundations in Lebanon could be characterized as charity associations mainly engaged in social services. Some are secular, but many are associated with a religious sect. Increasingly, foundations are formed by wealthy individuals in the name or memory of a family member. These newer foundations have a variable mix of social and political agendas, according to most Lebanese observers.

Private individual/family-based philanthropy generally is established by elites or return migrants who have amassed wealth abroad. Many but not all are highly involved in politics. A sad reality is that the frequency of political assassinations means that a number of these foundations are set up posthumously.

Among the most prominent role models for individual philanthropic giving was the late businessman and prime minister, Rafik Hariri. Despite his legacy as a controversial figure, few doubt the impact of the Hariri Foundation on the sustainability of higher education for students across the sectarian spectrum, or his repeated investments in the rebuilding of Lebanon through periods of war and destruction. Stories are told of Hariri's representatives going from village to village to identify talented young Lebanese and make scholarships available to them for study abroad during the worst years of the civil war.

Grant-making Foundations
The Hariri Foundation

The Hariri Foundation was founded in Lebanon by the late Rafik Hariri. Its mission is to make education a means for the development of Lebanon's youth. It is a grant- and loan-making institution that has responded to dire national needs stemming from the civil war and its aftermath. The foundation started its mission in Sidon in 1979. Then, it was called the Islamic Institute for Culture and Higher Education, but it has carried its present name since 1984, when it moved its central offices to Beirut. It opened offices in Tripoli and Bekaa, in addition to those in Sidon, in an attempt to facilitate the giving of grants and loans to individuals countrywide seeking education at the tertiary level, regardless of religious affiliation. It also opened offices in Paris, London, and Washington, DC, to keep in close contact with student protégés enrolled in nearly one hundred universities in Western Europe, North Africa, Canada, and the United States.

Throughout its life, the Hariri Foundation has supported a hundred and thirty thousand students from Lebanon with a cumulative budget of more than USD 1 billion. This is the largest private organization in Lebanon, and it has played a major role in building the educational sector. The Hariri family is the sole sponsor of the foundation, with no additional funding. The foundation also has the following projects:

- *The University Loan Program*: Up to June 1996, around thirty-two thousand students were granted loans.
- *Special English Training*: This makes it possible for students to over come the language barrier as a prerequisite for university admission abroad.
- *Preparatory Year Program*: The program helps students continue their education in French either in Lebanon or in France.
- *University Student Training*: The Hariri Foundation has sent 144 university graduates, mainly engineers, to be retrained and kept abreast of new developments in their fields after intensive English training.
- *Medical Training Program*: This is a program for Lebanese doctors who have completed their university education abroad and wish to continue their specialization in Lebanon.
- *Career Planning and Guidance*: The foundation provides information for job seekers on job availability and the needs of the labor market in various fields of specialization. In addition, a career guidance program exists that offers career counseling.
- *Funding and Renovating Secondary Education Facilities.*
- *The University Institute of Technology*: The foundation, in collaboration with Lebanese University and the Ministry of Higher Education in France, contributed the construction of this institute.

- *Kafar Falous Complex*: Founded in 1979, it contains a high school, a university, a school for the training of nurses, and a hospital. The university college is known as Sidon Institute for University Studies and is under the administration of St. Joseph University.

Operating Foundations
Oum al-Nour

Established nearly twenty years ago, Oum al-Nour is one of the oldest Lebanese operating foundations to be funded through profits from the Debanne family businesses. The organization has a focused commitment to helping people overcome drug addiction in order to attain a healthy society.

The organization recognizes the issue of drug addiction as a complex personal and societal problem, and it maintains extensive programs to rehabilitate and follow up with individual addicts. In addition to its prevention and treatment programs, it works on building a skilled staff that applies the latest scientific tools and methods and adapts them to Lebanese society.

Oum al-Nour has a multidisciplinary team composed of counselors, ex-drug addicts/peer counselors, psychologists, social workers, sociocultural workers, psychotherapists, recreation therapists, doctors, and lawyers.

Social Service Associations
The Lebanese Welfare Association for the Handicapped

The Lebanese Welfare Association for the Handicapped (LWAH) is a nongovernmental, nonprofit organization registered with the Ministry of the Interior under the notification and information no. 92/A.D. It was established in 1984 by Randa Assi Berri.

After the civil war, the number of disabled persons in Lebanon increased tremendously and the lack of basic services for this demographic was apparent. Beyond that, for all levels of society, whether young or old, it was clear that services ranging from medical and psychological aid to financial and social aid were needed. Thus, with a mission to improve the quality of life for people with special needs and to enhance their dignity, independence, and productivity, LWAH developed services for their reintegration into society.

The main objectives of the association include providing full rehabilitation services to the disabled, including diagnosis and treatment, physical rehabilitation, and psychosocial, educational, and vocational rehabilitation; ensuring the process of social integration of the disabled; and promoting and supporting the rights of the disabled. LWAH also works on some projects related to community development, agriculture, advocacy, sports activities, and awareness campaigns, but its primary capacity is for rehabilitation services. Services it offers include diagnosis and treatment, physical rehabilitation, psychosocial rehabilitation, and educational rehabilitation. After the war with Israel in July 2006, LWAH delivered prosthetics and orthotics to ninety-seven landmine, cluster munitions, and war victims, as well as eighty hearing aids to those suffering from hearing disabilities.

The Social Welfare Institution of Lebanon

The Social Welfare Institution of Lebanon (SWI) was started in 1917 as a small orphanage concerned with the condition of orphans distressed by the First World War. In 1932, having grown into a larger operation, the orphanage was named Dar al-Aytam al-Islamia. Forty years later, the organization was renamed the Social Welfare Institution after targeting a much larger portion of orphaned children.

Today, SWI provides diversified specialized services in over twenty-five locations, including Beirut and its suburbs, the Bekaa, Aramoun, Shimlan, Wadi al-Zaineh, Akkar, Kitirmaya, and Syr al-Dinnieyeh. It has forty-nine operating institutions.

Religious Associations
Fondation Père Afif Osseiran

The Fondation Père Afif Osseiran (FPAO), established in the 1960s by Reverend Father Afif Osseiran, was set up to rehabilitate minors from underprivileged backgrounds and troubled families, with the goal of reintroducing them into society.[11] The Foyer de la Providence, officially recognized by the Lebanese government in 1967, became a free boarding and technical school. Its main mission is to provide education and technical skills to disadvantaged and problematic young boys, regardless of religious or political affiliation. The home offers young boys a real family atmosphere and helps them maintain relations with their parents. They receive free accommodation, food, extracurricular activities, and psychological and medical follow up. In addition, the school offers them an education and instruction with specialized proficiency in carpentry, car mechanics, general mechanics, building electricity, and welding. The certificate of professional aptitude (CAP) and the Professional Certificate Brevet (BP) can be obtained through the school, along with official diplomas from the National Office for Employment for technical training. As soon as the children get their diplomas, the foundation helps them find jobs. In special cases, it directs particularly gifted students to institutes that offer them the opportunity to pursue their education further. The foundation serves about 150 children each year.

Minors in Conflict with the Law

In January 2004, FPAO, in partnership with Terre des Hommes, took charge of a program established by Terre des Hommes called Minors in Conflict with the Law (MCL). The program, in operation since 1993, consisted of follow-up on the social and professional integration of young former prisoners. In 2005, FPAO took sole charge of the program. Places of intervention include the prison of Roumieh (juveniles wing); Union for Protecting Childhood in Lebanon (UPEL) (Fanar); and the regions of Burj al-Barajneh, Saïda, and Tripoli.

The objective of the program is the rehabilitation and reintegration of juveniles in conflict with the law through a multidimensional approach. In the prison at Roumieh, rehabilitative services are offered by way of psychological support, educational support (including literacy classes and grade levels), improvements in the conditions of detention (e.g., hygiene, medical care, and food), and sports and leisure activities. The program works with an expected results approach. This includes improving the circumstances of detention, educational and psychological rehabilitation, social and professional reintegration, and the proper implementation of Law 422.* The number of beneficiaries through the expected results approach has been approximately 275 minor prisoners each year and 250 ex-prisoners living in the regions of greater Beirut, Saïda, and Tripoli.

Individual Philanthropy
The René Moawad Foundation

The René Moawad Foundation (RMF) was created on November 22, 1991, exactly two years after the assassination of President René Moawad, a Christian Maronite, who was killed seventeen days after being elected president of the Lebanese Republic. As a member of parliament and minister in various cabinets both before and during the civil war, he believed in the unity of the Lebanese people and actively strove for civil peace, dialogue, national unity, and the equality of all citizens.

Since its creation by his spouse, Member of Parliament Nayla Moawad, and other prominent Lebanese public figures, RMF has implemented development projects to support the disadvantaged in society. In this spirit,

---

* Law 422 of 2002 (Protection of at Risk Children or Children Violating the Law).

RMF provides medical care to the poor; develops agriculture and rural enterprises; conducts literacy campaigns and vocational training; encourages public political participation; promotes democratic values; and protects the environment. The foundation supports projects under several broad headings:

- *Education*: RMF's educational activities are delivered through individual projects and/or the foundation's established centers, which target youth and working children in particular. The main objectives are establishing equal access to basic education for the disadvantaged and developing the capacities of youth.
- *Human rights*: RMF's activities in human rights and democracy began in 1994 and are focused on women and youth. Since 2004, RMF has expanded its project of creating human rights clubs in schools with the Rights Education and Awareness for Children and Teens (REACT) project for raising awareness on human rights and democracy among youth, while continuing to offer numerous work shops for youth on democracy and human rights.
- *Economy*: RMF's economic and development activities mainly target rural women and the war-affected population. The Business Development Center is under construction in Tripoli to serve entrepreneurs and employees in small and medium-size enterprises. The main objectives of the projects include development and promotion of social services and capacity building of community-based organizations (mainly women's associations); increasing employment through vocational training in sectors of high growth; and supporting civilians in war-torn areas.
- *Agriculture*: RMF pursues a dual action plan in combating the severe problems confronting the agricultural sector in Lebanon. First, it supports the sector by improving the socioeconomic conditions of farmers and increasing their competitiveness. Second, RMF promotes environmental protection by encouraging public awareness of existing problems and the adoption of ecologically sound agricultural practices.
- *Health*: RMF's objectives and activities in the medical field focus on the provision of health services to the most disadvantaged and to those living in the poorest and most remote villages in northern Lebanon. Services are centered mainly in the community clinic in

Zgharta, which offers specialized and general medical consultation services and a dental clinic at reduced costs as well as other forms of financial aid. The clinic also maintains a laboratory and a pharmacy. RMF also runs a mobile dispensary service and public health prevention programs and awareness campaigns.

Issam Fares Foundation

Founded in 1987 by Issam M. Fares, deputy prime minister of the Lebanese Republic, the Fares Foundation is active in several fields of human and social development in Lebanon. The foundation pays particular attention to underprivileged groups, communities, and regions and includes programs and services in health, education, humanitarian aid, culture, infrastructure, research, and conferences. It implements about half of its activities, while the other half is implemented by other organizations and institutions in cooperation with the foundation. The foundation was established in order to organize and channel donations of Issam Fares in an organized and strategic way. The Fares Foundation's current areas of programming include:

- *Health:* The foundation has developed a general public health program that includes the Michael Issam Fares Clinic in Beino, Akkar, and the Mikhayel Gerges Fares Clinic in West Talabbas, Akkar. Each clinic includes doctors who specialize in general medicine, pediatrics, cardiology, urology, and ophthalmology, as well as a pharmacy that offers free medications. The foundation provides material support to other clinics around the country. It participates in vaccination campaigns in cooperation with the Ministry of Health. Among many other contributions, the foundation sponsors health awareness campaigns in schools in cooperation with various nongovernmental organizations (NGOs), as well as a series of health lectures and conferences in universities and medical centers.

  - *Education:* The foundation provides various forms of aid to educational institutions so that these institutions may play their role effectively. The foundation also supports and participates in the renovation and rehabilitation of many public and private schools in Akkar and northern Lebanon, as well as provides equipment for libraries, laboratories, and other school and university needs. It also assists in literacy campaigns that include adults and children, and it sponsors training workshops in various fields.

- *Social and cultural programs:* The foundation has adopted two different ways of addressing social and cultural issues in Lebanon: through general social services and promoting "the spirit of cooperation." It focuses on strengthening civil society and on invigorating cultural and sporting activity and all that encourages people to meet and interact. The foundation also provides help and support to a number of associations that focus on the needs of the handicapped, orphans, the elderly, and other marginalized groups. It supports the holding of artisanal exhibits that create incentives to promote local production and marketing. It also sponsors scouting camps and sporting tournaments and other youth activities, as well as musical festivals and concerts. The foundation supports many municipal councils, educational institutions, and NGOs in their attempts to invigorate cultural life and the preservation of cultural heritage. In 1996, it provided assistance to the victims of the Israeli attacks in southern Lebanon.
- *Infrastructure development:* The Fares Foundation has undertaken its own projects in the area of infrastructure development, as well as offered support to municipalities and other local institutions in their efforts to develop the infrastructure of their communities. It has been active in building and asphalting new roads, rehabilitating old roads, and providing street lighting, sidewalks, and other necessities.
- *Conferences and research:* The foundation sponsors a number of scientific and cultural lectures and conferences. It also sponsors the publication of books and studies on Akkar, Lebanon, the Middle East, and the relationship of Lebanon with the global community. Although the foundation's main activities are in Lebanon, it accords a significant importance to projecting a positive picture of Lebanon to the world.

On an international level, the Issam M. Fares Center for Mediterranean Studies at Tufts University in the United States focuses on Lebanese and Middle Eastern affairs. In addition, there is the annual Issam Fares Lecture Series, which has featured presentations by such major figures as former United States President George H.W. Bush, former British Prime Minister Margaret Thatcher, former French President Valery Giscard d'Estaing, former United States Secretary of State James Baker, former United States Senator George Mitchell, former United States Secretary of State General Colin Powell, and former United States President Bill Clinton.

Family Foundations

Safadi Foundation

Although the Safadi Foundation was officially established in 2001, it has been operating unofficially in northern Lebanon for more than fifteen years with a focus on youth development. Recently, the foundation has been separated from a more political entity. It traces its roots to the civil war that lasted from 1975 to 1990. During this period, state services collapsed, leaving a vacuum in the provision of social, health, and welfare services to Lebanese citizens. In order to reduce the burden faced by the public, the foundation's founder and honorary president, Mohammed Safadi, began to provide support for institutions, both governmental and nongovernmental, to enable them to continue meeting people's basic needs.

While its roots are in humanitarian or charitable work, the foundation's success in its early years developed into a commitment to developmental issues. The last four years have been critical in the evolution of the foundation. Its orientation and work methods have changed from those of a charitable institution to those of a broad-based development agency. This period witnessed a regional series of workshops entitled "Toward a Comprehensive Development Plan for North Lebanon."

The foundation's focus and methodology is based on the following values and core principles: All people are equal in dignity and rights, regardless of gender, race, religion, or beliefs. Individual development is the starting point for developing societies. The individual is the means and the end of improving the quality of life. Participation is the prerequisite for empowering all social sectors, including women and young people, and particularly children. Finally, consolidating cooperation among various stakeholders in society (official, private, and civil) is a fundamental precondition for successful development programs.

The foundation is undertaking programs in interfaith dialogue, agricultural extension, microclimate weather stations (with the United Cooperative in al-Joumeh-Akkar), women's empowerment programs, programs to improve marketing for poor fishermen, a tourism training center, youth programs, and alternative education schools.

Makhzoumi Foundation

The Makhzoumi Foundation, established in 1997 by Fouad Makhzoumi, is a private Lebanese nonprofit organization that contributes through its programs to civil society development.

The foundation sees its mission as working toward a more evolved Lebanese civil society through:
- Human resource development
- Self-responsibility and independence
- Environmental preservation
- Education and quality healthcare

Its programs are focused on five areas:
- *Civic centers*: The foundation provides trainees with educational, technical, and vocational skills.
- *Agriculture and environment*: It aims to preserve and care for the environment through sustainable agriculture and the management of natural resources.
- *Micro-credit*: It recognizes the importance of micro-credit as a beneficial tool for community development.
- Adult and child awareness activities including projects such as Public Awareness on the Concept of Democracy and Let's Talk.
- *Healthcare*: The foundation is building a healthcare network that provides citizens with medical care at the least possible cost in doctors' private clinics and access to insurance policies at attractive premiums, covering 100 percent of hospitalization. It has opened community clinics that offer up-to-date equipment and medical care.

Broadly Sponsored Associations
The Children's Cancer Center of Lebanon

Established in April 2002, the Children's Cancer Center of Lebanon (CCCL) is a unique regional center for the comprehensive treatment of pediatric cancer. An affiliate of St. Jude Children's Research Hospital in Memphis, Tennessee, in the United States, the center works in close association with the American University of Beirut Medical Center. While CCCL is completely dependent on donations, it maintains a state-of-the-art center for treating and curing children with cancer in Lebanon, at no cost to patients and without discrimination.

The CCCL employs various methods of fundraising, including:
- *Sponsor a Child*: As a child's sponsor, one may change the life of a sick child by sponsoring his or her one-year treatment for USD 30,000, paying monthly, quarterly, or annually. Child sponsorship can be for one year or more, as the average period for the treatment

of pediatric cancer is two to three years, depending on the child's age and circumstances. Today, more than four hundred patients from all backgrounds are being treated at CCCL.

- *Naming a Facility*: Naming a facility or space at the outpatient unit after an individual or a corporation is the most incorporated and institutionalized form of donation.
- *Give Hope*: This method allows the donor to choose the amount he or she wishes to donate on a monthly basis.
- *Partner in Life*: This is a corporate partnership whereby employees of corporations can make donations.
- *Math-a-thon*: Math-a-thon, initiated in 2003, is an educational program targeted at school students of grades three through seven, whose ages range from eight to fourteen years old. It is designed to be an educational learning experience for the students and is relatively easy to conduct.
- *Occasions gifts*: Donations to CCCL can be made in the name of a new-lywed couple or a newborn baby, or to commemorate other occasions.
- *Corporate sponsorships*: Companies give support within a marketing strategy.
- *Annual gala dinners*: The CCCL annual gala dinner is the corner stone of the organization's yearly fundraising efforts.

Conclusion

Because of a number of constraints on data collection, it was not possible to cover Lebanon's philanthropic landscape fully. Researchers were struck by the resilience and determination of those they did meet, who have sustained the sector through many years of uncertainty, often at substantial personal risk. A new generation of business leaders and philanthropic actors are consciously deciding to operate through the creation of secular Lebanese rather than sectarian institutions.

The study did not cover the networks of social service provision tied to militia and political groups, although it is widely believed that these are significant and growing in some instances. The weak presence of the government has both contributed to a climate of relative independence for the civil sector and strengthened the role of philanthropic institutions in basic service provision. Despite many cases where constituents subscribing to particular religious or political groups are the principle beneficiaries of philanthropic organizations, the trend is toward more all-inclusive programs and impacts.

Lebanese are proud of their ability to persevere and rebuild their society repeatedly. They believe in the merits of an open, entrepreneurial society where there is still care for a neighbor's welfare. They also increasingly recognize the enduring problems caused by underdeveloped notions of citizenship and a weak sense of belonging to a nation. These are challenges that a rising generation of philanthropists must face.

Notes

1. Gross domestic product and population figures are taken from IMF data. Estimates start after 2004. The population and religion breakdown is from NationMaster.com.
2. Freedom House 2007. http://www.freedomhouse.org.
3. Ibid.
4. Some estimates are as high as 350,000. See Freedom House 2007.
5. March 14 Alliance is named after a key date in the Cedar Revolution, which was a series of mass demonstrations and civic movements for greater independence and democracy after the assassination of Rafik al-Hariri.
6. Freedom House 2007.
7. World Bank. Republic of Lebanon. Economic Assessment of Environmental Degradation due to July 2006 Hostilities Report No. 39787-LB. Document of the World Bank. http://www.worldbank.org.
8. Economist Intelligence Unit Country Profile 2007:19.
9. Conversation with a past candidate for Lebanese parliament.
10. Khalil 2004:17–20, 28–30.
11. See Fondation Père Afif Osseiran, Foyer de la Providence, http://www.reincude.org/

References

Economist Intelligence Unit. 2007. Country Profile: Lebanon.

Freedom House: Lebanon 2007. http://www.freedomhouse.org.

International Monetary Fund. 2007. World Economic Database (Lebanon) April. http://www.imf.org.

Khalil, Abdullah. 2004. *A Comparative Guide on Laws: Relating to Establishing an Arab Fund (Endowment or Cash Deposit): To Extend Financial Support for Social Justice Programs in the Arab Region.* Cairo: Ford Foundation.

World Bank. 2007. Republic of Lebanon Economic Assessment of Environmental Degradation Due to July 2006 Hostilities. Sector note, report no. 9787-LB. World Bank, October 11.

6

The State of Kuwait

Mahi Khallaf

Overview

Kuwait is a country with a long history of philanthropy that goes back to the seventeenth century, before the formal establishment of the state of Kuwait. Since the discovery and mass production of oil, philanthropy in Kuwait has seen a consistent increase in volume of giving and a noticeable expansion in forms of philanthropy. Despite the country's small population size, it has myriad philanthropic initiatives ranging from organizations engaged in traditional Islamic philanthropy, such as Beit al-Zakat, to innovative, state-of-the-art philanthropic institutions, such as the Kuwait Foundation for the Advancement of Science.

Country Background

Modern History

Prior to the twentieth century, Kuwait was a semi-autonomous province that fell loosely under the jurisdiction of the Ottoman Empire. It was settled by several Bedouin tribes, and livelihoods in Kuwait consisted mainly of pastoralism and sea trading. European mercantilism in the eighteenth century allowed the establishment of a more sedentary lifestyle, as people began setting up trading centers and developed shipbuilding, pearling, and fishing industries.

In 1899, as European influence strengthened in the region, the ruler of Kuwait signed a treaty with the United Kingdom accepting British protection over Turkish control. Kuwait fell under British jurisdiction until 1961, when the United Kingdom and Kuwait mutually agreed to terminate the treaty and Kuwait became an independent nation.

Kuwait at a Glance[1]

Country size	17,820 sq. km.
Population (2006)	3.1 million
National	*33%*
Non-national	*69%*
GDP (2006)	USD 96.1 billion
GDP PPP (2006)	USD 61.6 billion
Industry	*56%*
Oil and gas	*42%*
Services and other	*44%*
GDP per capita (2006)	USD 31,051
GDP per capita PPP (2006)	USD 19,909
HDI ranking	33/177
Religious groups	Muslim 85% *(Sunni 70%, Shia 30%)*, Other 15%
1 Kuwaiti dinar (KWD)	USD 3.66

Boundary conflicts over disputed oil fields led to a devastating occupation of Kuwait by Iraq in 1990. An international outcry followed, which Iraqi leaders did not heed. In January 1991, a United States-led and United Nations-backed aerial bombing campaign was launched in Kuwait and Iraq. The first Gulf War ended in March 1991 with the successful expulsion of the Iraqi army from Kuwait and the return of the Kuwaiti royal family from self-exile in Saudi Arabia. A period of reconstruction followed.

The Political Scene

Kuwait has been ruled by members of the al-Sabah family from the Bani Utub tribe since 1752. Leadership alternates between two branches of the family, the Bani Salem and the Bani Jabr. Succession is not strictly hereditary, but rule remains in the al-Sabah line.

Members of parliament are, for the most part, independent or linked to tribal or family interests. In May 2005, the Kuwaiti parliament passed a law that gave women full suffrage rights, including the right to vote and to run for office. A month later, the first female cabinet minister, Massouma al-Mubarak, was appointed.

The Political Scene

Type of Government
Constitutional emirate headed by Emir Sheikh Sabah al-Ahmad al-Jabir al-Sabah, who acceded to the throne in February 2006. The Council of Ministers makes up part of the executive branch and is headed by a prime minister chosen by the emir. The current prime minister, Sheikh Nasser Muhammad al-Ahmad al-Sabah, is the emir's nephew.

National Legislature
The National Assembly, or Majlis al-Umma, first established in 1963, sits for four-year terms and is the oldest directly elected parliament among the Persian Gulf Arab countries. It has the power to ratify laws enacted by a decree from the emir, yet is somewhat vulnerable to the executive, having been dissolved by the emir four times since its establishment, and suspended twice for an extended period of time.

Legal System
The emir appoints all judges and oversees judicial promotions and renewals of judicial appointments. *Shari'a* law is the basis for a significant source of legislation.

Several key issues continue to polarize the positions of the executive and the National Assembly without major headway, including public sector salary levels linked to oil revenue; electricity and water shortages; disagreements over privatization and foreign investment in the oil sector; and the need for economic restructuring pertaining to social welfare and the distribution of national income. Reform is challenging because the majority of the active population is employed in the public sector, which gives citizens little reason to seek change. Although political groupings exist, formal political parties are prohibited in Kuwait and calls for their legalization have become more pronounced since 2004.

The media operates with relative freedom by regional standards. This is attributed in part to a relatively pluralistic political tradition. International pressure over censorship arose after the Gulf War in 1991, and in March 2006, the government enacted a revised press law that protects newspapers from closure without court order.[2]

The Economy

Oil, the country's principal resource, was discovered in 1938, but was developed aggressively only after the Second World War. In 1950, Sheikh Abdullah al-Salim al-Sabah set modern-day Kuwait on a fast-paced development track by instituting a program of public works and educational development fueled by petroleum revenues. These measures transformed Kuwait's infrastructure while simultaneously introducing a comprehensive system of welfare services for the native population. The expansion of the petroleum sector throughout the 1960s allowed for an extensive redistribution of income through public expenditure and a land compensation scheme.

Early budget surpluses allowed the country to develop an investment strategy, buying into Japan and many of the five hundred leading American companies.[3] Fiscal and balance of payment surpluses from the 1980s allowed Kuwait to create the Reserve Fund for Future Generations (RFFG), whereby 10 percent of Kuwait's annual revenue is saved and invested for future generations. Likewise, the General Reserve Fund was set up to mitigate the volatility of the international oil market.

Despite the constant stream of oil revenue, Kuwait has experienced relatively slow growth. This is attributed to high government consumption, combined with relatively low domestic investment compared with other countries in the region. Domestic investment has been declining since the mid-1990s.

The Kuwaiti economy today is highly dependent on the petroleum sector, which accounts for around 95 percent of merchandise export earnings, up to 85 percent of budget revenue, and over 50 percent of nominal gross domestic product.[4] Budget revenue is subject to the volatility of the oil market. Wages and salaries in public sector employment accounted for 30 percent of actual fiscal spending in 2006–2007.[5] State spending has been an integral part of the domestic economy since the onset of oil production.

As in other small Gulf countries in the region, native Kuwaitis have been a minority since the 1960s as a result of the demand for foreign labor. Kuwaiti nationals dominate the public sector, as 86 percent of all Kuwaiti employees work in the public sector and 75 percent of all public sector workers are Kuwaiti. The private sector is small by regional and international standards. Higher-than-market-value wages and job security make public sector work attractive.

According to a recent report by the United Nations Conference on Trade and Development, Kuwait's high per capita income, modern infrastructure, stable political environment, and large proven reserves of crude oil offer

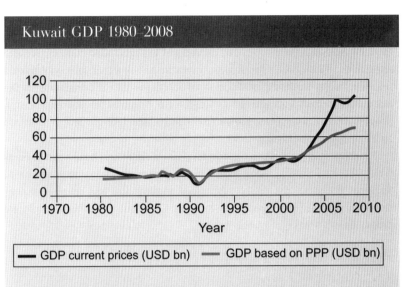

Source: International Monetary Fund, World Economic Outlook Database, April 2007.[6]

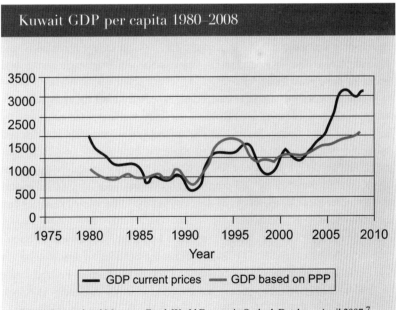

Source: International Monetary Fund, World Economic Outlook Database, April 2007.[7]

sizeable potential for foreign direct investment. While the National Assembly passed a law in 2001 allowing 100 percent foreign ownership in eleven different sectors,[8] state control of oil and gas has precluded competitive and attractive opportunities for foreign investment.[9] Another law was passed that authorizes limited participation of international oil companies in the petroleum sector, and an economic reform proposal in the exploration process known as Project Kuwait will introduce foreign investment into four northern oilfields.

Revenue from oil allows for ample social welfare and health services, as well as free education, along with a highly subsidized housing program. In addition, the state essentially guarantees employment and retirement pensions to Kuwaiti citizens. The long-term viability of these economic programs is a source of public debate.

Philanthropy in Focus
The Culture of Giving

The culture of giving is deeply rooted in the Islamic practices of the small population of Kuwait. Traditional Islamic forms of philanthropy can be traced back to at least 1695, to a mosque known as Bin Bahr that was set up as a *waqf*. In 1921, the *waqf* system was institutionalized through the creation of a government department for the management of *awqaf*. The Ministry of Awqaf and Islamic Affairs, created in 1942, was charged with developing the *waqf* culture in Kuwait. In 1993, an independent body, the Kuwait Awqaf Public Foundation, was established to manage *awqaf* and promote their growth.

Since the country's independence and especially after the start of active extraction of oil, the wealth of Kuwaiti nationals has increased substantially and so has their giving. Individual philanthropists are many in Kuwait and have donated substantial amounts of money for charitable, political, cultural, and social purposes, not just in Kuwait but also abroad. Members of the Kuwaiti ruling family and prominent businesspeople have set an example for other wealthy members of the community. Only a few examples can be given here:

- In 2007, His Highness Emir Sheikh Sabah al-Ahmed al-Sabah donated around USD 6.7 million for the building of a new wing for Islamic art and architecture in the Louvre Museum in France.
- In 2007, His Highness Sheikh Salem al-Ali al-Salem al-Sabah donated KWD 100 million to the Zakat House to be spent on the needy among Kuwaitis.

- His Highness the late Sheikh Gaber al-Ahmed al-Gaber al-Sabah was a generous contributor to the Louvre and other cultural projects worldwide. He was named world philanthropist of the year in the late 1990s.
- Sheikha Hussa al-Sabah founded the Dar al-Athar al-Islamiyya in Kuwait City, which houses one of the world's greatest collections of Islamic art.
- The poet and businessman Sheikh Abdul Aziz Saud al-Babtain, a philanthropist with a passion for reviving Arab poetry and culture, institutionalized his giving through the Abdul Aziz Saud al-Babtain Prize for Poetic Creativity Foundation, which was established in Egypt in 1989 and subsequently expanded to include branches in Kuwait and Tunisia. The foundation recognizes and produces outstanding literary Arab works; awards the annual Forefathers of al-Bokhary award, a USD 100,000 grant to bridge the cultural gap between Arabs and Islamic countries that were part of the former Soviet Union; and offers scholarships for Muslim students from around the world to study at Egypt's al-Azhar University. The foundation's achievements include the establishment of the Babtain Central Library for Arab Literary Work and the Babtain Library at Jerusalem University in support of Palestinian students.

In addition to individual giving, a substantial portion of Kuwait's oil-generated wealth has been directed to the establishment of large-scale philanthropic endowments and funds, often with support from the state. Both religious and nonreligious channels of giving have developed since the early 1950s. Perhaps the earliest example of 'modern' organized philanthropy in Kuwait, where individual philanthropists pooled their resources for the public good, is the People's Committee for Donation Collection (al-Lajna al-Sha'biya li-Jam' al-Tabarru'at). The committee was established in December 1954 by a group of wealthy Kuwaiti individuals under the leadership of HH Sheikh Sabah al-Ahmed al-Gaber al-Sabah, who was head of the Social Affairs Department at the time. The committee has provided substantial funds over the years to Arab and Islamic countries, as well as to Kuwaitis after the Iraqi invasion.

The Legal Environment for Philanthropy

Kuwaiti law allows for the registration of associations and philanthropic institutions as public welfare societies or clubs engaged in social, cultural, religious, or sports activities. By virtue of Cabinet Decree 74 of 1999, associations and philanthropic institutions must direct their activities toward charitable deeds or public service and are prohibited from seeking commercial gain or profit. The same decree allows public charities to advance research and funding for the promotion of scholarship.

A minimum of ten founding members is required for the establishment of any society or club, and the society is required to have a managing board. Clubs or societies are prohibited from "interfering in politics and religious conflicts or provoking fanaticism, sectarianism and racism."[10] They also are prohibited from joining societies or obtaining funding outside the country without the prior approval of the Ministry of Social Affairs and Labor, the authority responsible for the registration and monitoring of welfare societies and clubs. Kuwaiti civil society organizations (CSOs) wishing to operate abroad must coordinate their activities through the Kuwaiti Foreign Ministry.[11]

Endowment-based philanthropic organizations *(mabarrat)* are created by ministerial decree. A *mabarra* should be endowed with a minimum of KWD 50,000 deposited in a Kuwaiti bank account and should be set up as a separate financial entity from the business or wealth with which it is affiliated. It also should own the premises from which it operates.

A total of 110 organizations are currently registered with the Ministry of Social Affairs. The ministry may reject an application to register a welfare society or club, but it must state the reason for the rejection. The ministry maintains records of each society or club, monitors the accounting and financial practices of each, and is charged with assisting these organizations "in achieving their goals in serving society," provided they conform to the conditions stated in Law 24 of 1962. Monetary assistance by the state for cultural or social development purposes can be allocated to associations from the ministry's budget.

In the wake of 9/11, Kuwaiti giving came under scrutiny in Washington over concerns that charity funds collected in Arab countries were being used to finance terrorism abroad. The highly publicized debate that ensued about the legitimacy of Kuwaiti CSOs involved in philanthropy affected the fundraising abilities of all Kuwaiti CSOs, as well as their public image. The Kuwaiti government introduced stricter regulations for the collection of donations, and donation boxes were removed from all public places, which undermined a popular and widespread method of public giving. A new department within the Ministry of Social Affairs, the Department of Charitable Societies and Philanthropic Organizations, was established in 2001 to regulate CSOs, and ministry staff underwent training in the United States.

Institutionalized Philanthropy

Two types of CSOs in Kuwait engage in philanthropy: *mabarrat* and public interest organizations, which are nonprofit associations whose activities focus primarily on gender and health issues and the provision of social services, but which also maintain a philanthropic arm through their *zakat* committees. Philanthropy also is carried out by organizations that have quasigovernmental legal status, such as the House of Zakat and the Kuwait Awqaf Public Foundation. Organizations of this kind play an important role in channeling religiously motivated individual giving.

The state also has played a leadership role in stimulating nonreligious institutions, through, for example, the creation of an institute for science and technology funded annually through a percentage of the profits of registered Kuwaiti corporations. This model of corporate contribution is feasible largely because of the absence of national tax burdens on the private sector in Kuwait. New tax legislation currently under consideration could have a substantial impact on many aspects of corporate and individual giving by the business community in the country.

Mabarrat

There are approximately thirty-eight *mabarrat* registered with the Ministry of Social Affairs. A *mabarra* usually is endowed by high net worth individuals who wish to give back to society but to do so anonymously. Accordingly, it was difficult for the author to get financial information about these organizations, as staff members were less ready to speak about financial models or precise expenditure figures. Different forms of *mabarrat* exist, including:

- Individually endowed organizations set up by high net worth individuals to support those in need in Kuwait and around the world. Examples include Mabarrat Sheikh Sabah al-Salam and Mabarrat Sheikh Abdullah Mubarak al-Sabah, which are described below.
- Family-endowed organizations that cater to the needs of family members, such as marriage needs, financial support, and schooling fees. One example is Mabarrat Dashti.
- Business-related philanthropic organizations endowed by a business entity. These are rare in Kuwait. The most well-known and long-standing business-endowed organization is Mabarrat al-Maarify, which was established in 1976 and runs programs in Iran, Morocco, China, Afghanistan, Syria, and Pakistan.

Mabarrat Sheikh Abdullah Mubarak al-Sabah

Mabarrat Sheikh Abdullah Mubarak al-Sabah was established in 1992 by
parliamentary decree. The organization, which was set up with an endowment by the sheikh, works in Kuwait and in more than twenty countries
around the world, including Arab and Islamic countries. Its main objectives
are to support those in need; build mosques, religious schools, orphanages,
and freshwater wells in Islamic countries; provide in-kind contributions for
health and educational purposes; support student scholarships; build and
donate premises for newly established public interest organizations; and
build community centers that subsidize wedding parties.

Public Interest Organizations

Kuwaiti public interest organizations (PIOs) engage actively in philanthropic activities through their *zakat* committees. Around seventy-two
organizations are registered as such. PIOs have managed to gain the trust of
Kuwaiti citizens over the years; hence, *zakat* committees are able to raise
considerable amounts of money for charitable purposes.

Prior to 9/11, the Ministry of Social Affairs provided financial support to
all PIOs in the amount of KWD 12,000, and *zakat* committees operated
freely. Stricter regulations introduced after 2001 require PIOs to obtain the
ministry's approval a month in advance of launching donation campaigns.
The ministry has stopped its financial support of new organizations, but, in
return, has loosened the prerequisite that organizations own their premises
in order to be established. Despite the resultant tensions between government and civil society, a high level of collaboration between the two sectors
still exists. This was apparent from the author's discussions with ministry
officials and civil society representatives.

By and large, PIOs are transparent in reporting on their expenditures
and programs. Because they need to establish public trust in order to raise
funds, they, unlike *mabarrat*, are willing to share details of their work with
the public. They also are keen on maintaining a high profile in the media.
The post-9/11 climate that resulted in stricter government monitoring of
CSOs appears to have made these organizations more willing to work in
the spotlight.

The Women's Cultural and Social Society

The Women's Cultural and Social Society (WCSS) was the first women's
society established in Kuwait. Founded in February 1963 by a group of
Kuwaiti women, the society's main objective is to promote the development

of women in all fields, encourage their participation in community activities, and increase their awareness of their rights and obligations to ensure their effective contribution to society. A seven-member board of directors, elected every two years by the general assembly, administers the society. The society has eight different committees whose activities focus on culture, social affairs, health, preschool, political rights, the media, support to Palestine, and fundraising. Fundraising is undertaken through the *zakat* committee, which was established in 1981 to collect and distribute *zakat* contributions in Kuwait in accordance with *shari'a* rules. The committee's objectives are to:

- Provide economic support and assistance to needy Kuwaiti and non-Kuwaiti families residing in Kuwait
- Assist families that are unable to secure educational opportunities for their children, through the payment of school fees
- Offer financial assistance to hospital patients in need and to house bound patients who are unable to work and do not have an income;
- Provide care for poor orphans, as well as widows and divorced women who need to earn a livelihood
- Provide food supplies to families in need

The *zakat* committee is headed by a group of women with considerable fundraising capabilities and staffed with four full-time employees who review applications and monitor the use of funds. The committee coordinates its work with the Ministry of Social Affairs and other philanthropic entities in Kuwait to ensure that the funds reach those truly in need. According to the committee head, the committee has disbursed over KWD 100,000 in the past year alone, and more than a thousand families have received assistance since its establishment.

The Association for Social Reconstruction

Established in 1977, the Association for Social Reconstruction (Jam'iyat al-Islah al-Ijtima'i) contributes to social welfare and promotes the concept of social solidarity through its social support activities, foremost among which is the administration of *waqf* and *zakat*. The association's Zakat Committee, which has eighteen branches distributed in Kuwait's six governorates, disburses *zakat* funds to their rightful beneficiary groups *(al-masarif al-shar'iya)* as specified in Islam. The Zakat Committee Network coordinates the activities of the branches and liaises with the Ministry of Social Affairs and the Zakat House. As of 2005, 115 full-time staff members have managed the operations of the branches around Kuwait, supported by 114 volunteers. Between 1977 and 2005, the association disbursed a total of KWD 27 million, benefiting 716,914 people. In 2005, the association set up new endowment funds to support the needy in Kuwait.

Government-led Philanthropic Initiatives

The Kuwaiti government has built a strong track record in initiating and managing successful and highly institutionalized Islamic philanthropic entities. These entities are quasigovernmental in the sense that they are government initiated and supported although they are not managed directly by government. The two main entities that deserve attention are the Kuwait Awqaf Public Foundation and Zakat House.

Kuwait Awqaf Public Foundation

The Kuwait Awqaf Public Foundation (al-Amana al-'Amma li-l-Awqaf) was established in November 1993 by emiri decree to take on the Ministry of Awqaf's duties of managing and developing endowments. The foundation is relatively independent from the government in its decision-making process and the utilization of funds. It aims to raise awareness of *awqaf* and ensure high standards of *waqf* management, with the purpose of developing the Kuwaiti community culturally, socially, and economically. A quarter of the endowed money or property is disbursed in accordance with the wishes of the endower.

One of the main activities of the Kuwait Awqaf Public Foundation is the creation of funds to finance development initiatives that serve its goals. So far, eight funds have been established: 1) the fund for disabled and marginalized groups; 2) the fund for cultural and intellectual thought; 3) the fund for the study of the Quran; 4) the education fund; 5) the family fund; 6) the environmental fund; 7) the health fund; and 8) the fund for mosque maintenance. These funds are financed primarily through *waqf* earnings, but also through individual and CSO donations. The foundation actively networks and collaborates with government bodies, public interest organizations, and other funds that operate in areas that complement its work.

The foundation is innovative in its approach to development, going beyond the traditional Islamic notion of *waqf*. In 1994, for example, the foundation led a fundraising campaign with the aim of setting up the first center for educating autistic children in the Arab world. Time Endowment, another interesting initiative, aims to raise awareness of the importance of volunteering time for the benefits of others.

Zakat House

Zakat House *(Beit al-zakat)* is a pioneering initiative to revive *zakat* as an important pillar of Islam. Established in January 1982 by virtue of Law 5 of 1982, it was declared a public entity with an independent budget. It is supervised by the Minister of Awqaf and Islamic Affairs.

Over the twenty-three-year period from the date of its establishment to the end of 2005, the organization benefited more than 102,900 families in Kuwait through USD 1,053,038,633, disbursed as follows:

Areas of Giving	Amounts Collected (in KD)	Percentage
Zakat funds	85,339,000	30
Seasonal charitable giving	27,496,000	10
Kuwaiti government contributions	72,428,000	25
Sadaqa jariya	11,539,000	4
Orphan support	38,367,000	13
Charitable projects	20,480,000	6
Charity investment	33,480,000	12
Total	**289,169,000**	**100**

An additional KWD 25 million-plus were allocated to the numerous projects implemented by Zakat House abroad in support of orphans, the poor, education, and the building of Islamic centers and mosques, among others. Zakat House's Cairo branch, established two decades ago and officially endorsed by Egyptian Presidential Decree 60 of 2006, has implemented over four hundred projects throughout Egypt in the health, education, and religion domains.

Both the Kuwait Awqaf Public Foundation and Zakat House are successful examples of government-led initiatives that have managed to maintain their autonomy despite their affiliation with the Kuwaiti government. Both organizations are highly professional in the day-to-day management of their activities and appear committed to the creation of knowledge about Islamic philanthropy. They are well connected internationally and act as models worthy of emulation in other parts of the Islamic world.

While both organizations are rooted in traditional Islamic practices, they have been active in modernizing their work to keep up with contemporary realities and global trends. The Kuwait Awqaf Foundation, for example, has pioneered innovative methods such as using mobile phones to raise endowment funds through short messages. These mass fundraising activities encourage the public to give to charitable causes and to become more engaged in volunteer work.

Corporate Philanthropy

Corporate philanthropy in Kuwait is undertaken, for the most part, through specialized units within a business rather than through a separate entity. Most companies have launched corporate social responsibility (CSR) departments geared toward the care or development of Kuwaiti society. Understanding of CSR in Kuwait has not developed to the point of building on core business strengths, but it is moving in that direction.

Zain

Zain (formerly MTC-Vodafone) hopes to have a sustainable impact on society through its CSR activities. In 2006, the organization was involved in a number of health and environmental projects, including Beit Abdullah, a home for children with cancer. In 2007, Zain supported an environmental awareness campaign in collaboration with cooperative supermarkets to encourage shoppers to switch from plastic bags to paper bags. Zain also has instituted strict environmental codes within its offices and has a strong CSR strategy vis-à-vis its employees in Kuwait and around the world.

The National Bank of Kuwait

The National Bank of Kuwait (NBK) is active in the Kuwaiti community and in other communities around the world. It supports health, education, and sports initiatives. In 2007, for example, the bank donated a KWD 3 million hospital for underprivileged children to the Ministry of Health to manage. The bank supports the activities of CSOs and has initiated its own employee volunteering programs, through which staff actively participate in community initiatives.

The Kuwait Foundation for the Advancement of Science

The Kuwait Foundation for the Advancement of Science (KFAS) is a private, nonprofit organization established by emiri decree in 1976 and managed by a board of directors chaired by the emir of Kuwait. The foundation's objectives are to finance research in basic and applied sciences; support projects of national priority; recognize and award prizes for outstanding scientific achievement at the national, regional, and international levels; organize scientific symposia and conferences; enrich the Arabic language library by publishing journals, books, and encyclopedias; and promote scientific and cultural awareness.

The foundation receives financial contributions from Kuwaiti shareholding companies, which amounts to 1 percent of their net annual profits. In 2006, the National Bank of Kuwait alone contributed USD 6 million to KFAS. Through the huge funds at its disposal, the organization has been able to provide research grants, fellowships, and awards to Kuwaitis, as well as to individuals and institutions around the world.

Conclusion

Kuwait is a country with vibrant traditions of giving. Since the 1970s, Kuwait has produced excellent models of updated and institutionalized forms of giving. The model of sustained corporate contributions for scientific research could be expanded to other sectors and adapted in other parts of the region. Likewise, the example of productive relations between CSOs and government oversight bodies could be used as a model and bears further analysis. Transparency and management professionalism are distinctive marks of the Kuwaiti experience. As investment levels increase in Kuwait, levels of corporate engagement also can be expected to rise. Like many of the countries included in this study, Kuwaiti philanthropists are just beginning to grapple with the different tools necessary to shift from a predominantly charitable to a more strategic approach in their giving.

Notes

1. Population and gross domestic product (GDP) figures taken from International Monetary Fund data and the Economist Intelligence Unit. The breakdown of religious groups is taken from NationMaster.com.
2. Freedom House 2007.
3. Europa World Online 2008:19, 21.
4. Economist Intelligence Unit Kuwait Country Profile 2007:22.
5. Economist Intelligence Unit Kuwait Country Profile 2007:25.
6. Estimates start after 2004.
7. Estimates start after 2004.
8. Economist Intelligence Unit Kuwait Country Profile 2007:22.
9. International Monetary Fund 2005:15--16.
10. International Center for Not-for-Profit Law. Law on clubs and public welfare societies (Law 24 of 1962). http://www.icnl.org.
11. Information taken from Law 24 of 1962 on Clubs and Public Welfare Societies, Ministerial Decree 48 of 1999 on the Basic Model Organizations of Charitable Institutions, and the cabinet's Decree 74 of 1999 Concerning the System of Public Charities.

References

Economist Intelligence Unit. 2006. "Country Profile: Kuwait."

Economist Intelligence Unit. 2007. "Country Report: Kuwait."

Europa World Online. 2007. "Kuwait." Routledge.

Freedom House. 2007. "Country Report: Kuwait."

International Center for Not-for-Profit Law. "Law No. 24 of the Year 1962 on Clubs and Public Welfare Societies." http://www.icnl.org. Retrieved 30 November 2007.

International Center for Not-for-Profit Law. "Ministerial Decree No. 48 of 1999 on the Basic Model Organizations of Charitable Institutions." http://www.icnl.org. Retrieved 30 November 2007

International Center for Not-for-Profit Law. "The Cabinet's Decree No. 74 of 1999 Concerning the System of Public Charities." http://www.icnl.org. Retrieved 30 November 2007.

International Monetary Fund. 2005. "Kuwait: Selected Issues and Statistical Appendix." International Monetary Fund Country Report No. 05/234.

Pfeifer, Karen. 2002. "Kuwait's Economic Quandary." *Middle East Report* 223:10–13.

Tétreault, Mary Ann. 2003. "Advice and Dissent in Kuwait." *Middle East Report* 226:36–39.

7

The State of Qatar

Mahi Khallaf

Overview

Despite its small size and population, Qatar has managed in the last ten years to create a dynamic economy and a progressive state apparatus in comparison to many of its neighbors. Its unprecedented economic growth is built upon massive natural gas reserves, but its strides in governance and social progress might not have been predicted. Native Qataris number only around two hundred thousand and they have the same austere Wahabi social and religious background as Saudi Arabia. Yet, in the decade since HH Emir Sheikh Hamad Bin Khalifa al-Thani assumed power, he has managed to transform the country, introducing positive reforms in governance, public participation, and education and laying the groundwork for a sustainable economy in the face of eventual resource depletion.

With the leadership of the emir and the first lady, Her Highness Sheikha Mozah Bint Nasser al-Missned, the face of philanthropy in Qatar has been transformed rapidly away from a traditional reliance on tribal loyalties and individual acts of charity to an increasing focus on sustainable endowments. Today, an emerging cluster of foundations operates programs with well-defined strategic objectives and an array of global partnerships to achieve their aims. Corporate social responsibility (CSR) is emerging as a potential force for dynamic change, albeit more slowly. A major focus of philanthropic investments in Qatar is education at all levels.

Country Background

Qatar at a Glance[1]

Country size	11,437 sq. km.
Population (2006)	838,000
Nationals	*24%*
Non-nationals	*76%*
GDP (2006)	USD 52.7 billion
GDP PPP (2006)	USD 27.7 billion
Oil and gas	*62%*
Finance, insurance, real estate	*8%*
Manufacturing	*7%*
Construction	*5%*
Trade, restaurants, hotels	*4%*
Transportation and communications	*3%**
GDP per capita (2006)	USD 62,914
GDP per capita PPP (2006)	USD 33,049
HDI ranking	46/177
Religious groups	Muslim 78%, Christian 9%, Other 14%
1 Qatar Rial (QAR)	USD 0.27

Note: Figures taken from the Economist Intelligence Unit.

Modern History

Before its independence in 1971, Qatar fell under the jurisdiction of Great Britain as a British protectorate. His Highness Sheikh Khalifa Bin Hamad assumed leadership after deposing his cousin within the first year of independence. The economy faltered under his long tenure due to abuse of petroleum reserves for private benefit. The country's current head, HH Emir Sheikh Hamad Bin Khalifa al-Thani, came to power in 1995 in a bloodless coup, deposing his father as a result of conflicting views on foreign policy and national development.

The Political Scene

Type of Government
Emirate led by Sheikh Hamad Bin Khalifa al-Thani based on the June 2005 constitution. The national government consists of a Cabinet led by the prime minister, currently Hamad Bin Jasim Bin Jabir al-Thani.

National Legislature
The Consultative Council, or the Majlis al-Shura, is undergoing reforms following the launch of the new constitution. The current Majlis al-Shura, with 35 seats directly appointed by the emir, plays only an advisory role. Guidelines for the new Majlis al-Shura include two-thirds of a 45-member parliament elected by the voting public and one-third subject to appointment by the emir. Elections are slated to take place before the end of 2008. The new council will be vested with the competence to pass or reject the state budget, monitor the function of the government, and question ministers. Although the council's legislative powers have been strengthened, the emir still retains the power to block or veto legislation.

Legal System
The legal system is based on Islamic and civil law codes. Islamic law governs family and personal matters. Judges, the majority of whom are foreign nationals, are appointed and removed by the authority of the emir.

Early on, HH Sheikh Hamad explored the possibility of some political participation for citizens. The idea of a municipal council functioning as a consultative body for the Ministry of Municipal Affairs and Agriculture was announced in 1997. In 1998, a law was issued for the establishment of the council, and in 1999, elections were held, making Qatar the first state of the Gulf Cooperation Council (GCC) to introduce universal suffrage for a body of participatory policy making. A second election was held in April 2003.

The 2005 constitution providing for these changes was approved by 97 percent of eligible voters in a referendum.[1] The constitution managed to broaden political participation without challenging major features of the existing power structure. It provides for a separation of the executive, legislative, and judicial branches of government, with executive authority remaining in the hands of the emir and his council of ministers. The constitution further guarantees freedom of expression, religion, and association, as well as provides for the establishment of an independent judiciary and a new forty-five-member consultative council.

The Middle East is at a crossroads of democratic change. Qatar has enacted multiple reforms voluntarily, which makes it one of the most politically progressive states in the region. Political and economic pressures have not been the cause of political liberalization, but rather the result of a conscious top-down decision. A tacit social contract exists whereby the state provides social and economic welfare in exchange for political loyalty and slowly expanding participation. With regard to its external affairs, close ties with the United States and vast resource wealth have afforded Qatar more influence and freedom in forging its foreign policy than other countries of comparable size in the region.

Shortly after coming to power, HH Sheikh Hamad instigated one of the boldest media moves in the region with the launch of al-Jazeera, an Arabic-language satellite news channel that defied accepted practices of heavy censorship in the region and put Qatar on the map as a Middle East media hub. Al-Jazeera now has both Arabic and English outlets and is one of the most popular (and controversial) Arabic-language satellite television channels in the region.

The media and government share a unique relationship whereby the state generally refrains from direct censorship while al-Jazeera and other media outlets practice a degree of self-censorship, particularly concerning Qatar and the Thani family, who have provided funding since its inception. The five leading newspapers are owned by or have boards that include members of the royal family and other notables.[2] In a move to signal the regime's dedication to freedom of expression, the Ministry of Information was abolished in 1998.

The Economy

As elsewhere in the Gulf region, oil and natural gas resources have spearheaded the development of the country. Oil was discovered in 1939 and has functioned as an engine for growth. The population jumped from sixteen thousand in 1949[3] to an estimated 907,229 by July 2007.[4]

The country's economic policy has focused on liberalization, encouragement of foreign investment, and economic diversification. Oil and gas comprise more than 60 percent of gross domestic product, roughly 85 percent

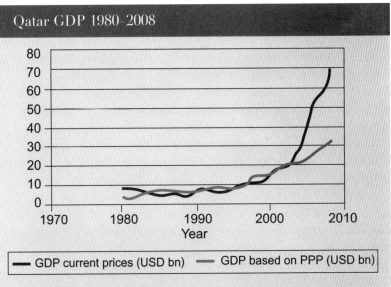

Source: International Monetary Fund, World Economic Outlook Database, April 2007.

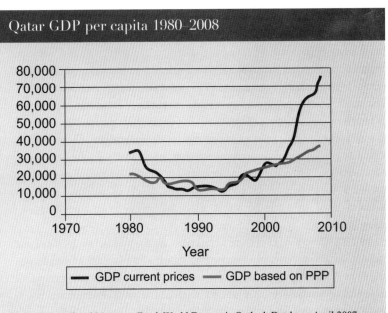

Source: International Monetary Fund, World Economic Outlook Database, April 2007.

of export earnings, and 70 percent of government revenues. These natural resources have afforded Qatar one of the fastest-growing and highest per-capita incomes in the world. According to 2007 estimates, current output is sustainable for twenty-three more years, and this relatively short window is a key motivation for developing new avenues of sustainable growth.

Since Qatar's hydrocarbon sector was opened to foreign investment in the early 1990s, the country's global market share of crude oil reserves has quadrupled. Qatar's proven natural gas reserves are the third-largest in the world and comprise 5 percent of the global total. The country has managed to attract huge amounts of foreign investment, becoming the world's largest liquefied natural gas producer in 2006. Cheap and available gas reserves have encouraged the development of petrochemical projects by foreign firms. A forward-thinking five-year plan is underway to develop and expand the gas sector, which entails some austerity in the short term in exchange for longer-term benefits.

Having noted the transitory nature of a natural resource-based economy, the country's leadership is tapping into investment income in the form of international stock market investments, which in 2007–2008 accounted for 20 percent of revenue.[5] Other diversification projects include tripling local steel production and increasing petrochemical production projects, both facilitated by the availability of cheap energy. With the country enjoying sustained economic growth, construction continues unabated, yet a shortage of building stock still exists. The housing shortage has sent rents and inflation soaring and minimized the availability of affordable housing, which was a major contributing factor to an almost 15 percent inflation rate in 2007.[6]

The government continues to create a climate favorable to foreign investment as a major cornerstone of economic policy. A recently announced cut in corporation taxes from 35 percent to 12 percent is expected to attract more foreign investment, particularly in the nonhydrocarbon sectors.[7] Direct foreign investment and ownership without a compulsory local partner or sponsor are the result of reforms and new investment laws. In a similar spirit, the government is in the process of opening up the telecommunications sector.

Nearly all Qatari workers are employed in the public sector, and the country is hugely dependent on imported labor. The Ministry of Labor was reestablished and expanded in order to deal with external allegations of poor work conditions and failure to meet international standards. New labor laws that came into effect in 2005 expanded some protections, but more are required.[8]

In a push to distinguish itself from its neighbors, Qatar seeks to develop its comparative advantage as a knowledge hub of the Middle East and is making major investments in the field of education, largely through an accelerated program to build educational institutions in the country. The basic educational structure is being reformed with a focus on creating labor that can compete at the international level. High-profile foreign universities like Cornell and Georgetown have been invited to establish branch campuses in Education City.

Philanthropy in Focus
The Culture of Giving
Qatar's philanthropic initiatives have evolved from tribal practices, a culture of giving back to others that springs from the deep influence of Islamic teachings, as well as from a small but dynamic civil society sector that has taken shape over the years. The rise of civil society activity in Qatari society can be traced to the time prior to the discovery of oil resources, when citizens banded together to provide much-needed social services on an ad hoc and reactive basis. The first civil society organization (CSO) to register under Law 2 of 1974 was the Qatari Organization for Caring and Rehabilitating Persons with Disabilities. Soon after, the Qatari Red Crescent was established and gained international recognition in 1981. Over the years, charitable CSOs grew in number in Qatar, taking up work that focused on the development of Qatari society but also increasingly targeting those in need in other parts of the world.

The extraordinary economic growth over the past two decades has generated wealth that, in turn, has stimulated an increase in philanthropic activity. By far the strongest catalyst for Qatari philanthropy was the coming to power of HH Emir Sheikh Hamad in 1995. With the aid of HH Sheikha Moza, Qatar's philanthropic initiatives expanded rapidly.

The Legal Environment for Philanthropy
Organized civil society came into existence through Law 2 of 1974, which was enacted to regulate the activities of emerging CSOs. Laws governing social and philanthropic organizations were revised in 2004. Associations are defined as groups formed to perform a humanitarian, social, cultural, scientific, professional, or charitable activity not motivated by material gain or political goals. Associations and private associations fall within the jurisdiction of the Ministry of Civil Service and Housing Affairs. The ministry reserves the right to inspect documents and records.

A minimum of twenty founding members is required to set up an association, each of whom must be a Qatari national and over eighteen years of age, not have been convicted of a crime against honor or decency, and have a good reputation. A decision taken by the council of ministers can allow for the involvement of non-Qatari citizens, but their number should not exceed 20 percent of the total membership.

Associations are required to register their location, activities, purpose, bylaws, annual financial figures, conditions of membership, and duties and rights of members, as well as their procedures for withdrawal, expulsion, and termination of membership. Registration must include the name, nationality, and place of residence of each founding member.

Associations must have prior approval from the Minister of Civil Service and Housing Affairs for fundraising. All funds must originate from within the state of Qatar. Private associations, similar in concept to private foundations, must depend solely on self-generated funds. They may not receive assistance from the government, but they can accept local grants and donations.

The Ministry of Civil Service and Housing Affairs has the authority to dissolve an association based on membership of fewer than twenty persons, violation of the provisions of stipulated laws, or involvement in political activities. The ministry also reserves the right to expel managers of associations under certain conditions. Falsified information on documents, conducting banned activities, misuse of funds, or continued participation in association activities after dissolution can result in imprisonment and fines.

Given the restrictive nature of some of these legal measures, a few Qatari-based foundations are resorting to special emiri decrees to ensure their independence and/or to enhance the international nature of their operations.

Institutionalized Philanthropy

Influenced by local and global trends, institutionalized philanthropy in Qatar has evolved over the years. Four different forms can be distinguished: philanthropic initiatives that evolve into operating CSOs, grant-making foundations, charitable CSOs that operate a philanthropic arm, and corporate philanthropy.

Philanthropic Initiatives as Operating CSOs

Qataris have a strong sense of responsibility toward their society, and high net worth individuals have set up personal philanthropic initiatives as a way of channeling their *zakat* contributions. These philanthropic initiatives have evolved into full-fledged CSOs. They are formally registered as professional CSOs with experienced staff and in-house programs of service.

The Qatar Foundation for Education, Science, and Community Development

"Today we plant seeds—strong roots for a better future."
—HH Sheikha Mozah Bint Nasser al-Missned

The Qatar Foundation for Education, Science, and Community Development was founded in 1995 by HH Sheikh Hamad. It was registered as a nonprofit organization to exemplify the value and importance of education, science, and community development. HH Sheikha Moza serves as the chairperson of the foundation and personally guides it with a long-term vision. The Qatar Foundation is financed through a generous endowment by HH Sheikh Hamad and HH Sheikha Moza. The foundation operates many different initiatives under its flagship project, Education City, through affiliates, and in partnership with other institutions.

Education City is an 8-million-square-meter cluster of elite learning centers and cutting-edge research facilities, including five campuses of world-class universities (Virginia Commonwealth University, Weill Cornell, Texas A&M University, Carnegie Mellon University, and Georgetown University). These universities cater to Qatari nationals, as well as students from all over the world, offering scholarships to outstanding students. Education City supports advanced research to foster the creation of new knowledge and technologies, promote the development of existing industries, and inspire new opportunities and sectors. Its Community Health and Development Program focuses on research on Qatar society, as well as on the Middle East region, and targets children via a children's educational television channel.

Through Education City, Qatar is hoping to position itself as an international center for educational excellence. It also hopes to invest in the people of Qatar and the region, positioning itself as a recognized leader in international cooperation and crosscultural understanding. Qatar Foundation's partners and affiliates include:

- *The Doha Debate*: A public forum for dialogue and freedom of speech in Doha that is chaired by the well-known British Broadcasting Company (BBC) broadcaster Tim Sebastian and is broadcast live monthly, both locally and on BBC World News.

- *Reach Out to Asia (ROTA)*: A nongovernmental organization (NGO) chaired by Her Excellency Sheikha Mayassa Bint Hamad al-Thani and founded in 2005 with a primary focus on community development projects in Asia. ROTA promotes global responsibility for basic quality primary education for children and adults.
- *Fitch*: A global design company with studios in Qatar. Through a unique collaboration with the Qatar Foundation, the partners focus on the design of dynamic branded consumer experiences and the education and implementation of best practice design in the region.
- *Al-Shaqab Stud*: A company that is world famous for its champion racing horses. It was owned by HH Sheikh Hamad before being donated to the Qatar Foundation. Al-Shaqab Stud includes a riding academy and a world-class equestrian academy.

The Qatar Foundation began as a personal initiative of the royal family, but over the years and under the leadership of HH Sheikha Moza, it has evolved into a national institution leading Qatar's educational development. One might call it a philanthropic conglomerate—one to which many branches of the Qatari government are committed.

Grant-making Foundations

Qatar boasts a number of recently established grant-making foundations built on the Islamic concept of *waqf*. These foundations serve the needy not just among Qatari nationals but also among non-Qatari residents of the country. They are highly institutionalized, each with a cadre of professional staff that manages all aspects of the foundation's work.

The Sheikh Jassem Bin Gaber Bin Mohamed al-Thani Charity Foundation

The Sheikh Jassem Bin Gaber Bin Mohamed al-Thani Charity Foundation was established in 2001 with the mission of supporting Qataris in need, as well as non-Qataris residing in Qatar. Sixty percent of its funds are dedicated to the support of Qatari nationals, while 40 percent are dedicated to resident non-Qataris. The foundation supports persons with special needs, the sick and elderly, widows, divorced women, and orphans, as well as outstanding students. The foundation also builds mosques and centers for religious education and hospitals, and provides humanitarian assistance to victims of natural disasters and wars.

The foundation, which is governed by Law 8 of 1998 and reports to the Qatari Agency for Charitable Work, relies on its own funds and does not fundraise or solicit donations from the public. Funds available to the foundation are generated from dedicated income from the *waqf* allocated by the late Sheikh Jassem, which represented approximately one-third of his total wealth. The *waqf* property is made up mainly of buildings and apartment blocks that are maintained and rented out. Their revenue is utilized to operate the foundation. The sons and daughters of the late Sheikh Jassem also provide financial support to the foundation.

The foundation provides financial support to its beneficiaries, as well as some in-kind support (representing 10 to 20 percent of dedicated funds) in the form of food stamps, meat products, stationary and school bags, and furnishings for mosques. During financial year 2005–2006, the foundation received a total of 3,052 applications for support and disbursed 1,821 grants using a computerized system to evaluate and select the grantees. A total of USD 2.6 million went toward supporting the needy.

The Sheikh Eid Bin Mohamed al-Thani Charitable Foundation

The Sheikh Eid Bin Mohamed al-Thani Charitable Foundation was established in 1995 upon the death of Sheikh Eid, who was known for his commitment to charitable giving in Qatar and abroad. The foundation administers an endowment of one-third of the late sheikh's fortune, which is directed to charitable work targeting the poor and needy. Operating in similar fields as the Sheikh Jassem Foundation, the Sheikh Eid Foundation also provides international support to victims of disaster and war. In 2004, the foundation spent over USD 6.79 million on its activities in Qatar and around the world.

The Sheikh Eid Foundation supports a cultural center established in 2000 to benefit the Qatari people and encourages others to create endowments, managing them on their behalf. In 2004, four new *awqaf* were established, valued at a total of USD 1.3 million. The foundation has developed professional management structures and outreach tools, including both a Web site and extensive annual reports. In a region where financial information often is not disclosed to the public, the foundation posts its financial reports on its Web site.

The Sheikh Jassem Bin Gaber Bin Mohamed al-Thani and Sheikh Eid Bin Mohamed al-Thani Charitable Foundations are impressive examples of grant-making organizations rooted in the Islamic concept of *waqf*. The founders' visions have developed into strong institutions with management practices that ensure the sustainability of these philanthropic initiatives.

Other professionally managed grant-making foundations are emerging, endowed by high net worth Qataris. Although one can count only a few, their number and impact is significant in relation to the size of the country. Because of their large assets and their professionally managed operations, they are able to work effectively not only in Qatar but also internationally. Humanitarian relief and short-term support to those in need will always have a place in the philanthropic goals of a society. One expects that, in time, some of these institutions will enter into more strategic fields and alliances that could harness their potential for generating major social advances.

Charitable CSOs that Operate a Philanthropic Arm

Some of the oldest social service delivery CSOs in Qatar are involved in philanthropic initiatives that are not the main activity of the organization but rather one of its secondary objectives. These types of CSOs conduct fundraising campaigns that rely on altruistic sentiments, religious giving obligations, and CSR. The CSOs utilize the funds raised to provide services to those in need within Qatari society, in alignment with their objectives.

Many charitable CSOs in Qatar operate a philanthropic arm. They rely on public support and engage others in their philanthropic activities by developing strong programs and building trust over time. These charities are well known to Qatari society and their activities are visible through fundraising campaigns in public spaces and through frequent reports in the media. They are innovative in their approach to philanthropy and tailor their programs to public demand. Charitable CSOs are becoming increasingly similar in operation to community foundations in other parts of the world, in that they leverage a large number of modest donations, fulfill community social needs, and create solidarity and a sense of belonging among those engaged in their activities. Unlike many community foundations, their scope of operations extends beyond Qatar to the international arena.

Qatar Charity

Qatar Charity (QC) has a longer history than most foundations. It was established in 1980 by a group of Qatari notables in order to support the neediest groups, whether within or outside Qatar. The foundation places great emphasis on cooperation, professionalism, innovation, and quality.

The organization operates locally through nine offices in Qatar, as well as externally, covering more than forty countries in Africa, Asia, and Europe through its branches and partnerships with other NGOs. The organization's four fields of focus are: family, women, and children; education and culture; productive projects; and investment and *waqf.*

Perhaps the most innovative of the Qatar Charity's activities is its *waqf* program, which has the dual purpose of honoring parents and supporting the needy. The foundation encourages donors to create endowments in the name of a parent, with the proceeds going to orphans, destitute families, the elderly, divorcees and widows, poor students, and young men preparing to marry.

QC has a strong presence in Qatari society; in fact, the organization maintains high visibility through media advertisements and booths and posters at shopping malls. The better part of the organization's funds is collected through fundraising drives that solicit contributions from the Qatari people.

Qatar Red Crescent
Perhaps the most prominent organization in this category is the Qatar Red Crescent, which was established in 1982. Although the Qatar Red Crescent focuses on providing relief for victims of disaster and war in Asia and Africa, its Social Work Department is involved in philanthropy for Qatari citizens and residents. The department provides financial grants and in-kind contributions through two programs, one targeting families in need and the other directed at sick people who cannot afford healthcare. In 2005, a total of QAR 3 million was disbursed through both programs.

Corporate Philanthropy
Corporate philanthropy is becoming more evident in Qatar, largely in the form of CSR initiatives launched by private as well as public companies. Prominent examples are:

- *Qatar Telecom (Qtel)*: The company is providing support to Qatari civil society and government through sponsorship schemes. It donated USD 1.5 million to the Qatar Foundation to bolster the foundation's scholarship program. Additionally, Qtel donated QAR 300,000 to the Qatar Center for Voluntary Activities to support its social and economic development activities.
- *Intilaqah Qatar*: An educational program launched by a group of local and multinational corporations operating in Qatar, led by Salam International, Qatar Shell, the Social Development Center, the College of the North Atlantic–Qatar, Microsoft, and HSBC, to help young Qataris explore business start-ups as a viable career choice by assisting them to acquire the necessary skills to be successful entrepreneurs.

- *RASGAS:* A Qatari liquid gas joint stock company that invests in health, education, and sports activities in collaboration with civil society and government initiatives through its CSR program, launched in 2006.
- *Qatar National Bank (QNB)*: A bank that implements its CSR activities through the Social Development Center and Reach Out to Asia. QNB's employee engagement program encourages all employees to engage actively in social work, volunteering, or public relations.

These examples suggest a budding CSR culture within Qatar's flourishing business sector that holds much promise. To date, however, few businesses have elected to establish philanthropic foundation arms, electing instead to contribute financially and in-kind to worthy CSOs or Qatari foundations.

Conclusion

Since 1995, Qatar has embarked on a fast journey of development and modernization under the leadership of HH Sheikh Hamad. In a little over a decade, Qatar has witnessed impressive economic growth that has led to a boost in the culture of giving in the country. Qatar's charitable activities include both traditional and creative modes of channeling philanthropy. Since these philanthropic initiatives are relatively recent, perhaps the main recommendation that could be made is that they focus on continued growth and diversification. Like-minded initiatives should establish productive avenues of communication among themselves to ensure the effectiveness of their giving and to avoid duplication.

In addition to their generous programs of emergency humanitarian aid and support to the poor and needy, Qatari philanthropies, given the public trust they enjoy, could develop rights-based initiatives. These would need to address sensitive but important issues such as the status and rights of non-Qatari residents. Initiatives of the kind could build on innovative programs like the Doha Debates, helping young Qataris to learn and practice participation and good citizenship. The newly formed Arab Democracy Foundation, a regional grant-making organization founded and hosted in Qatar, is a promising development.

The momentum corporate philanthropy has gained over the past few years needs to be maintained, with greater emphasis placed on institutionalization. Currently, most CSR initiatives take the form of financial donations or in-kind contributions to worthy causes, but the author expects that companies increasingly will seek to align their core business activities with goals and programs that engage the entire work force and supply chain in addressing sustainable development and attacking poverty at its roots. There is great scope in Qatar for businesses to partner with progressive public agencies and private donors in addressing major issues in a strategic manner. The project of fostering this socially responsive business climate would be an excellent one for commercial networks such as the S-Qatar Business Council.

Notes
1. Freedom House 2007.
2. Ibid.
3. International Monetary Fund and the United States Library of Congress Federal Research Division's Qatar data.
4. United States Central Intelligence Agency World Fact Book.
5. Ibid.
6. Economist Intelligence Unit 2007:3.
7. Economist Intelligence Unit 2007:9.
8. Freedom House 2007:4.

References
Economist Intelligence Unit. 2007. "Country Report: Qatar."

International Center for Not-for-Profit Law. "The Qatari Law of Associations and Private Institutions." http://www.icnl.org. No. 12 of 2004. Retrieved 30 November 2007

Freedom House. 2007. "Country Report: Qatar."

Metz, Helen Chapin. 1994. "Qatar," Library of Congress Country Studies.

Qatar, in Europa World Online. London: Routledge. American University in Cairo. http://0-www.europaworldcom.lib.aucegypt.edu:80/entry. Retrieved 5 December 2007.

United Nations Commission on Sustainable Development. 2002. "Qatar Country Profile."

8

The United Arab Emirates

Dina H. Sherif

Overview

The United Arab Emirates (UAE) has gone to great lengths to modernize and diversify its economy in order to become a powerful competitor in the global market. Strong work ethics and an ambitious vision have laid the foundation for remarkable growth. These efforts are paying off, as Dubai is established not only as the financial hub of the region but also as one of the emerging financial hubs of the world. Other emirates are following the example of Dubai in economic diversification and modernization. The rapid economic growth of the UAE over the past four decades has led to substantial accumulation of wealth among the ruling families and leaders in the private business sector.

As with all of the societies of the Arab region, the UAE benefits from a strong culture of giving rooted in tribal traditions and religion. The late twentieth century saw that culture of giving begin to be institutionalized separate from initiatives that fell directly under the Ministry of Awqaf (endowments). More recently, philanthropy has increased in both scope and depth, with the state and ruling families setting an example through the social investing of their personal wealth. The establishment of initiatives like International Humanitarian City (IHC), a home for international and Arab organizations working for human welfare, signaled the UAE's commitment to supporting social development and the public good. In the last five years, organizations such as the Emirates Foundation (a public–private initiative), the Mohamed Bin Rashid Al Maktoum Foundation (a personal initiative of the ruler of

Dubai), and the Arab Science and Technology Foundation (heavily supported by the ruler of Sharjah) have followed on its heels.

One can safely say that the culture of giving in the UAE has grown to be a multibillion-dollar industry, with funds socially invested both within and outside the country. As is shown below, pressure is being applied by many quarters for this investment in public welfare to demonstrate clear and measurable returns.

Country Background

United Arab Emirates at a Glance[1]	
Country size	83,600 sq. km.
Population	4.3 million
National	*20%*
Non-national	*70%*
GDP (2005)	USD 130.3 billion
GDP PPP (2005)	USD 128.0 billion
Agriculture	*3%*
Industry	*51%*
Crude oil production	*27%*
Manufacturing	*13%*
Construction	*8%*
Services	*47%*
GDP per capita (2006)	USD 33,397
GDP per capita PPP (2006)	USD 29,142
HDI ranking	41/177
Religious groups	Muslim 96% *(Sunni 80%, Shia 16%)*, Other *(includes Christian, Hindu)* 4%
1 UAE dirham (AED)	USD 0.27

Modern History

Under British protection since 1892, the emirates were loosely tied to the United Kingdom by a series of treaties until 1971, when seven emirates—Abu Dhabi, Dubai, Sharjah, Ras al-Khaimah, Ajman, Fujairah, and Umm al-Quwain—combined to form a confederation.

The UAE has gained much attention for navigating progressive economic policies in a traditionally conservative culture. Economic interest in the area developed in the second part of the twentieth century with the discovery of oil in 1958. Before the discovery of oil, economic activity was concentrated in pearling and fishing. The remaining part of the population earned its livelihood from agriculture, rural handicrafts, and herding.

Strong growth performance based on oil exports in the 1970s and early 1980s precipitated the development of physical and social infrastructure. From the 1980s onward, volatile oil prices were the source of uneven but continuous growth. Abu Dhabi and Dubai are currently the economic powerhouses driving the country, providing a high standard of living and level of security to all the emirates.

The Political Scene

Type of Government
Federation of seven emirates with a provisional constitution renewed every five years from 1971 until 1996, at which point it was formally codified. The current president is HH Khalifa bin Zayed Al Nahyan, ruler of Abu Dhabi. The prime minister and vice president is HH Mohamed bin Rashid Al Maktoum. The Supreme Council of Rulers is comprised of the hereditary rulers of the seven emirates and is the highest national authority. The Supreme Council elects the Council of Ministers, an executive body (cabinet) headed by the prime minister.

National Legislature
Federal National Council (FNC) made up of a 40-member body that is largely consultative. Half of the members are elected and the other half are appointed.

Legal System
Federal court system is in accordance with the 1971 constitution. Criminal, civil and commercial matters fall under the jurisdiction of secular courts. Family and religious disputes are adjudicated under Islamic courts.

The political power of the country rests almost completely with the hereditary leaders of the seven emirates, with particular power concentrated in the capital, Abu Dhabi, and in Dubai. The ruler of Abu Dhabi, His Highness Sheikh Khalifa Bin Zayed al-Nahyan, became the UAE's second president upon the death of his father, His Highness Sheikh Zayed Bin Sultan al-Nahyan, in 2004. The posts of prime minister and vice president are traditionally held by the ruler of Dubai. His Highness Sheikh Mohammed Bin Rashid Al Maktoum assumed these positions in January 2006 upon the passing of his brother.

Few challenges exist to undermine the status quo in the political environment. There is no organized political opposition, as political parties and pressure groups are not permitted. Positions within the government tend to be determined by tribal loyalties and economic power. The ruling families are generally popular and well regarded within their emirates, so inhabitants tolerate a degree of political control in exchange for economic and internal security. Foreign guest workers are the most likely group to exert pressure for reforms, and recent strikes and other labor actions are forcing a revision of policies regarding their contracts and work conditions.

The Economy

Liberal economic policies continue to contribute to strong growth, although the volatile price of oil, upon which a large share of the country's revenue depends, creates an unpredictable revenue stream. Economic growth can be attributed to several factors: government investment in infrastructure, which boosted general economic activity and private investment; a relatively stable domestic environment; availability of capital and few capital controls; and relatively cheap labor from neighboring Arab countries and the Indian subcontinent.

At 27 percent of the gross domestic product (GDP), according to 2005 figures, oil production is a key source of revenue and the principal source of government income, which ultimately funds public sector expenditure. The UAE is in the process of vigorously diversifying its economy. By the 1990s, non-oil exports and non-oil GDP exceeded oil exports for the first time since the oil boom began. As a result, the economy of the UAE is considered the most diversified in the Gulf region.

High levels of wealth within the country have contributed to considerable domestic investment. Public investment, providing infrastructure and services needed by other sectors, is expected to continue stimulating growth. Private investment rose from 7 percent of GDP from 1975 to 1985

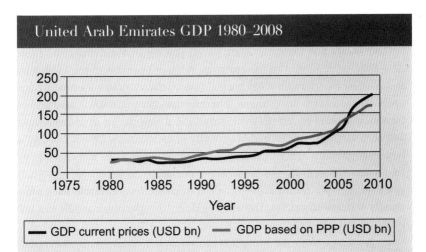

Source: International Monetary Fund, World Economic Outlook Database, April 2007.[2]

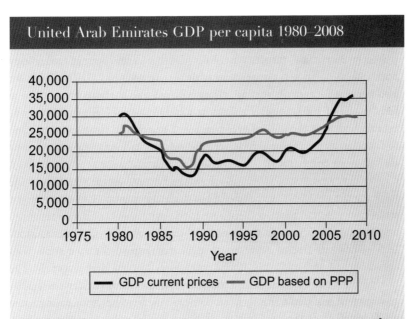

Source: International Monetary Fund, World Economic Outlook Database, April 2007.[3]

to 12 percent from 1996 to 1998. From 2000 to 2005, private investment fell to an average of 10 percent.

Abu Dhabi and Dubai account for 80 percent of the national revenue. Abu Dhabi, the largest of the emirates, holds 90 percent of the UAE's oil and gas reserves, though it has been slower to diversify its oil economy and open up to foreign investment. The city has been a main proponent of increased private sector involvement in the development of infrastructure and core services. The second-largest city of the emirates, Dubai, boasts the largest population. Only 3 percent of petroleum and natural gas deposits are found there, however, and these are expected to be exhausted in twenty years' time.[4] As a result, economic diversification has occurred much more rapidly and, in the process, Dubai has successfully positioned itself as a hub for trade and services.

In order to encourage foreign investment, the government has created a series of rapidly expanding free economic zones in which designated areas enjoy relaxed economic jurisdiction vis-à-vis the rest of the country. Dubai, envisioned as a world business hub, has successfully profited from the Jebel Ali Free Zone (JAFZ), which was established in 1980. Offering business and tax incentives to corporations, it hosts some twenty-five hundred firms from over a hundred countries. The success of JAFZ led to the development of two additional free zones, Dubai Internet City (DIC), established in 1999, and Dubai Media City (DMC), established in 2001. DIC targets emerging markets as an Internet technology park operating in a tax-free zone with few restrictions. DIC allows for 100-percent foreign ownership, along with tax and customs benefits up to fifty years. In 2003, the Dubai International Financial Center (DIFC) was established with the aim of creating a self-regulating financial free zone to function as the regional base for leading international banks and financial services companies.

The development of DMC has stimulated debate on the freedom of the media in the UAE. The government has made the guarantee to international news and entertainment content providers, publishers, music companies, and production firms that the content of their news and information products will remain free of government regulation, provided they comply with certain broad and relatively liberal guidelines of taste and propriety. The pledge has been heeded, with relatively few infractions. Conversely, the government has kept a firm grip on domestic media output, tolerating some mild criticism of the government at times, but disallowing any negative coverage related to Islam, with punishable consequences.

Like other countries in the Gulf, the UAE is highly dependent on foreign labor. Expatriates make up a high proportion of the labor force—2.5 million out of 2.7 million—which means nationals make up less than 10 percent of it. Nationals hold 80 percent of the jobs in the public sector/civil service and only 2 percent of jobs in the private sector.[5] A major effort is underway to train and place young nationals in key positions in the labor force. Currently, because of pressure from striking foreign workers, work hours and other conditions in the construction sector are being improved.

The UAE has positioned itself as the financial powerhouse of the Middle East, with liberalized open markets and an amalgam of nationalities building careers and homes within its borders. The UAE prides itself on being visionary, constantly pushing itself to be a top competitor globally. Taking the emirate of Dubai as an example, the country has often exceeded its growth targets. In a speech on the Dubai 2015 Strategic Plan, the UAE prime minister and ruler of Dubai HH Sheikh Mohamed Bin Rashid Al Maktoum said:

> When I announced my Vision for Dubai in the year 2000, I spoke of economic aims for the year 2010. The reality is that not only have these aims been realized, but they have been realized in half the time. In the year 2000, the plan was to increase GNP to USD 30 billion by 2010. In 2005, that figure was exceeded, with GNP reaching USD 37 billion. The plan also included an increase in income per capita to USD 23,000 by the year 2010. In 2005, the average income per capita reached USD 31,000. In other words, we realized in five years economic achievements beyond those which were planned for a ten-year period.[6]

The achievements in Dubai are reinforced by similar growth in its oil-rich sister emirate, Abu Dhabi.

Philanthropy in Focus
The Culture of Giving

The end of the twentieth century witnessed an exponential growth of private wealth in many parts of the world, not least in the Arab region. With this global increase in wealth has come an increase in philanthropy. While a strong culture of giving always has existed in the UAE, derived mainly from religious motivations, little strategic philanthropy has emerged until recently. For the most part, giving in the UAE can be said to be of a charitable nature, with scant emphasis on intrinsic social change. The philanthropic landscape in the UAE is undergoing a transformation. Many state officials and wealthy individuals are changing the face of their giving, with sustainable impact being at the core of their focus. There is evidence of an emerging trend toward attacking core problems in ways that are strategic, creative, and sustainable.

The turn of the century has seen continuous growth in wealth for the UAE. The percentage of high net worth individuals based in the UAE has been on the rise. According to Hilal al-Marri, managing director of the Dubai World Trade Center, wealthy UAE families, which often exceed a net worth of USD 100 million, give in ways that are increasingly developmental rather than charitable, but not necessarily institutionalized. Many families have established education endowments that are used to sponsor emirati citizens of lower income through school, with the hope that this will eventually bring all citizens to a high standard of living. A number of families also have invested in the developing world, specifically Sub-Saharan Africa, through the building of schools and hospitals. Some of the families known for their traditions of giving include the Futaim family, the Owais family, and the Mutafik family. At the forefront of giving are ruling families like al-Nahyan, Al Maktoum, and al-Qassimi, which set an example of philanthropic giving in the UAE.

For the most part, giving is done quietly and discreetly through personal channels. Recently, a new focus has emerged on institutionalizing philanthropy through the creation of professionally managed foundations, such as the Emirates Foundation and the Mohamed Bin Rashid Al Maktoum Foundation. Although institutionalized philanthropy has become more apparent in the UAE since the turn of the century, other examples date back to the early 1990s, such as the Sultan Bin Ali al-Owais Cultural Foundation.

While it is still too early to tell where unprecedented growth and development will take the UAE, one thing remains certain: the incredible accumulation of wealth brings with it responsibilities, obligations, and duties that the UAE is now under pressure to act upon. The government and high net worth citizens have begun to think critically about how that wealth can be harnessed to bring about positive social change, not only in the UAE but also in the region. Many believe it imperative that their giving be invested in the younger generation to sustain the achievements of today. Furthermore, the UAE has currently established itself as a hub for regional dialogues on Arab philanthropy and corporate social responsibility (CSR), attempting to promote itself as a thought leader in the region.

The Legal Environment for Philanthropy

Private associations, nongovernmental organizations (NGOs), and public interest associations are all governed by Federal Act 6 of 1974, which stipulates that foreigners may not join such associations. Incorporation of associations requires the approval of the Ministry of Social Affairs, which has the authority to reject applications, merge and dissolve associations, and control their activities. The ministry's approval must be obtained for extending grants, fundraising, receiving and distributing funds to and from abroad, and for conferences or meetings abroad. According to Article 182 of the Penal Code, a court may dissolve an illegal association or organization and confiscate its properties and belongings.[7]

Nongovernmental or nonprofit organizations that have been established by emiri decree are not subject to the abovementioned laws and enjoy greater flexibility with regard to the raising and use of funds. This method of establishing relatively independent foundations is becoming increasingly common throughout the Gulf region.

Institutionalized Philanthropy

The overall culture of giving in the UAE is complex once one moves beyond the religiously obligated individual *zakat* contributions. For the purposes of this chapter, the author will consider only indigenous giving. The conceptual framework of this local philanthropy is a diverse multibillion-dollar 'growth industry' derived from a variety of providers, including: 1) foundations established by individuals and supported by their personal wealth; 2) public-private partnership foundations dedicated to a specific cause and financed by both the public and private sources; 3) community-based philanthropy; 4) charity organizations that are partly philanthropic in nature; and 5) private equity firms as an example of corporate-led philanthropy. These are the categories that defined data collection for this chapter.

Individual-based Foundations
The Mohamed Bin Rashid Al Maktoum Foundation
The Mohamed Bin Rashid Al Maktoum Foundation was launched in May 2007 with an endowment of USD 10 billion,[8] making it the largest foundation in the Arab region and among the largest in the world. The main focus of the foundation is education and knowledge creation in the Arab region, with a specific emphasis on youth.

In his launch speech at the World Economic Forum in Jordan, HH Sheikh Mohamed Bin Rashid Al Maktoum said the foundation will finance and manage a wide range of initiatives, such as establishing high-quality research programs and research centers, supporting research in universities across the region, and providing scholarships to allow students to attend leading universities and institutes. Other activities he highlighted include leadership programs for Arab youth in government, the private sector, and NGOs that focus on instilling in them a sense of citizenship and social responsibility, and initiatives that encourage innovation and entrepreneurship throughout the region and, ultimately, create significant new employment opportunities for the region's youth.

According to Her Highness Princess Haya Bint Al Hussein, the wife of HH Sheikh Mohamed Bin Rashid Al Maktoum, this personal initiative, supported by the sheikh's own wealth, stemmed from a vision that socially investing in the education of youth will enhance and sustain the efforts underway for Arab growth and development. Conversely, if youth in Dubai, for example, are not empowered, the work that has gone into making Dubai what it is today will not endure in the long term.[9] Yasar Jarrar, former executive dean of the Dubai School of Government and strategy advisor to the executive office of Dubai, highlighted the foundation's belief in the importance of combining access to and production of knowledge with employment opportunities for Arab youth as basic prerequisites for the region's sustained growth and development.[10]

In addition to giving grants where possible, the foundation will launch and manage its own initiatives, working in partnership with other organizations to achieve its mission. Currently, the foundation is in the process of launching key activities, hiring staff, and identifying its long-term strategies.

The Sultan Bin Ali al-Owais Cultural Foundation
Named after Sultan Bin Ali al-Owais, the Cultural Foundation was established by Emiri Decree 4, dated March 21, 1994. It is run by a board of trustees of seven to fifteen members who are qualified in the fields of administration, science, and culture. A general secretariat acts as the foundation's executive arm. The foundation's financial resources consist of funds provided by the founder and financial contributions through endowments, wills, grants, and donations approved by the board.

The foundation is known for the Sultan Bin Ali al-Owais Award for Scientific and Cultural Achievement. The USD 100,000 award is presented every two years to individual Arab litterateurs, intellectuals, writers, artists, and scientists who have served Arabic culture and who have had a significant impact on their respective fields. Winners of the award are able to publish their works through the foundation. In addition, the foundation has established a library specializing in modern Arabic literature to spread cultural and intellectual consciousness. The library has about forty thousand titles in the arts and humanities. It includes works translated into Arabic.

Many similarities can be drawn between the Sultan Bin Ali al-Owais Foundation and the Abdel Hameed Shoman Foundation in the Hashemite Kingdom of Jordan, both of which are dedicated to the publishing and promotion of Arabic literature. Each of these foundations has made significant contributions to the field, and it would be interesting to see a joint initiative between the two foundations bridging the Gulf and Mashreq regions of the Arab world.

Public–Private Partnership Foundations
The Emirates Foundation

The Emirates Foundation was established in 2005 by emiri decree and inspired by His Highness Sheikh Mohammed Bin Zayed al-Nahyan, the crown prince of Abu Dhabi. The foundation is a nationwide initiative led by a private- and public-sector partnership. It functions on pooled resources raised through the private and public sectors.

The vision of the Emirates Foundation is to improve the quality of life of all people in the UAE. Through a variety of projects that stimulate intellectual and social growth, the foundation aims "to increase access to cultural, educational and technological resources, and foster increased participation in civic life."[11]

The foundation designs and implements its own projects and makes grants to individuals and organizations. As an operating foundation, its goal is to establish pilot projects and evaluate the progress of the foundation through these projects. Through 2007, the key programs of the foundation included Tawteen and Takatof. Meaning 'localization' in Arabic, Tawteen brings together representatives from government, business, education, and civil society from the UAE and the wider Arab world to address persisting social and cultural obstacles, advise youth on meaningful careers, and engender self-development in the UAE. Takatof aims to help find creative solutions to community needs by promoting the spirit of volunteerism as a way of life in the Arab world. Takatof is meant to create a sense of commitment to volunteering, an essential factor in bringing together a community. Beginning in 2008, the foundation's grant-making is to increase significantly with the launch of more than fifty projects in science and technology, education, the environment, arts and culture, public awareness, and social development.

In late 2007, the UAE government pledged to match all private sector donations for the foundation's endowment and to cover all its administrative expenses as a way to assure private donors that their contributions are used strictly for projects. This innovative funding mechanism defines the Emirates Foundation as a mix of state-led philanthropy and corporate philanthropy, which is a unique example of a public-private partnership working together for the good of the UAE.

The Arab Science and Technology Foundation

The Arab Science and Technology Foundation (ASTF) was established in 2000 by a decree issued by His Highness Sheikh Sultan Bin Mohammed al-Qassimi, the governor of Sharjah, who also donated USD 1 million to the foundation as start-up funds. Since it was established by royal decree, the foundation is not governed by the UAE NGO law, so it can function in a relatively flexible manner and is allowed to receive funds from abroad. Over the past three years, the foundation has received an annual USD 1 million from Abdel Latif Jameel of Saudi Arabia.

As its name suggests, the objective of the ASTF is to promote scientific research and technology in the Arab region. Specifically, the foundation provides a forum for Arab scientists worldwide (currently 2,784 from both outside and within the Arab world) to network and engage in proactive dialogue through annual conferences on Arab science and technology. In addition, it provides funding for innovative research and promotes investment in technology. Based on research results, ASTF plays the role of middleman between scientists and investors, encouraging investors to support the innovative ideas evolving from research. To date, the foundation has published 883 scientific papers, organized eight conferences and twelve workshops, and has a database of 2,297 Arab scientists from within the Arab world associated with its work.[12] A significant accomplishment has been its financing of ten scientific research projects from around the Arab world amounting to over USD 300,000 during its third funding cycle (July–December 2006). These include projects in the fields of biotechnology, drugs and medicine, intelligent systems and robotics, the environment, energy, water, agriculture, material science, and more.

Another interesting initiative of the foundation is a technology venture capital fund launched in 2005 known as Arab Technology Ventures (ATV). The fund's authorized capital is USD 5 million. ATV invests in Arab technology-based ventures in the fields of information technology, telecommunications, biotechnology, pharmaceuticals, new materials, nanotechnology, and new engineering technology, among others.

ASTF is a grant-giving organization, but it has yet to establish an endowment, which means that the organization constantly struggles to cover the costs of the activities it would like to implement. The Arab region currently lags behind the rest of the world, only investing 0.02 percent of its GDP on scientific research. With a proper endowment, the foundation could play an expanded role in promoting science and technology in the Arab world.

The Dubai Harvard Foundation for Medical Research

Established in partnership with Harvard University, the Dubai Harvard Foundation for Medical Research supports cutting-edge collaborative research and the establishment of sustainable research centers and education programs to promote innovation in medical practice. The foundation has set up the Dubai Healthcare City to revitalize and intensify medical research in the Middle East and thereby address the region's most pressing health problems.

The foundation's endowment of USD 100 million, which is managed by Harvard University, was gathered from a number of prominent Arab donors in the region, including Their Highnesses Prince Walid Bin Talal of Saudi Arabia and Sheikh Mohamed Bin Rashid Al Maktoum of Dubai.

The strategic partnership with Harvard University focuses on building the research capacity of Arab scientists. Arab scientists are sent to Harvard to train with the university's top medical researchers and then return to the region to carry out their own research in collaboration with a partner scientist at Harvard. The foundation's first research grant was issued in August 2007.

Community-based Philanthropy

Dubai Cares

Launched in September 2007 during Ramadan by HH Sheikh Mohamed Bin Rashid Al Maktoum, Dubai Cares seeks to bring the Dubai community together in support of one cause: primary education for children in developing countries. Around USD 500 million were raised through a combination of individual and corporate donations, and this amount was matched by the sheikh, creating a total of USD 1 billion dedicated to primary education in developing countries. Following this success, a decision was made to turn Dubai Cares into an independent institution, with its own dedicated endowment derived from funds collected annually. Dubai Cares will not be an operating foundation; it will have an annual plan for grant giving (the amount depending on the return from the endowment).

The institution will work in collaboration with credible partners such as UNESCO, Care International, and Save the Children. Dubai Cares is an example of a broad-based initiative that can be transformed into a large-scale community foundation dedicated to raising local community funds in Dubai for the resolution of regional problems. It will be interesting to see how this initiative further institutionalizes giving and continues to inspire the local population of Dubai (both Emiratis and expatriates) to be philanthropic and think beyond themselves to the problems of other communities.

Charity Organizations as Philanthropic Institutions

If we take the working definition of philanthropy as the institutionalized pooling and distribution of resources with the goal of building capacity, sustainable financing, and expertise for long-term societal benefit, then a number of organizations in the UAE that qualify as charity organizations should, in fact, be categorized as philanthropic institutions, as well. While all of them are motivated by Islamic principles and teachings and often rely on *zakat* and *sadaqa* contributions as their main financial resource, the majority also are endowed with *awqaf* in the form of land and other fixed assets allocated by the state or by wealthy individuals. This gives the organizations financial sustainability and enables them to function partially as grant-giving entities, often with a focus on one sector or on the welfare of a specific group in society, such as children or women. These organizations, which often predate the newer foundation models, include Al Maktoum Foundation, the Mohamed Bin Rashid Charitable Humanitarian Foundation, Beit al-Khair Society, and the Dubai Autism Center. Beit al-Khair, for example, is endowed, receives large-scale private sector support, and is, in some cases, a grant giver. While its stated mission is to alleviate poverty in the UAE, Beit al-Khair primarily reduces the immediate wants created by poverty, as opposed to seeking permanent solutions. All of these organizations are supervised by the Ministry of Awqaf, which oversees their distribution of resources and ensures that the resources are contributing to the public good.

Clearly, the Ministry of Awqaf in the UAE and the charity organizations that fall under its jurisdiction play a large role in the philanthropic sector. These organizations donate their charitable funds in the UAE, as well as to organizations in other countries in the Arab region and beyond. They are increasingly venturing beyond short-term charity to development arenas such as education, healthcare, and income generation. With the exception of Beit al-Khair and Al Maktoum Foundation, this study was not able to profile and fully assess 'charity organizations' in the UAE. This is an area that needs further research and documentation. It is important for these organizations to contribute to the growing professional networks of philanthropic institutions.

Beit al-Khair

Beit al-Khair is an International Organization for Standardization (ISO) certified *gam'iya khayriya* established in 1989 by Juma al-Majid, a well-known Emirati philanthropist, and a group of fellow businessmen. The organization finances its activities through *awqaf* in its name, individual donations from al-Majid and fellow board members, and corporate donations. Beit al-Khair is the largest charity organization in the UAE, with over a hundred employees and two hundred volunteers. The organization was established to support Emirati families who are beneath the poverty line. Seeking to reduce the impact that poverty has on underprivileged groups, it focuses on providing relief aid to those in need, including the poor, widows, divorcees, patients, families of prisoners, disabled nationals and nationals with special needs, orphans, and students, among others. Beit al-Khair collaborates with several other organizations in the UAE, such as the Al Maktoum Charity Organization and Red Crescent Society.

Al Maktoum Foundation

Al Maktoum Foundation was established in 1996 in Dublin, Ireland. Since then, its activities have expanded to more than sixty-nine countries. In January 2000, the foundation set up its main office in Dubai. Like Beit al-Khair, Al Maktoum Foundation falls under the jurisdiction of the Ministry of Awqaf in Dubai.

Through a yearly stipend, occasional donations, and the dividends on its endowments, the foundation funds several entities in the UAE, including schools, orphanages, and centers for the handicapped and disabled. In addition, the foundation participates in hosting Ramadan meals and Quranic memorization courses.

The foundation is active in fourteen Arab countries: Palestine, Lebanon, Jordan, Iraq, Egypt, Morocco, Mauritania, Sudan, Tunisia, Yemen, Qatar, Bahrain, Somalia, and the Comoros. Its activities in these countries include the establishment of schools, financing the purchase of medical equipment and computers, building mosques, and sponsoring orphanages and orphans. The foundation also is active in countries in Asia and Africa. Its activities in Asia focus on financing the education of individual students, establishing schools and information technology centers, organizing pilgrimages, and building and heating mosques. In Africa, the foundation sets up schools, universities, and women's centers, in addition to providing financial support for teachers, doctors, and Muslim preachers. The foundation has funded activities in Europe, including the establishment of a center for Islamic studies (the Islamic College in London), centers for Arabic studies, Muslim women's and student's associations, and various other cultural centers.

The organization's budget for 1997–2002 was approximately USD 29,971,885.

Private Equity Firms

The growth of private equity in the UAE has been on the rise since the start of the twenty-first century. The UAE is now home to some of the largest private equity firms in the Arab region and the world. While the philanthropic work of other private equity firms, such as Dubai International Capital and Egypt's Citadel Capital, have not been documented in this study, private equity firms are poised to become leaders in targeted social investment. The face of private equity in the Arab world has changed, with private equity firms based in the region rapidly growing and becoming competitive with the global 'big shots.' These firms have set stringent and ambitious standards when it comes to the maximization of returns on financial investments. When they invest their money socially, they often are quite generous with the amounts allocated. However, they have not yet become as stringent and as ambitious when it comes to benchmarking and ensuring a return on their social investments as they are with their financial investments. The author expects to see a rapid evolution of social giving, as well as investing, among such private sector firms in the near future.

Two of the largest private equity firms in the UAE, Abraaj Capital and Ithmar Capital, are given as examples here of different approaches with regards to philanthropy.

Abraaj Capital

Abraaj Capital is one of the leading private equity firms in the region, currently managing assets amounting to USD 4 billion. Abraaj's chief executive officer recently was named among the fifty most influential private equity personalities in the world. According to Mustafa Abdel Wadood, the company's managing director, while Abraaj does not publicize any of its giving outright, upper management at Abraaj believes that giving back to the community should be something that all employees feel compelled to do. Following that philosophy, Abraaj established the Community Partnerships Program, which is managed by a committee of employees (on a voluntary basis) and promotes the overall culture of giving among members of the firm. Employees are encouraged to donate money from their salaries and annual bonuses to the program. The sum of money collected is augmented by a general sum donated by the firm as a whole, which is again matched by the CEO. Until now, the committee has focused mainly on donating to humanitarian relief and charity-related causes. According to Abdel Wadood, the recent establishment of the Mohamed Bin Rashid Al Maktoum Foundation has inspired many, Abraaj included, to give more thought to how they can contribute strategically to more long-term change.

Ithmar Capital

Ithmar Capital is essentially a family-run private equity firm, and while it is not as large as Abraaj in terms of assets under management, it is experiencing rapid growth. Ithmar's approach to giving is motivated by the family's Islamic beliefs and is distinctly different from that of Abraaj. It dedicates 5 percent of its shares to *zakat* and *sadaqa*. Profits derived from that amount annually are put into a nonprofit sister company led by the women of the family.

The company was established to manage the distribution of the funds in accordance with what is considered appropriate *zakat* and *sadaqa*. This approach has led to a more structured management and distribution of the family's giving. According to Faisal Belhoul, the company's managing director, Ithmar invests its money in sectors that build human capital, such as health and education, as "no business should exist without investing in social sectors and the upgrading of human capital."[13]

Conclusion

Gulf states like the UAE are notable for the ways in which people have revamped and invigorated traditional channels of giving, such as *waqf* and charitable associations, while also launching large-scale and strategic foundations like the Mohamed Bin Rashid Al Maktoum Foundation and the Emirates Foundation. As with technology, sometimes the benefits of being a so-called latecomer can be great in terms of capitalizing on the accumulated knowledge and lessons learned from those who already have been in the practice for years.

One thing is certain: If the accumulation of wealth and private equity has dominated the mindset of Emiratis for the past several decades, how to use that wealth for public benefit now seems to be high on their list of priorities as they determine the regional role they wish to play in the decades to come. For this sector to grow and flourish in the UAE, as with every other country in this study, a supportive legal framework that facilitates independence and good governance of foundations will be required. As it stands, the UAE foundations profiled in this chapter were established by emiri decree or placed in the category of charity organizations that must abide by a law drafted in the 1970s. This points to an important area for policy work that will be needed if the sector is to grow and have its desired impact in the UAE, the region, and beyond.

Notes

1. Population and gross domestic product (GDP) figures taken from International Monetary Fund (IMF) data. GDP estimates start after 2004. GDP per capita estimates begin after 2004 and GDP per capita purchasing power parity (PPP) estimates begin after 2003, based on existing IMF data. GDP PPP reflects the weight of GDP in relation to the purchasing power of other countries. The human development index (HDI) is derived from United Nations development reports and is the measure of life expectancy, literacy education, and standard of living. The breakdown of religious groups is taken from http://www.Nation-Master.com.
2. Estimates start after 2004.
3. Estimates start after 2004.
4. UAE Oil and Gas. http://www.uae.gov.ae/Government
5. Library of Congress Federal Research Division 2007:13.
6. Business Intelligence Middle East 2007.
7. Khalil 2004:20–21.
8. The foundation's endowment currently is being managed by Dubai Holding.
9. Personal interview with HRH Princess Haya Bint Al Hussein, Dubai, October 2007.
10 Personal interview with Yasar Jarrar, former executive dean of the Dubai School of Government and strategy advisor to the executive office of Dubai, Dubai, October 2007.
11. Taken from the Emirates Foundation Web site.
12. Information taken from ASTF's "About Us" section on its Web site.
13. Personal interview with Faisal Belhoul, Dubai, June 2007.

References

Economist Intelligence Unit. 2006. "Country Profile: United Arab Emirates."
Economist Intelligence Unit. 2007. "Country Report: United Arab Emirates."
Freedom House. 2004. "Country Report: United Arab Emirates."
Global Investment House. 2007. "United Arab Emirates Economic & Strategic Outlook." http://www.globalinv.net.

Khalil, Abdullah. 2004. A Comparative Guide on Laws Relating to the Establishment of an Arab Fund (Endowment or Cash Deposit) to Extend Financial Support for Social Justice Programs in the Arab Region. Cairo: Ford Foundation.

Library of Congress Federal Research Division. 2007. "Country Profile: United Arab Emirates (UAE)."

Merrill Lynch. 2007. "World Wealth Report."

"Mohammed Bin Rashid Unveils Highlights of Dubai Strategic Plan." 2007. *Business Intelligence Middle East*, February 4.

United Arab Emirates. Oil and Gas. http://www.uae.gov.ae/Government

Moving Forward

*Barbara Lethem Ibrahim
and Dina H. Sherif*

The dearth of published material on Arab philanthropy might lead to the conclusion that the sector is inactive or unimportant in the region. Our data collection efforts over the past year refute that proposition. The very pervasiveness of charitable giving at all levels of society renders it a taken-for-granted aspect of life. Until recently, the forms and motivations for giving had their roots in religious or cultural practices that were centuries old and relatively unchanging. While those forms of charity persist and, in fact, are on the rise today, we also see emerging trends that suggest a move beyond charity toward more sustainable social change. This has variously been labeled as 'the new philanthropy,' venture philanthropy, and strategic philanthropy. It is characterized by a desire to address the root causes of social ills and to target resources effectively, by leveraging the involvement of other actors and creating sustainable models of intervention.

In each of the eight countries covered in this volume, we found this new breed of philanthropist. Most are engaged in institution building rather than relying on their individual efforts. They are beginning to know each other and to exchange information about what works and how to use their influence to bring others into the field. It is for these reasons that we have speculated that this dynamic moment in Arab philanthropy may presage the birth of a new social movement. Our field researchers reported back from each country a sense of passion and urgency among the people and the institutions they documented. Philanthropists operate within an awareness of the immense scope of the problems they need to address and the realization that public institutions alone are not capable of effectively solving deep social ills.

While the 'withdrawal of the state' is now a familiar theme in neoliberal discourse, nearly all countries of the Arab world have experienced recent phases in which government action was assumed to be the panacea for development. Today, even in the wealthiest nations, that assumption is being replaced by a more balanced understanding of the need for civic participation in public life. While some aspects of the welfare state remain in the Gulf states, these countries are among the most energetic in exploring the utility of partnerships among government, business, and private philanthropy. It is this formula that seems to be attracting the energies and talents of the new breed of civic actors, among them the new philanthropists. What had been an isolated assortment of philanthropic organizations is shaping itself into an emergent sector.

The obstacles to achieving greater effectiveness in philanthropy remain daunting. They include civil strife, war, underdevelopment, and struggles to improve governance. The Arab region is challenged by its problems, some of which are exacerbated by external actors. At the same time, the region is in possession of great resources of wealth and talent waiting to be unleashed. Throughout our research, we heard people speak in terms of a crossroads. They believe that attempts to forge indigenous routes to Arab problem solving are cumulating toward a "tipping point." For the emerging Arab philanthropic sector to flourish, there must be changes in the way philanthropies are regulated by government. Increased information sharing and transparency will need to characterize the field itself going forward. The findings presented in this volume affirm the potential of Arab philanthropy, and the fact that in several places it appears to be firmly in a growth trajectory.

While still incomplete, the research presented in this volume provides a first-of-its-kind map of the landscape of institutionalized private giving in the Arab region. To round out that picture, subsequent studies need to include other Arab countries and to cover the important elements of diaspora philanthropy; new trends in faith-based philanthropy, particularly Muslim philanthropy; and emerging pan-Arab foundations. In addition, further analysis is needed of the impact of philanthropy on its target communities—both its intended and its unintended consequences.

Regional Trends

Based on what we have learned, a number of broad trends can be identified. Among the most important is an increase in citizen activism among successful and affluent business leaders. They are bringing innovation to the usual targets of philanthropic giving, as well as the vast resources of their wealth. We have called them citizen business leaders in recognition of their determination to leverage change at a societal level and to use the talents and energies of the civil society sector to carry out their visions for change. This is a class that previously would have kept its contact with government at an instrumental level to benefit their private sector ventures. Now, they are being drawn in as advisors, cabinet ministers, and partners in a variety of economic and social development spheres. Its members are discovering, as philanthropists, that one of the most effective ways they they can assist poor or disadvantaged groups is by using their clout to provide access to public goods and services otherwise difficult to obtain. They also bring management and financial savvy to the programs they support. Partnerships between these philanthropists and civil society organizations (CSOs) are likely to be beneficial far beyond the amounts of cash contributed.

While it is fair to say that the average Arab businessperson is still operating at the level of donations to discreet projects and local sponsorships that advance his or her business reputations, a more systemic approach to social action is emerging among business elites in all of the countries studied. Their giving tends to be focused on major social problems, such as youth unemployment or poverty, and to be designed in ways that encourage large-scale impact. They are impatient with traditional forms of intervention that are more charitable in nature, preferring to ask how much lasting change they can leverage with their inputs. Most of these leaders are finding ways to institutionalize their giving, usually through a grant-making foundation or an operational nongovernmental organization (NGO). As levels of wealth continue to grow in the region, we expect that these high-profile individuals increasingly will serve as role models for others to enter the field of philanthropy for change.

A second major driver of enhanced philanthropic giving comes from members of reformist ruling families. These individuals are found in small Gulf countries, as well as in countries like Morocco and Jordan. Rulers almost by definition are able to diffuse ideas and act as strong role models for their citizens. They also have the advantage of being able to cut through red tape and security regulations that may inhibit others from acting effectively. These rulers' parents would have responded to individual petitions for help from citizens in need. As their countries grow in population and governance becomes more complex, present-day rulers are recognizing the limitations of that sort of face-to-face giving. A new generation of rulers in their forties and fifties are modeling ways of giving that are institutionalized, sustainable, and, in a growing number of cases, strategic. This is demonstrated by the rise in the number of endowed royal foundations over the past two to three years. Some are established to support work in the home country, but, increasingly, royal establishments have a regional scope (the Mohamed Bin Rashid Al Maktoum Foundation in Dubai) or work even further afield (Reach Out to Asia, Qatar).

A related trend is the important increase in public-private partnerships. Some Arab governments are coming to recognize the advantages of joint efforts with private philanthropists and corporations to address local challenges. The Hashemite Kingdom of Jordan provides an interesting example of how public-private partnerships are strengthening education reform. The country has seen the launch of a new initiative called Madrasati (My School), which links government, businesses, and citizens in the effort to upgrade public schools throughout Jordan. Another phenomenon worth noting is what we call public-private partnership foundations, an example of which is the Emirates Foundation based in Abu Dhabi, UAE. These initiatives pool the financial contributions of both a governmental or quasigovernmental entity and private donors who agree to conditions for supporting causes that maximize the impact of both.

Less well established but of great potential are institutions that pool small sums of money from a large number of givers, allowing for collective support of local communities and public support for social causes. We documented a number of these initiatives, calling them community foundations, though some reach beyond one geographic area. Community-based philanthropy is initiated by multiple donors who pool their financial resources together for a common local purpose. This type of philanthropy fosters solidarity and civic participation within a community by addressing its most pressing social needs. Examples include the King Hussein Cancer Foundation in Jordan, the Dalia Foundation in Palestine, Waqfeyat al-Maadi in Egypt, and Dubai Cares in the UAE.

Religion remains a strong motivator of giving across the region, providing multiple channels for believers to fulfill spiritual requirements, as well as for more voluntary giving. Endowed *waqf* institutions have grown in number and size in those countries that encourage them. With some exceptions, however, religiously motivated giving is largely personal and anonymous, an individual practice. The bulk of giving through religious channels can be characterized as charitable, although our study finds an increasing trend toward more developmental targets. Religion also appears to be inspiring greater levels of volunteerism in recent years, especially among young people.

Another interesting trend was noted as we reviewed the data from all eight countries. Women always have played a prominent role in traditional forms of NGO activities, but it was thought that new philanthropy was dominated by men, especially male business leaders. In fact, whether we looked at rulers or at business leaders, the role of women in creating strategic and effective Arab philanthropy is striking. Yousria Loza Sawiris was the founder of one of the first and largest of Egypt's modern private grant-making foundations. Among ruling families, Sheikha Mozah Bint Nasser, Queen Rania Al Abdullah, Princess Haya Bint Al Hussein, and Princess Mayessa are all founders or leaders of innovative philanthropic institutions. Others, such as Muna Abu Sulayman and Rima Khallaf, are chief operating officers of major Arab foundations. These are significant examples of women leaders who are pushing the philanthropic sector forward.

With the philanthropic sector becoming more institutionalized, proactive, entrepreneurial, and influential, expectations regarding the return on social investment have risen. Foundations are expected to go beyond showy press releases to demonstrate results. The civil society groups that want access to these growing sources of funding likewise need to improve their practices and internal governance. As one result, NGOs are becoming more transparent. They are under pressure to do a better job of measuring impact and reporting on their successes and failures. They still have a long way to go in terms of improving the standards of civil society work, but change is underway. More philanthropists are working in partnership with CSOs and offering management, analysis, and other services, as opposed to carrying out projects themselves.

Another major finding is the degree to which legal frameworks for citizen-led initiatives can enhance or hinder the work of philanthropy. In nearly all contexts, civil society legislation is far too restrictive to unleash the full participation of citizens in the development of their societies. Nationalization of assets or interference with the boards of private organizations stays in the public memory and inhibits those who might otherwise build up effective institutions within their home countries. Relying on emiri decrees or other exceptional legislation to establish new foundations is a stop-gap measure. These need to be replaced by reforms to existing laws governing CSOs and foundations that draw upon best practice from successful national models.

Modeling Change

In order for the philanthropic sector not simply to grow but also to realize its full potential for generating positive social change, all of society's sectors need to find more effective ways of partnering. The philanthropic sector, government, and civil society each have strengths needed by the other and can tackle important problems with a better mix of coordination, standards of quality, equity, transparency, and accountability.

The development of a professionalized civil society sector in the Arab world needs the expertise and resources of a strong indigenous grant-making sector. That sector's growth, in turn, is spearheaded by a vibrant private sector and the business community. Governments support both by creating enabling environments that do not overregulate, but instead help in the setting of standards for transparency and effectiveness. A strong civil society then can speak on the emerging concerns of the population and assist the government to meet basic needs. Both the private sector and civil society have knowledge and advocacy tools that would support governments in fulfilling their pledges for good governance.

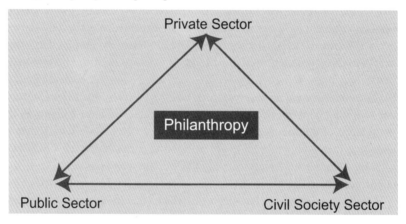

Strength at each point in this relationship will contribute to the solution of major social problems and the building of strong, viable nations. In many ways, philanthropy stands at the center of the model, providing resources and helping to balance the power and influence of the three sectors. As the region continues to accumulate wealth and create new cohorts of wealthy citizens, private philanthropy seems poised to become a major engine for change.

Recommendations

Based on the findings of this first phase of study, we offer some general recommendations that may help to unleash greater potential for the Arab philanthropic sector and enhance its effectiveness. The agenda is large and therefore will require efforts on the part of multiple actors. Some work needs to be undertaken at local levels, while other advances will be made through collaborations at the national or the regional level. Philanthropy is increasingly a global enterprise—cooperation will need to extend to the international level, to Diaspora groups, professional networks, and other resources that can enhance Arab philanthropy.

1. Create an Enabling Environment for Enhanced Philanthropy

In every country, both the potential and the obstacles inherent in laws and regulations were avidly discussed. Philanthropists are careful with their funds. They require legal structures that provide straightforward and non-intrusive relationships with regulatory authorities. Laws governing foundations and endowments must be reformed. Better training must be provided to mid-level authorities in Ministries of Awqaf and Social Affairs and related agencies. Increasingly, they must be able to handle complicated financial reports and understand concepts such as stock value, portfolios, and risk management.

The opportunities provided by reform of policies and laws are enormous in the area of creating incentives for philanthropy. These could take the form of income tax incentives for increased giving or customs and other forms of tax relief for registered foundations. Public bodies also may offer priorities in accessing goods or services to communities that are willing to pool their own local resources. This kind of creative partnering has been highly successful; for example, in anti-poverty programs in Latin America.

Neighboring countries have paved the way for effective legislation to revive important traditional forms of philanthropy such as the Islamic *waqf.* Turkey's reform of *waqf* legislation in 1981 led to positive competition among the wealthiest commercial families to endow private universities and scholarship programs across the country.

National dialogue between government and civil society can broaden the space for civic action and decrease over-regulation. Such forums for public dialogue would help in addressing sensitive issues, such as minority rights, poverty, or guest worker practices.

As the philanthropic sector grows, it should develop methods for self-monitoring. Governments can help by setting procedural and financial 'bottom line' standards of conduct. However, the promotion of ethical standards and best practices should be left to members of the philanthropic community, through mechanisms they create and maintain.

2. Professionalize the Philanthropic Sector

Along with self-monitoring, other steps can be taken to 'shorten the learning curve' for new foundations and to share professional standards among organizations in the sector. This would entail building effective networks for practitioners. Initiatives already underway include the Arab Foundations Forum, a membership network for organizations, and the Arab Forum for Social Innovation, an informal gathering of individual philanthropists. Future networks might focus on the needs of foundation executives or provide standards of practice for the field. In particular, the authors of this study believe that religious philanthropies and those with more secular identities have much in common and could benefit from greater interaction. Efforts could be made to bridge that communication gap where it occurs.

Documentation and analysis of trends is another area that could benefit the sector as a whole. Philanthropists are often like civil society activists— too engaged in their passion for a cause to take time out for assessment or research. Increasingly, however, these actors recognize the importance of sound impact evaluations, design of indicators to chart program progress, and so forth. Universities as well as private consulting firms should be encouraged to engage with philanthropy as an important area of study and teaching.

Training and technical assistance also would be of great service to the emerging philanthropic sector. Currently, this is rare in the region, but it is being provided by some financial services units and consulting groups among corporate clients. There is a gap in the provision of practical guidance for `families wanting to institutionalize their giving, build an endowment, or help a second and third generation take over leadership of family philanthropies. Short courses with targeted objectives are requested by foundation executives and board members alike. Topics that are particularly relevant include grant-making guidelines, setting ethical standards, measuring impact, and building strategic alliances.

New philanthropic instruments are proliferating in the region. Greater interaction between those involved in Islamic banking, for example, with those seeking to increase giving for a particular cause might prove beneficial. Achieving greater consensus over the allowable recipients of *zakat* funds also would open up wider avenues for giving. Innovative modes of fundraising from individuals should be investigated and promoted, including the use of Facebook and other social networking Internet sites, so that multiple small dominations can be mobilized for maximum effectiveness.

Foundations and civil society alike are in need of mechanisms to match donors with appropriate recipients of funding. This clearinghouse function currently does not exist in the region, which makes for inefficiencies and inequality in access to support. It is best done by a consortium of donor and civil society leaders with experience in building and funding quality programs. Online and electronic models could be adapted at the national level, and eventually by the entire region.

Finally, the philanthropic sector would be well served by the creation of resource hubs and an information clearinghouse for donors. This would become the repository for documentation like the present study and case studies of best practices in the field. Training materials, sample policy and procedure manuals, and similar practical tools should be made easily and widely available throughout the region. For this to be most effective, materials should be available online and translated where necessary into Arabic. The Gerhart Center at the American University in Cairo, and the Center for Development Services, Cairo, currently are building such resources.

3. Foster Effective Public Education about Philanthropy and Corporate Responsibility

One reason that the emerging philanthropic sector is invisible to many people is the dearth of media sources of information. Only the biggest donors or the most dramatic contributions are covered by print or electronic journalism. Alternatively, media coverage is framed by an outdated understanding of philanthropy as charity, and featured on the women's pages of newspapers or magazines. There also is a tendency to think of philanthropy in terms of 'kindness' rather than as strategic investments aimed at addressing social problems in a systematic manner.

Short courses, such as one recently offered at the American University in Cairo for mid-career journalists, could help to improve coverage of the field and alert journalists to the relevance of these stories as hard news. The Cable News Network (CNN) and other television outlets have shown leadership in highlighting the role of philanthropy in African and Arab social development.

More can be done to publicly recognize the contributions of exemplary philanthropic institutions and individuals. Prizes such as the one awarded by Mo Ibrahim in celebration of good governance in Africa could be adapted to recognize outstanding philanthropists in the Arab region. In order to encourage a new generation of philanthropists, awards can be established in universities and schools for students who show innovation and success in their philanthropic endeavors.

One reason that international corporations have been quick to adopt the practices of corporate social responsibility is the scrutiny they receive from stakeholders and the public. Arab companies are largely free of pressure to improve their environmental and social policies, improve labor conditions, and serve the poorest sectors of the market. Informed publics and alert media would be a positive influence on the business community and, at the same time, could highlight best practices and speed the adoption of innovation.

4. Foster a Culture of Civic Engagement and Social Responsibility among Arab Youth

For the philanthropic sector to flourish, it must have infusions of young energy and talent. Currently, a career in philanthropy is hardly a top priority for bright students or their parents. There are few career paths or role models to encourage young people to enter the field. On the other hand, youth community activism is growing around the region, and young Arabs today have a sense that they must build their own lives and societies without depending on state support. That commitment to service, seen in the rise of youth organizations in Egypt, Jordan, Palestine, and elsewhere, could be harnessed for the philanthropic sector.

Donors should be encouraged to partner with universities to increase the teaching and practice of community engagement and active citizenship. Business leaders could act as mentors to young activists and bring interns into their philanthropic endeavors. Youth job training and placement programs could include civil society and philanthropy as potential career paths for young applicants.

Businesses, schools, and universities could promote innovation and social entrepreneurship among youth. This is a short step from the successful business training efforts, such as Injaz, which have captured the imaginations of young people and business leaders alike. Universities could sponsor competitions for effective social investment business plans and encourage faculty and students to partner on research that addresses aspects of philanthropy.

Youth want to be taken seriously and they want to be heard. It would be refreshing to see younger members of the community serving on the boards of philanthropies and panels at conferences and representing organizations at regional and international meetings. Girls as well as boys can be encouraged to think of business careers and careers in executive management of philanthropies.

In conclusion, while many obstacles remain to the full emergence of philanthropy as a social movement, the opportunities are numerous and exciting. The potential impact of the trends noted above—a vast pool of new wealth, increased activism among business leaders, the empowerment of civil society, and the rising influence of private donors—are clear and need to be supported. In a region where poverty, substandard healthcare, lack of education, and youth unemployment are rampant, Arab philanthropists have a unique opportunity to join forces and make a difference.

That difference will come through not only investing funds on a social level but also making market forces work better for the poor, who continue to exist on the margins of Arab societies. Markets are booming today, but the benefits are felt by too few of the region's citizens. For the good of the region, it is imperative that these efforts are launched now. We hope that this study will serve as motivation to increase both strategic philanthropy and effective partnerships. Philanthropies in the Arab region may still be few in number, but as Martin Luther King Jr. noted, "Almost always, the creative dedicated minority has made the world better."

Glossary

'ata' igtima'i: Social giving. A term that tries to capture the idea of modern philanthropy.

'ata' khayri: Charitable giving, excluding obligatory *zakat* or *'ushr.*

birr/mabarra: Good or blessed acts.

citizen–business leaders: Emerging businessmen and women who apply their wealth and talents to social and public causes by founding non-profit associations or foundations, becoming outspoken advocates for social issues, serving as advisors to government, and so on.

community foundation: A philanthropy pooling many contributions toward services for a specific geographic area or population sub-group.

corporate foundation: A legally independent foundation created in the name of a for-profit company, and operated through a share of annual profits.

corporate social responsibility (CSR): CSR derives from the strategic decisions of corporate leaders to orient their businesses toward fair labor practices, protection of natural resources, and solutions to major social problems that expand the economy and therefore improve long-term business prospects. CSR posits a mutual benefit to businesses and society from corporate engagement in the long-term solution of pressing social problems.

Eid al-Adha: Feast of the Sacrifice. A religious festival celebrated by Muslims in commemoration of Ibrahim's (Abraham's) willingness to sacrifice his son. It is one of two major feasts celebrated by Muslims.

family foundation: A foundation established by private individuals in the name of the family or as a tribute to a family member.

fatwa: A religious edict or opinion on Islamic law issued by a scholar of Islam.

fi-sabil Allah: Following the cause of God. The seventh category of people entitled to receive *zakat* donations. It has been variously interpreted as supporting spiritual or militant *jihad* and funding the travel of those who cannot afford to perform the *hajj* pilgrimage.

grant-making foundation: A philanthropy channeling its financial resources to other groups in civil society, usually organized around one or more funding themes.

Hadith: Oral traditions relating to the words and deeds of the Prophet Muhammad.

Hajj: The fifth pillar of Islam, the pilgrimage to Mecca is an obligation to be carried out once in a Muslim's lifetime by every able-bodied believer who can afford to do so.

jihad: Literally 'struggle,' it is used to refer to the struggle to lead a righteous life (major *jihad*) and fighting/defending in the name of Islam (minor *jihad*).

mu'assasa: Legal term in some Arab countries for a private foundation.

operating foundation: A philanthropy that conducts its own in-house social or cultural programs.

philanthropy: The institutionalized pooling and distribution of private resources. Optimally, with the goal of building capacity, sustainable financing, and expertise for long-term societal benefit.

public–private partnership: Government service or private business venture including a social purpose, funded and operated through a partnership of government and one or more private sector companies. These schemes are sometimes referred to as PPP or P3.

qard hasan: Interest-free loans allowed under shari'a law, and created by the pooled donations of participating members. Generally granted to those who are facing emergency or personal crises.

sadaqa: 'Benevolence,' connoting voluntary charitable giving and beneficence of all types. It differs from *zakat* which is obligatory.

sadaqa jariya: Benevolent acts with an ongoing life, such as distributing religious books or tapes, making educational materials available, or planting fruit trees in a public square. *Waqf* is an important part of *sadaqa jariya.*

shari'a: The rules and laws of Islam, including laws governing all aspects of day-to-day Muslim behavior such as family affairs, relationships, business, politics, economics, hygiene, and social issues. Shari'a is rooted in the Quran and Hadith and comprises Islamic judicial decisions derived by generations of learned Muslim scholars.

shilla foundation: An Arabic term for a closely knit group of friends who provide mutual support. When two (or more) entrepreneurs or philanthropists partner with each other on the basis of trust and a common social goal, they form a *shilla* foundation.

strategic philanthropy: Defined as utilizing resources effectively to address the underlying causes of important social problems, and ultimately, to resolve them.

Sunna: The ways and deeds of the Prophet Muhammad, norms of behavior followed by Muslims.

takafful insani: Humanitarian solidarity; attempts to capture the idea of modern philanthropy.

'ushr: Religious tithing among Arab Christians. The practice of giving a tenth of one's wealth or income to those less fortunate in the community. Often accompanied by giving time for voluntary service to others.

venture philanthropy: An idea that borrows from venture capitalism by providing intensive funding, technical expertise, and strategic thinking to promising social enterprises with the expectation of results and accountability.

waqf (pl. awqaf) : Literally to stop, confine, isolate, or preserve in perpetuity, certain revenue or property for religious or philanthropic purposes. One of the oldest examples of an endowment.

zakat: The third pillar of Islam, the giving of wealth required of all believers. Often translated as 'alms' or 'charitable giving.'

zakat al-mal: One form of *zakat* on money, on trade, on merchandise, and so on.

Appendix

Selected Philanthropic Organizations, by Country*

The Arab Republic of Egypt

Alfanar Community Foundation
http://www.alfanar.org.uk
Email: info@alfanar.org.uk
18 al-Mansour Mohamed St.
Zamalek, Cairo 11211
Egypt
Tel: +2 (0)2 2735-3797
Fax: +2 (0)2 2735-5489

Al-Maadi Community Foundation
9 Uthman Buildings
Maadi, Cairo
Egypt
Tel: +2 (0)2 2525-5549
Office Mobile: (018) 172-2224

Al Noor Foundation
http://www.alnoor.org.eg
Email: alnoor@alnoor.org.eg
Tel: +2 (0)2 3363-1111
Fax: +2 (0)2 3363-9001

Dar al-Orman
Email: info@alorman.com
7 al-Hag Mossa St.
Al-Haram, Giza
Egypt
Tel: +2 (0)3 3383-1189

EFG Hermes Foundation
http://www.efghermesfoundation.org
Email: info@efghermesfoundation.org
58 al-Tahrir St.
Dokki, Giza 12311
Egypt
Tel: +2 (0)2 3336-4693
Fax: +2 (0)2 3338-3616

Egyptian Food Bank
http://www.egyptianfoodbank.com
Email: info@egyptianfoodbank.com
6 Nafoura St.
Cairo, Mokattam
Egypt
Tel: +2 (0)2 3508-0000

Sawiris Foundation For Social Development
http://www.sawirisfoundation.org/en
Email: info@sawirisfoundation.org
22 al-Montazah St.
Ground Floor
Zamalek, Cairo
Egypt
Tel: +2 (0)2 2736-2012 / 2736-6783 / 2736-4841
Fax: +2 (0)2 2736-2013

---

* This directory includes philanthropic institutions profiled in this report and does not claim to be comprehensive of all philanthropic organizations and initiatives in the eight countries included in this study or in other Arab countries. Efforts to compile a comprehensive directory are underway.

The Hashemite Kingdom of Jordan

Abdul Hameed Shoman Foundation
http://www.shoman.org
Email: ahsf@shoman.org.jo
P.O. Box 940255
Amman 11194
Jordan
Tel: +962 6 463-3627 / 463-3372
Fax: +962 6 463-3565

Jordan River Foundation
http://www.jordanriver.jo
Email: info@jrf.org.jo
P.O. Box 2943
Amman 11181
Jordan
Tel: +962 6 593-3211
Fax: +962 6 593-3210

King Hussein Cancer Foundation
http://www.khcc.jo
Email: info@khcf.jo

King Hussein Foundation and Noor Al Hussein Foundation
http://www.kinghusseinfoundation.org/khf.htm
Email: khf-nhf@nic.net.jo /
dhussieni@khf.org.jo / khf-nhf@khf.org.jo
P.O. Box 926687
Amman 11110
Jordan
Tel: +962 6 560-7460
Fax: +962 6 560-6994

Tkiyet Um Ali
http://www.tkiyetumali.org
Email: info@tkiyetumali.com
P.O. Box 4060
Amman 11131
Jordan
Tel: +962 6 491-6816 / 491-6800
Fax: +962 6 490-3686

Ruwwad
http://ruwwad.net/home
Email: info@ruwwad.net
Nathmi Abdel Hadi St.
Jabal Nathif, Amman
Jordan
Tel: +962 6 473-3313
Fax: +962 6 473-3315

The Kingdom of Saudi Arabia

Al-Mansouria Foundation
http://www.almansouria.org
Email: mcc@almansouria.org

The Coexist Foundation
http://www.coexistfoundation.net
Email: bridget.flavell@coexistfoundation.net
17-19 Bedford St.
London WC2E 9HP
UK

The Help Center
http://www.helpcenter.med.sa
Email: info@helpcenter.med.sa
P.O. Box 51890
Jeddah 21553
Saudi Arabia
Tel: +966 2 663-1113
Fax: +966 2 668-3109

King Faisal Foundation
http://www.kff.com
Email: info@kff.com
P.O. Box 352
Riyadh 11411
Saudi Arabia
Tel: +966 1 465-2255
Fax: +966 1 465-6524

Palestine: West Bank and Gaza Strip

Abdel-Mohsen Qattan Foundation
http://www.qattanfoundation.org

Email: info@qattanfoundation.org
P.O. Box 2276
Ramallah
Palestine
Tel: +972 2 296-0544
Fax: +972 2 298-4886

Al-Lod Charitable Society
http://www.allodpal.org
Email: infor@allodpal.org

Al-Quds Zakat Committee
http://www.khayma.com/sinan
Email: alzkah@hotmail.com
Al-Aqsa Mosque
P.O. Box 17420
Jerusalem
Tel: +972 2 228-7772
Fax: +972 2 228-7772

Burqa Zakat Committee
http://www.lzaka-burqa.org
Email: info@lzaka-burqa.org
Tel: +972 2 253-0699
Fax: +972 2 253-0699

Dalia Association
http://www.dalia.ps
Email: info@dalia.ps
P.O. Box 51822
East Jerusalem, via Israel
Tel: +972 (0)54 653-6671/+972
(0)598 824-8807

Faisal Husseini Foundation
http://www.fhf-pal.org
Dahiyat al-Bareed
P.O. Box 19
Bir Nabala
East Jerusalem
Tel: +970 2 234-2686
Fax: +970 2 234-5521

**Hani Qadoumi Scholarship
Foundation**
http://www.hq-sf.org
Email: info@hq-sf.org

Jawwal Community Fund
http://www.jawwal.ps
Al-Bireh:
P.O. Box 3999
Tel: +970 22 240-2440
Fax: +970 22 296-8636
Gaza:
P.O. Box 1300
Tel: +970 28 283-3220
Fax: +970 28 283-3322

Nablus Zakat Committee
http://www.zakat-nablus.org

Palestinian NGOs Network
http://www.pngo.net
Email: pngonet@pngo.net
Sabat Building
First Floor
Al-Masyoun
P.O. Box 2232
Ramallah
Palestine
Tel: +970 2 297-5320/1
Fax: +970 2 295-0704

Palestinian Red Crescent Society
https://www.palestinercs.org
Email: info@palestinercs.org
P.O. Box 3637
Al-Bireh
Palestine
Tel: +972 2 240-6515
Fax: +972 2 240-6518

**Patients Friends Society, Abu Raya
Rehabilitation Center**
http://www.kaburaya.org
Email: info@kaburaya.org
Tel: +970 2 295-7060/1
Fax: +970 2 295-7062

**The Scientific Foundation of Hisham
Adeeb Hijjawi**
http://www.sfohah.org
Email: he.lp@sfohah.org

P.O. Box 103
Amman 11810
Jordan
Tel: +962 6 581-4257 / 581-6072
Fax: +962 6 582-6861

The Society of In'ash El-Usra
http://www.inash.org
Email: usra@palnet.com
Society of In'ash El-Usra
P.O. Box 3549
Al-Bireh
Palestine
Tel: +972 2 240-1123/240-2876
Fax: +972 2 240-1544

Union of Charitable Societies
http://www.ucs-pal.org
Email: info@ucs-pal.org
Tel: +970 2 628-5870
Fax: +970 2 628-5870

The State of Lebanon
Fondation Pere Afif Oseiran
Email: fpao.mcl@idm.net.lb

Hariri Foundation
http://www.hariri-foundation.org.lb

Lebanese Welfare Association for the Handicapped
http://www.lwah.org.lb
Email: lwah@cyberia.net.lb
Mazra'a 1101-2010
Lebanon
P.O. Box 14-5011
Tel: +961 1 374-100/1/2
Fax: +961 1 374-033

Makhzoumi Foundation
http://www.makhzoumi-foundation.org
Email: info@makhzoumi-foundation.org
Ras Beirut
Al-Kaala Tower
Al-Kalaa St.

P.O. Box 13/5009
Beirut
Lebanon
Tel: +961 1 869-318 / 865-759 / 860-940
Fax: +961 1 863-949

Fares Foundation
http://www.fares.org.lb
Email: ffinfo@fares.org.lb
Fares Foundation Building
Maameltein Highway
Jounieh
Lebanon
Tel: 091 639-987/8
Fax: 091 639-991

Rene Moawad Foundation
http://www.rmf.org.lb
Email: rmf@rmf.org.lb
844 Alfred Naccache St.
Achrafieh
Beirut
Lebanon
BP: 468 Hazmieh
Tel: +961 1 613-367/8/9
Fax: +961 1 613-370

Safadi Foundation
http://www.safadi-foundation.org

The Lebanese Center for Policy Studies
http://www.lcps-lebanon.org
Email: osafa@lcps-lebanon.org

Carnegie Middle East Center
http://www.carnegie-mec.org
Email: psalem@ceip.org

Oum al-Nour
Email: Pascale.debbane@debbane-group.com

The State of Kuwait
Kuwait Awqaf Public Foundation
http://www.awqaf.org

Email: faq@awqaf.org
Lot 6, Al-Manqaf St.
P.O. Box 482
Al-Safa 13005
Kuwait
Tel: +965 804-777
Fax: +965 253-2670

**Kuwait Foundation for the Advance-
ment of Science**
http://www.kfas.com
Email: publicr@kfas.org.kw
P.O. Box 25263
Safat 13113
Kuwait
Tel: +965 242-5898, ext. 123
Fax: +965 241-5365

Zakat House
http://www.zakathouse.org.kw
Email, general:
zakat@zakathouse.org.kw
Email, external:
ead@zakathouse.org.kw
Email, information:
info@zakathouse.org.kw
Lot 6, Qatar St.
Al-Safa 23865
Kuwait
Tel: +965 224-0225

The State of Qatar
**Sheikh Eid Bin Mohamed al-Thani
Charitable Foundation**
http://www.eidcharity.net
Email: mail@eidcharity.net
Doha 22278
Qatar
Tel: +974 487-8071/487-8061/487-8051
Fax: +974 487-8081

Qatar Foundation
http://www.qf.edu.qa
Email: info@qf.org.qa
P.O. Box 5825
Doha
Qatar
Tel: + 974 492-7000

The United Arab Emirates
Abraaj Capital
http://www.abraaj.com
Emirates Towers Offices
Level 7
P.O. Box 504905
Dubai
UAE
Tel: +971 4 319-1500
Fax: +971 4 319-1600

Beit al-Khair Society
http://www.beitalkhair.com
Email: balkhair@emirates.net.ae
P.O. Box 55010
Dubai
UAE
Tel: +971 4 267-5555
Fax: +971 4 267-0762

**The Arab Science and
Technology Foundation**
http://www.astf.net
Email: info@astf.net
P.O. Box 27272
Sharjah
UAE
Tel: +971 6 505-0551
Fax:+971 6 505-0553

Dubai Cares
http://www.dubaicares.ae
Email: dubaicaresinfo@teo.ae
Offices Level 43, Office Tower,
Emirates Towers,
Sh. Zayed Rd.
P.O. Box 73311
Dubai
UAE
Tel: +971 4 330-4444
Fax: +971 4 330-4000

**The Dubai Harvard Foundation
for Medical Research**
http://dhfmr.hms.harvard.edu
Email: dhfmr@hms.harvard.edu

Boston:
One Renaissance Park, Suite 900
1135 Tremont St.
Boston, MA 02120
USA
Tel: +1 617-535-6510
Fax: +1 617-535-6410
Dubai:
P.O. Box 66566
Dubai
UAE
Tel: +971 4 362-2807
Fax: +971 4 362-4778

Emirates Foundation
http://www.emiratesfoundation.ae
Email: information@emiratesfoundation.ae
P.O. Box 111445
Abu Dhabi
UAE
Tel: +971 2 616-7777
Fax: +971 2 616-7788

Forsa-Insead
http://www.forsa.ae
Email: info@forsa.ae
P.O. Box 17000
Dubai
UAE
Tel: +971 4 375-9655
Fax: +971 4 375-9630

Ithmar Capital
http://www.ithmar.com
Email: info@ithmar.com
P.O. Box 5527
Dubai
UAE
Tel: +971 4 282-5555
Fax: +971 4 283-1155

Mohamed Bin Rashid Al Maktoum Foundation
http://www.mbrfoundation.ae

Sultan Bin Ali al-Owais Cultural Foundation
http://www.alowaisnet.org
Email: mail@alowaisnet.org
P.O. Box 14300
Dubai
UAE
Tel: +971 4 224-3111
Fax: +971 4 221-7839